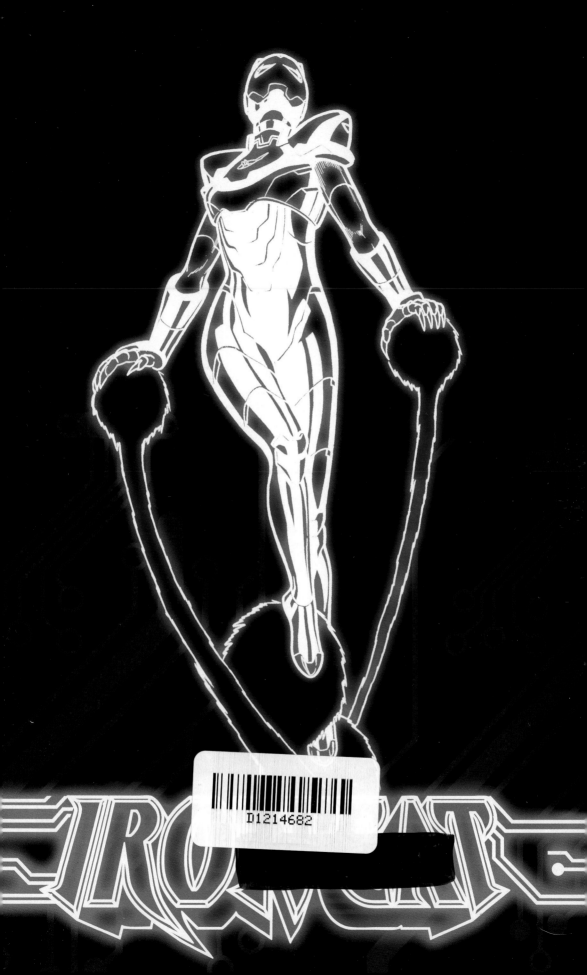

D1214682

IRON CAT

JED MacKAY
WRITER

PERE PÉREZ
PENCILER

PERE PÉREZ (#1-2, #4-5)
& JORDI TARRAGONA GARCIA (#3)
INKERS

FRANK D'ARMATA
COLOR ARTIST

PERE PÉREZ & FRANK D'ARMATA
COVER ART

VC's ARIANA MAHER
LETTERER

LINDSEY COHICK
ASSISTANT EDITOR

TOM GRONEMAN
ASSOCIATE EDITOR

DEVIN LEWIS & NICK LOWE
EDITORS

DANIEL KIRCHHOFFER ○ COLLECTION EDITOR
MAIA LOY ○ ASSISTANT MANAGING EDITOR
LISA MONTALBANO ○ ASSOCIATE MANAGER, TALENT RELATIONS
JENNIFER GRÜNWALD ○ DIRECTOR, PRODUCTION & SPECIAL PROJECTS

JEFF YOUNGQUIST ○ VP PRODUCTION & SPECIAL PROJECTS
SARAH SPADACCINI WITH CARLOS LAO ○ BOOK DESIGNERS
JAY BOWEN ○ SENIOR DESIGNER
DAVID GABRIEL ○ SVP PRINT, SALES & MARKETING
C.B. CEBULSKI ○ EDITOR IN CHIEF

IRON CAT. Contains material originally published in magazine form as IRON CAT (2022) #1-5. First printing 2022. ISBN 978-1-302-94697-5. Published by MARVEL WORLDWIDE, INC., a subsidiary of MARVEL ENTERTAINMENT, LLC. OFFICE OF PUBLICATION: 1290 Avenue of the Americas, New York, NY 10104. © 2022 MARVEL No similarity between any of the names, characters, persons, and/or institutions in this book with those of any living or dead person or institution is intended, and any such similarity which may exist is purely coincidental. **Printed in the U.S.A.** KEVIN FEIGE, Chief Creative Officer; DAN BUCKLEY, President, Marvel Entertainment; DAVID BOGART, Associate Publisher & SVP of Talent Affairs; TOM BREVOORT, VP, Executive Editor; NICK LOWE, Executive Editor, VP of Content, Digital Publishing; DAVID GABRIEL, VP of Print & Digital Publishing; SVEN LARSEN, VP of Licensed Publishing; MARK ANNUNZIATO, VP of Planning & Forecasting; JEFF YOUNGQUIST, VP of Production & Special Projects; ALEX MORALES, Director of Publishing Operations; DAN EDINGTON, Director of Editorial Operations; RICKEY PURDIN, Director of Talent Relations; JENNIFER GRÜNWALD, Director of Production & Special Projects; SUSAN CRESPI, Production Manager; STAN LEE, Chairman Emeritus. For information regarding advertising in Marvel Comics or on Marvel.com, please contact Vit DeBellis, Custom Solutions & Integrated Advertising Manager, at vdebellis@marvel.com. For Marvel subscription inquiries, please call 888-511-5480. **Manufactured between 11/11/2022 and 12/13/2022 by SEAWAY PRINTING, GREEN BAY, WI, USA.**

10 9 8 7 6 5 4 3 2 1

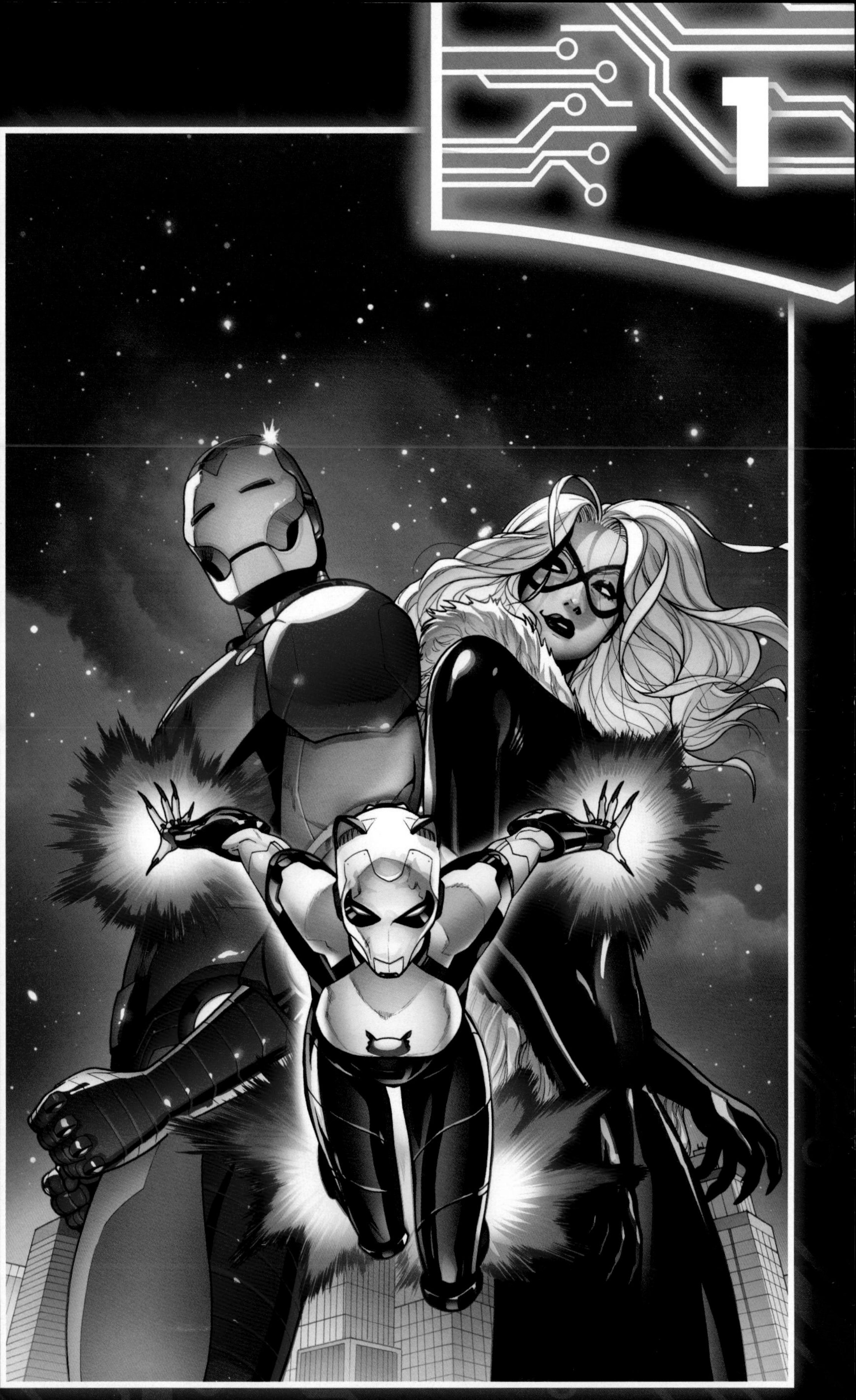
1

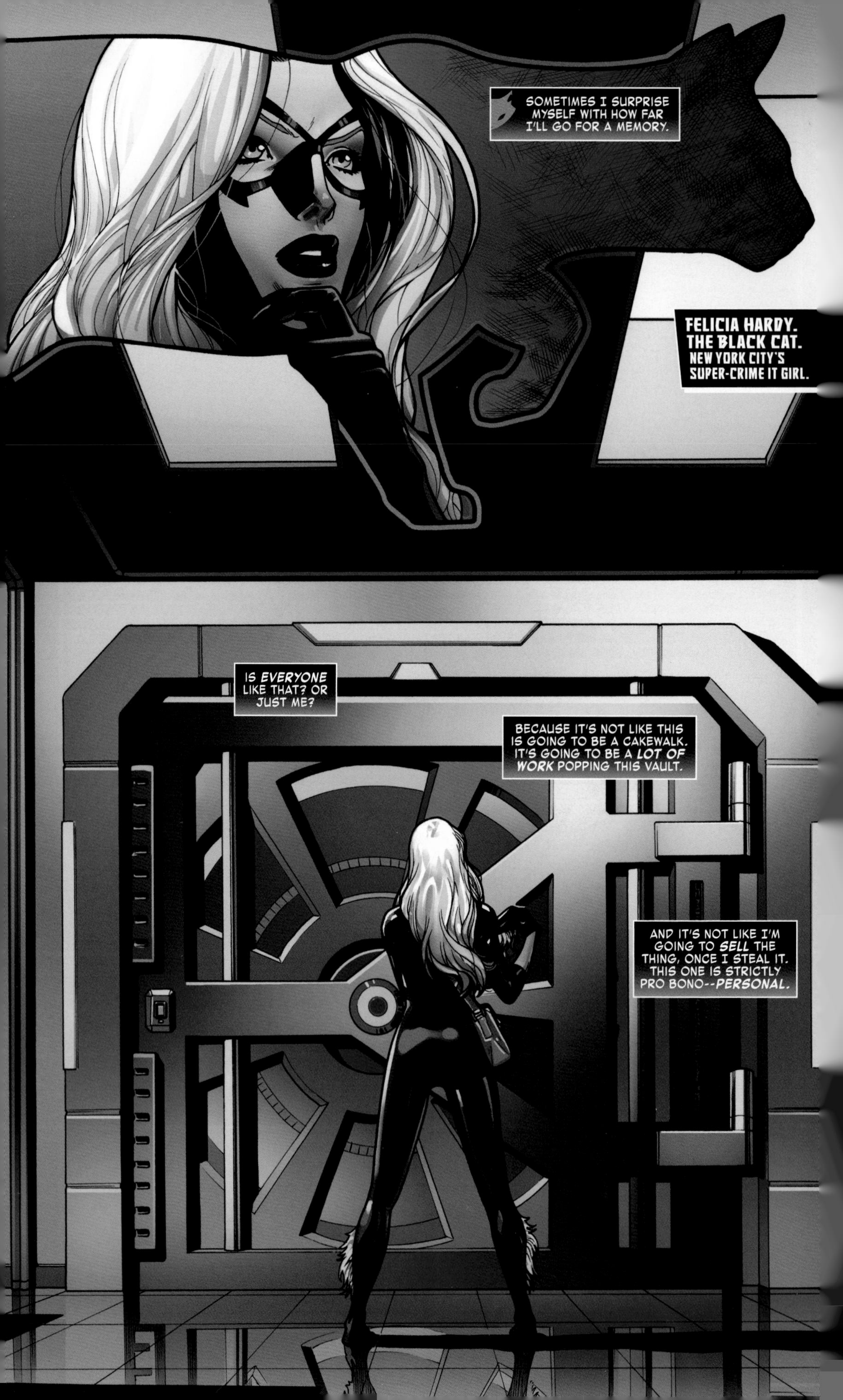
SOMETIMES I SURPRISE MYSELF WITH HOW FAR I'LL GO FOR A MEMORY.
FELICIA HARDY. THE BLACK CAT. NEW YORK CITY'S SUPER-CRIME IT GIRL.
IS EVERYONE LIKE THAT? OR JUST ME?
BECAUSE IT'S NOT LIKE THIS IS GOING TO BE A CAKEWALK. IT'S GOING TO BE A LOT OF WORK POPPING THIS VAULT.
AND IT'S NOT LIKE I'M GOING TO SELL THE THING, ONCE I STEAL IT. THIS ONE IS STRICTLY PRO BONO--PERSONAL.

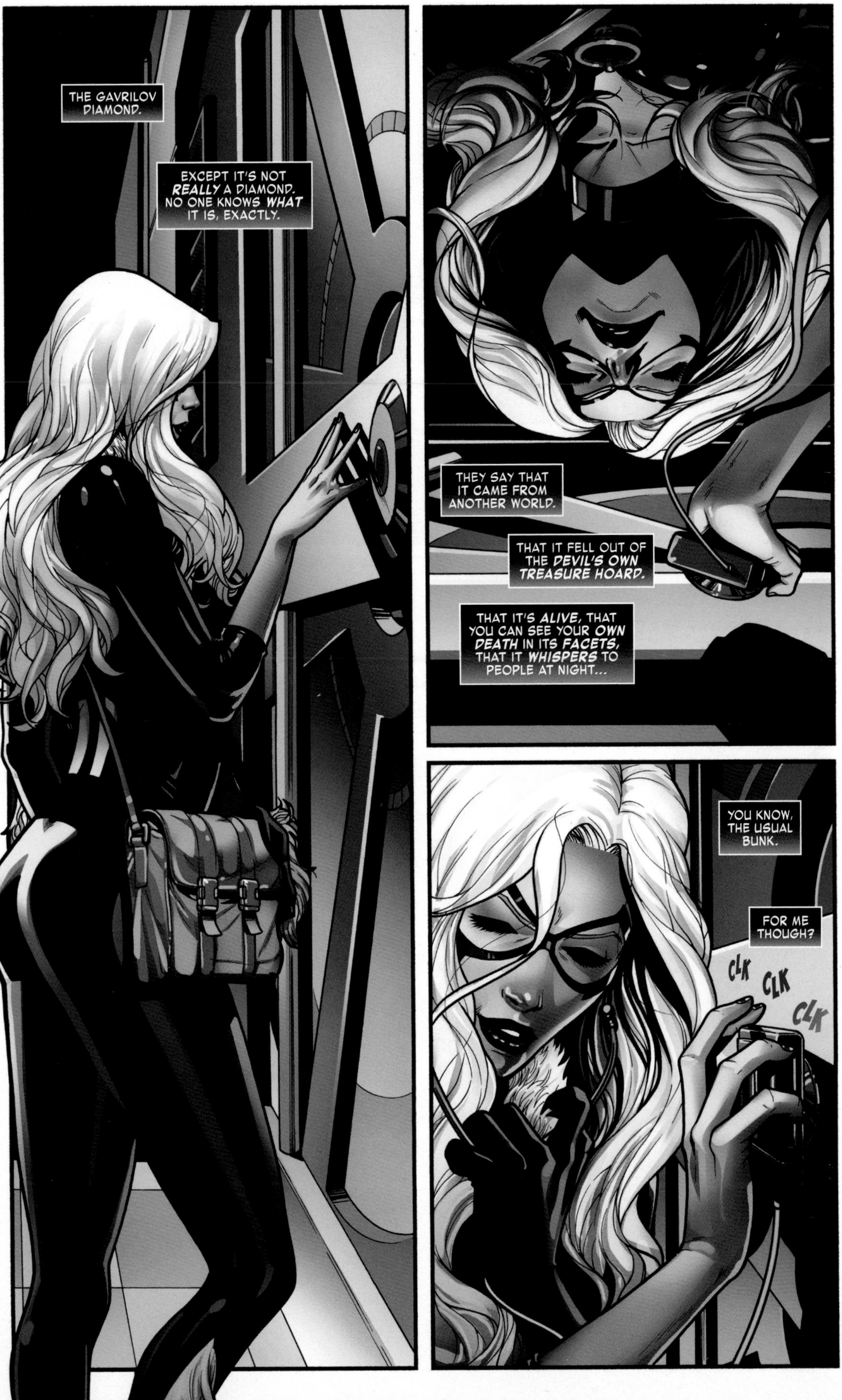
THE GAVRILOV DIAMOND.
EXCEPT IT'S NOT *REALLY* A DIAMOND. NO ONE KNOWS *WHAT* IT IS, EXACTLY.
THEY SAY THAT IT CAME FROM ANOTHER WORLD.
THAT IT FELL OUT OF THE *DEVIL'S OWN TREASURE HOARD.*
THAT IT'S *ALIVE,* THAT YOU CAN SEE YOUR *OWN DEATH* IN ITS *FACETS,* THAT IT *WHISPERS* TO PEOPLE AT NIGHT...
YOU KNOW, THE USUAL BUNK.
FOR ME THOUGH?
CLK
CLK
CLK

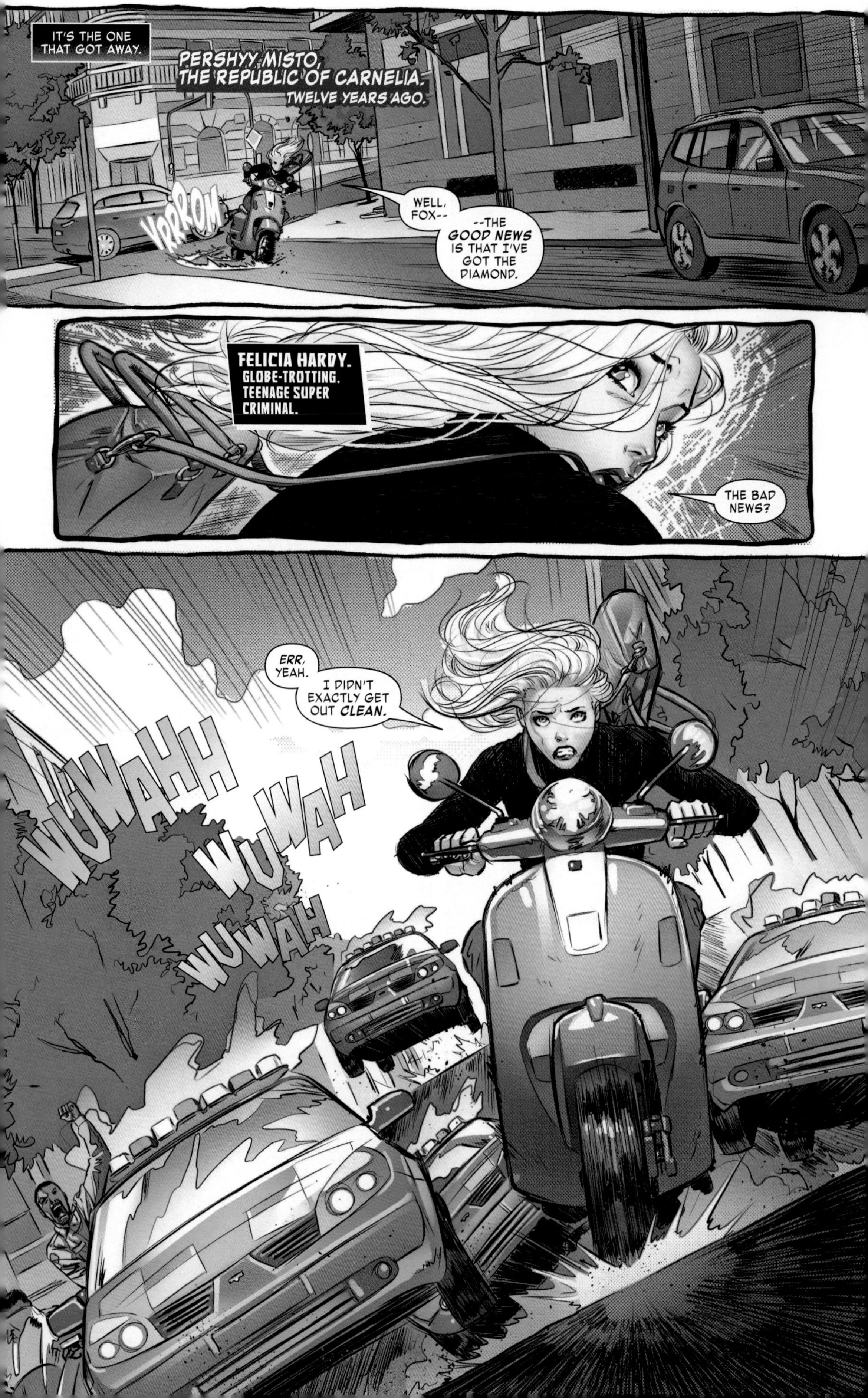
IT'S THE ONE THAT GOT AWAY.
PERSHYY MISTO, THE REPUBLIC OF CARNELIA.
TWELVE YEARS AGO.
VRRROM
WELL, FOX--
--THE GOOD NEWS IS THAT I'VE GOT THE DIAMOND.
FELICIA HARDY. GLOBE-TROTTING. TEENAGE SUPER CRIMINAL.
THE BAD NEWS?
ERR, YEAH.
I DIDN'T EXACTLY GET OUT CLEAN.
WUWAHH
WUWAH
WUWAH

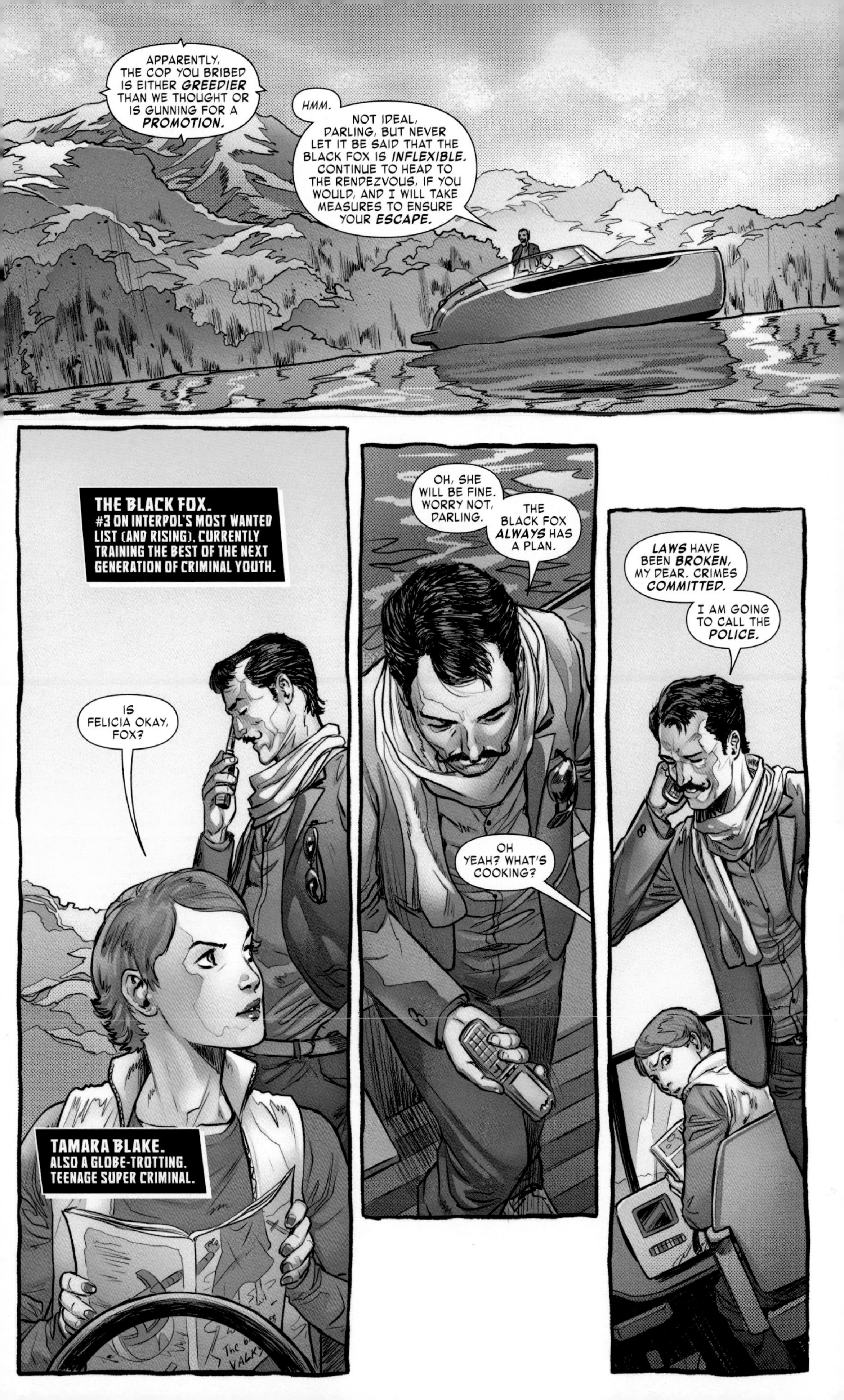
APPARENTLY, THE COP YOU BRIBED IS EITHER GREEDIER THAN WE THOUGHT OR IS GUNNING FOR A PROMOTION.
HMM.
NOT IDEAL, DARLING, BUT NEVER LET IT BE SAID THAT THE BLACK FOX IS INFLEXIBLE. CONTINUE TO HEAD TO THE RENDEZVOUS, IF YOU WOULD, AND I WILL TAKE MEASURES TO ENSURE YOUR ESCAPE.
THE BLACK FOX. #3 ON INTERPOL'S MOST WANTED LIST (AND RISING). CURRENTLY TRAINING THE BEST OF THE NEXT GENERATION OF CRIMINAL YOUTH.
IS FELICIA OKAY, FOX?
TAMARA BLAKE. ALSO A GLOBE-TROTTING. TEENAGE SUPER CRIMINAL.
OH, SHE WILL BE FINE. WORRY NOT, DARLING.
THE BLACK FOX ALWAYS HAS A PLAN.
OH YEAH? WHAT'S COOKING?
LAWS HAVE BEEN BROKEN, MY DEAR. CRIMES COMMITTED.
I AM GOING TO CALL THE POLICE.

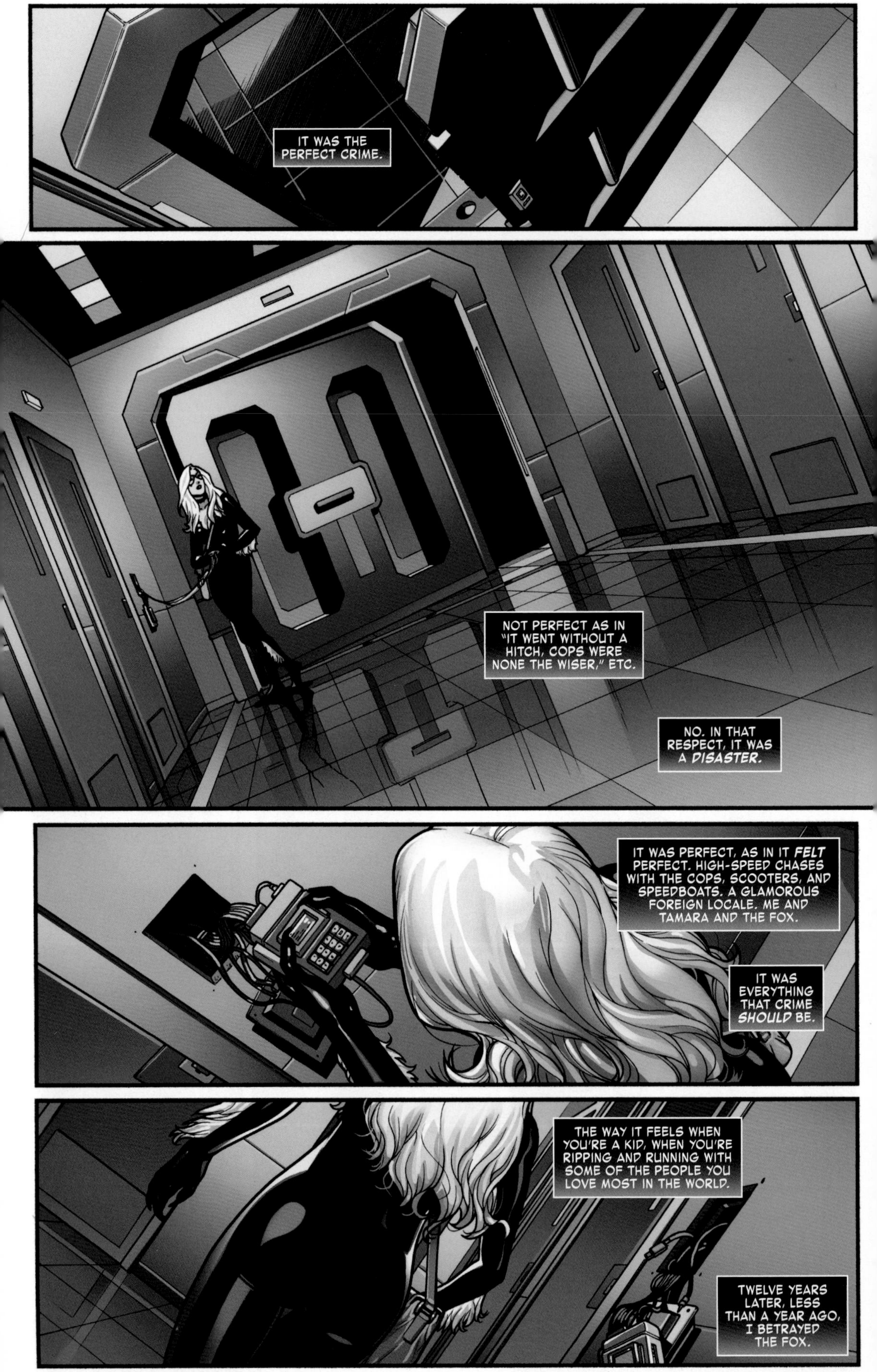
IT WAS THE PERFECT CRIME.
NOT PERFECT AS IN "IT WENT WITHOUT A HITCH, COPS WERE NONE THE WISER," ETC.
NO. IN THAT RESPECT, IT WAS A *DISASTER.*
IT WAS PERFECT, AS IN IT *FELT* PERFECT. HIGH-SPEED CHASES WITH THE COPS, SCOOTERS, AND SPEEDBOATS. A GLAMOROUS FOREIGN LOCALE. ME AND TAMARA AND THE FOX.
IT WAS EVERYTHING THAT CRIME *SHOULD* BE.
THE WAY IT FEELS WHEN YOU'RE A KID, WHEN YOU'RE RIPPING AND RUNNING WITH SOME OF THE PEOPLE YOU LOVE MOST IN THE WORLD.
TWELVE YEARS LATER, LESS THAN A YEAR AGO, I BETRAYED THE FOX.

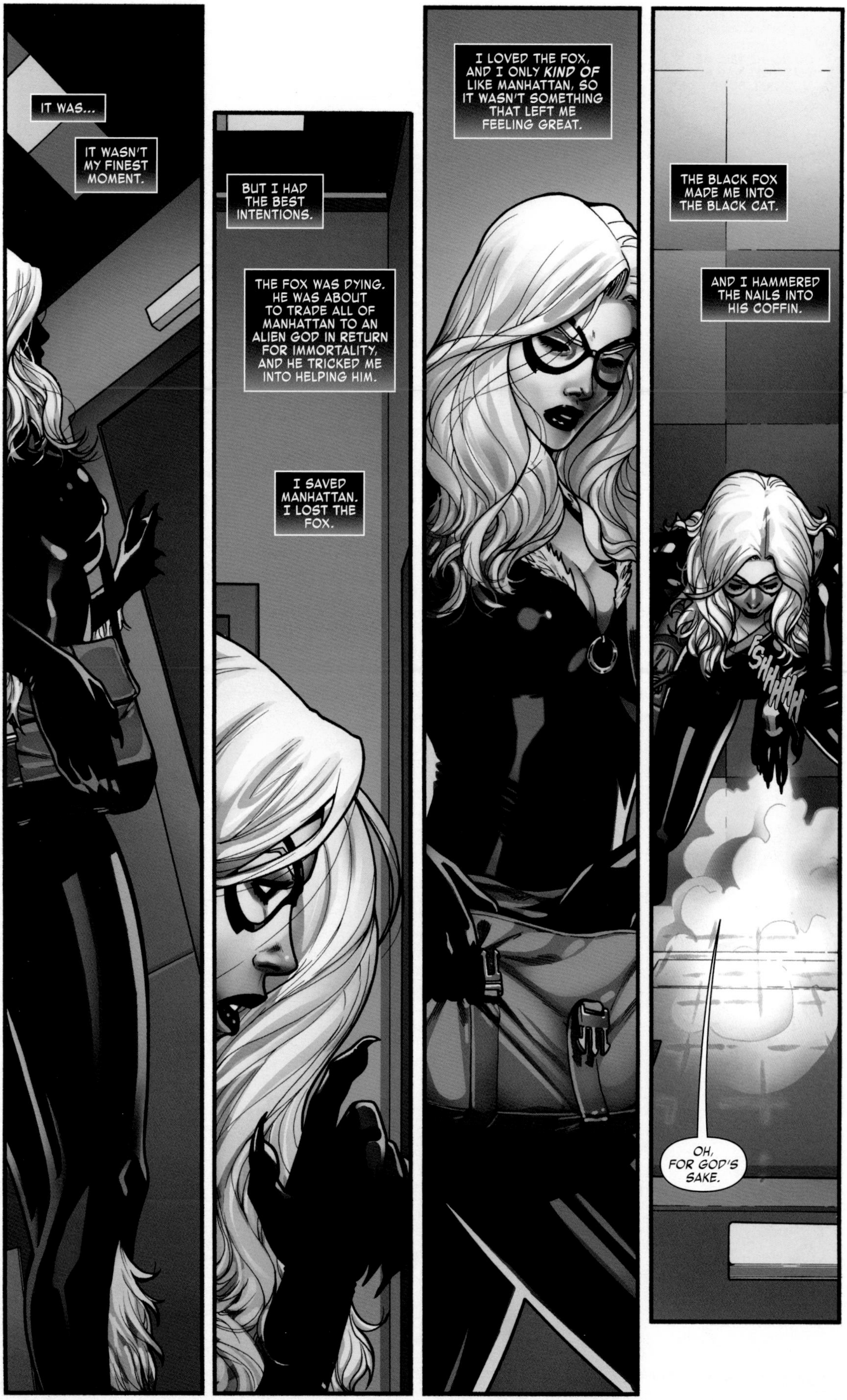

IT WAS...
IT WASN'T MY FINEST MOMENT.
BUT I HAD THE BEST INTENTIONS.
THE FOX WAS DYING. HE WAS ABOUT TO TRADE ALL OF MANHATTAN TO AN ALIEN GOD IN RETURN FOR IMMORTALITY, AND HE TRICKED ME INTO HELPING HIM.
I SAVED MANHATTAN. I LOST THE FOX.
I LOVED THE FOX, AND I ONLY KIND OF LIKE MANHATTAN, SO IT WASN'T SOMETHING THAT LEFT ME FEELING GREAT.
THE BLACK FOX MADE ME INTO THE BLACK CAT.
AND I HAMMERED THE NAILS INTO HIS COFFIN.
FSHHHHH
OH, FOR GOD'S SAKE.

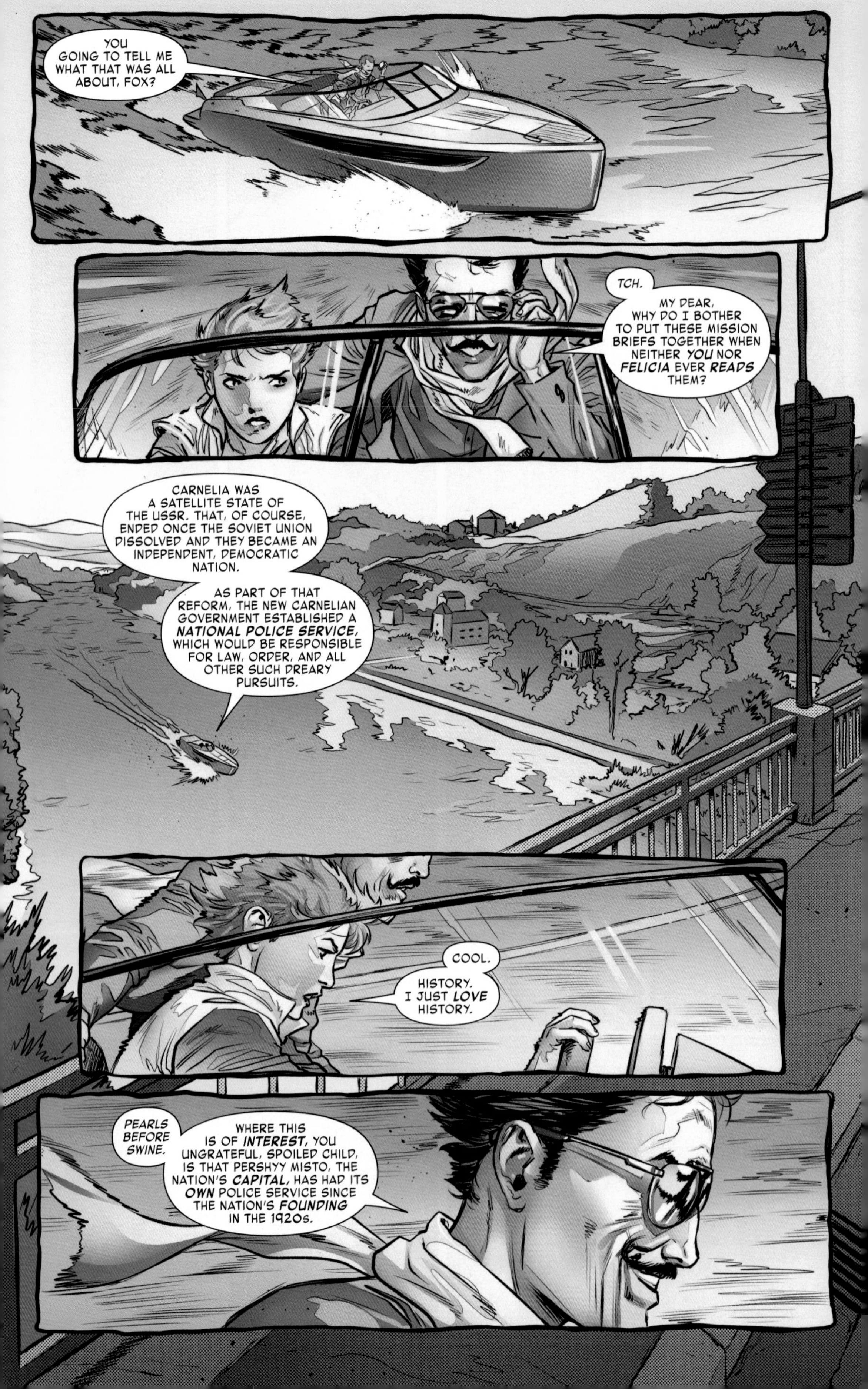
YOU GOING TO TELL ME WHAT THAT WAS ALL ABOUT, FOX?
TCH.
MY DEAR, WHY DO I BOTHER TO PUT THESE MISSION BRIEFS TOGETHER WHEN NEITHER *YOU* NOR *FELICIA* EVER *READS* THEM?
CARNELIA WAS A SATELLITE STATE OF THE USSR. THAT, OF COURSE, ENDED ONCE THE SOVIET UNION DISSOLVED AND THEY BECAME AN INDEPENDENT, DEMOCRATIC NATION.
AS PART OF THAT REFORM, THE NEW CARNELIAN GOVERNMENT ESTABLISHED A *NATIONAL POLICE SERVICE,* WHICH WOULD BE RESPONSIBLE FOR LAW, ORDER, AND ALL OTHER SUCH DREARY PURSUITS.
COOL.
HISTORY. I JUST *LOVE* HISTORY.
PEARLS BEFORE SWINE.
WHERE THIS IS OF *INTEREST,* YOU UNGRATEFUL, SPOILED CHILD, IS THAT PERSHYY MISTO, THE NATION'S *CAPITAL,* HAS HAD ITS *OWN* POLICE SERVICE SINCE THE NATION'S *FOUNDING* IN THE 1920s.

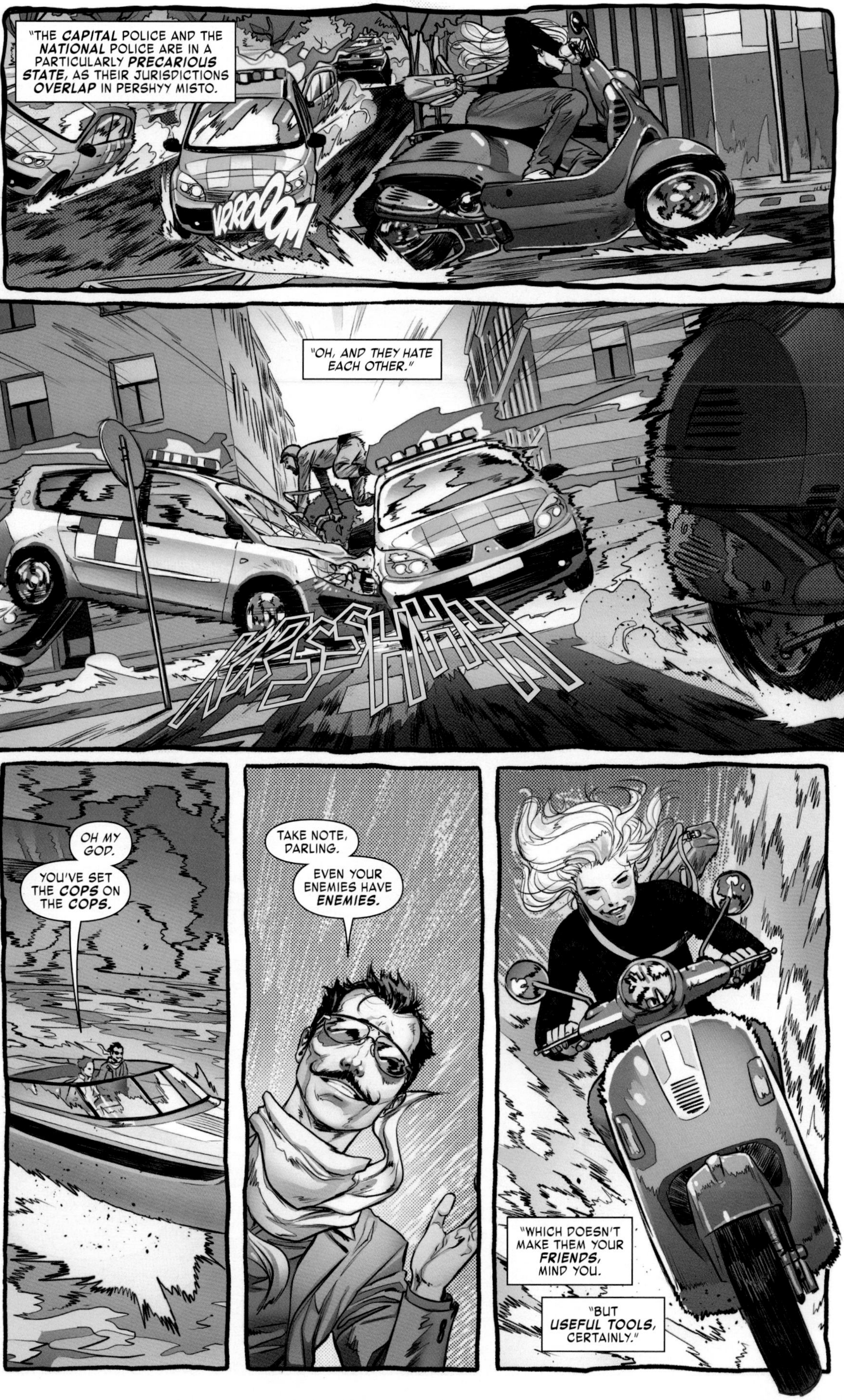
"THE CAPITAL POLICE AND THE NATIONAL POLICE ARE IN A PARTICULARLY PRECARIOUS STATE, AS THEIR JURISDICTIONS OVERLAP IN PERSHYY MISTO.
VRROOOM
"OH, AND THEY HATE EACH OTHER."
OH MY GOD.
YOU'VE SET THE COPS ON THE COPS.
TAKE NOTE, DARLING.
EVEN YOUR ENEMIES HAVE ENEMIES.
"WHICH DOESN'T MAKE THEM YOUR FRIENDS, MIND YOU.
"BUT USEFUL TOOLS, CERTAINLY."

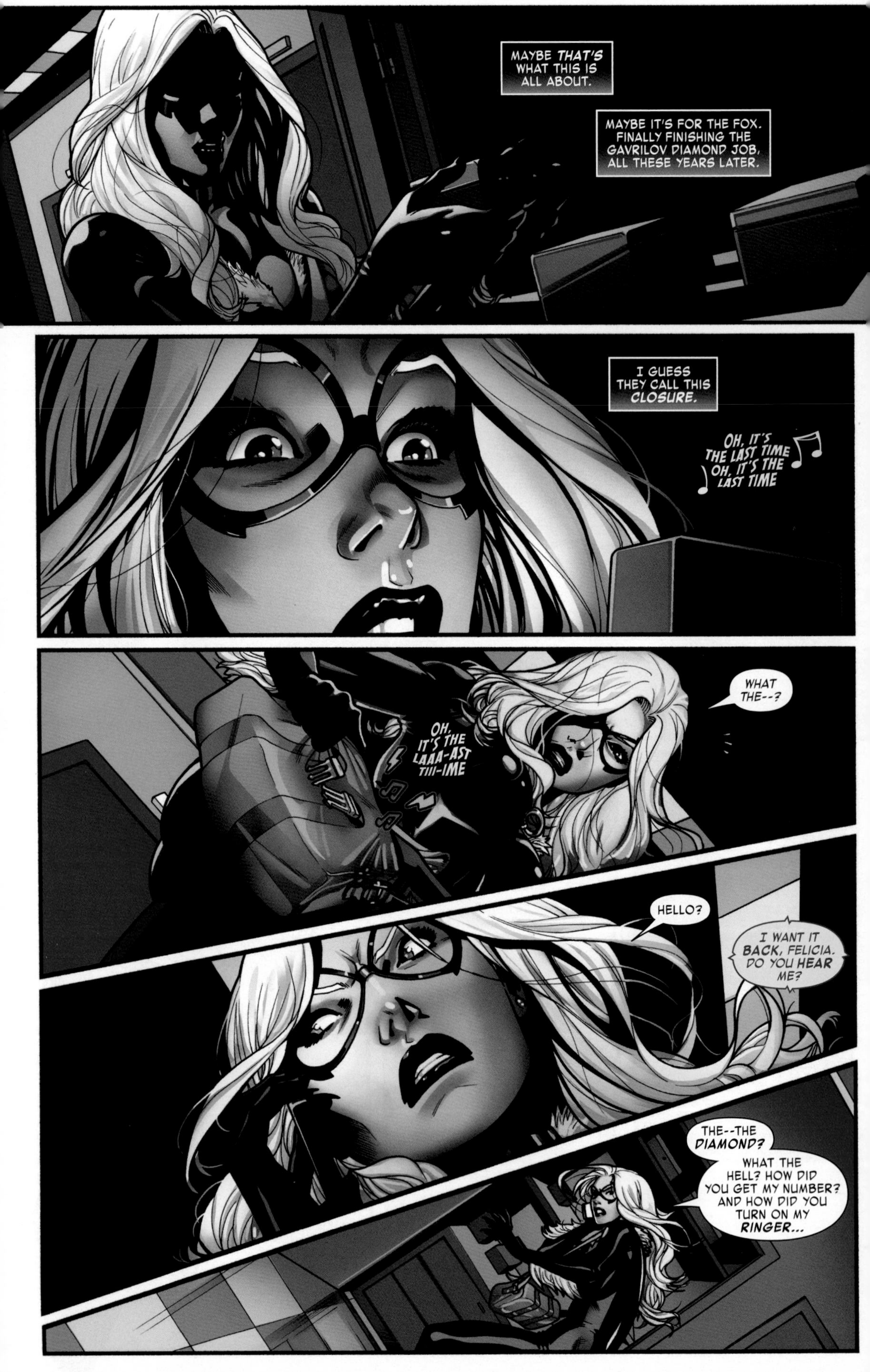
MAYBE THAT'S WHAT THIS IS ALL ABOUT.
MAYBE IT'S FOR THE FOX. FINALLY FINISHING THE GAVRILOV DIAMOND JOB, ALL THESE YEARS LATER.
I GUESS THEY CALL THIS CLOSURE.
OH, IT'S THE LAST TIME OH, IT'S THE LAST TIME
WHAT THE--?
OH, IT'S THE LAAA-AST TIII-IME
HELLO?
I WANT IT BACK, FELICIA. DO YOU HEAR ME?
THE--THE DIAMOND?
WHAT THE HELL? HOW DID YOU GET MY NUMBER? AND HOW DID YOU TURN ON MY RINGER...

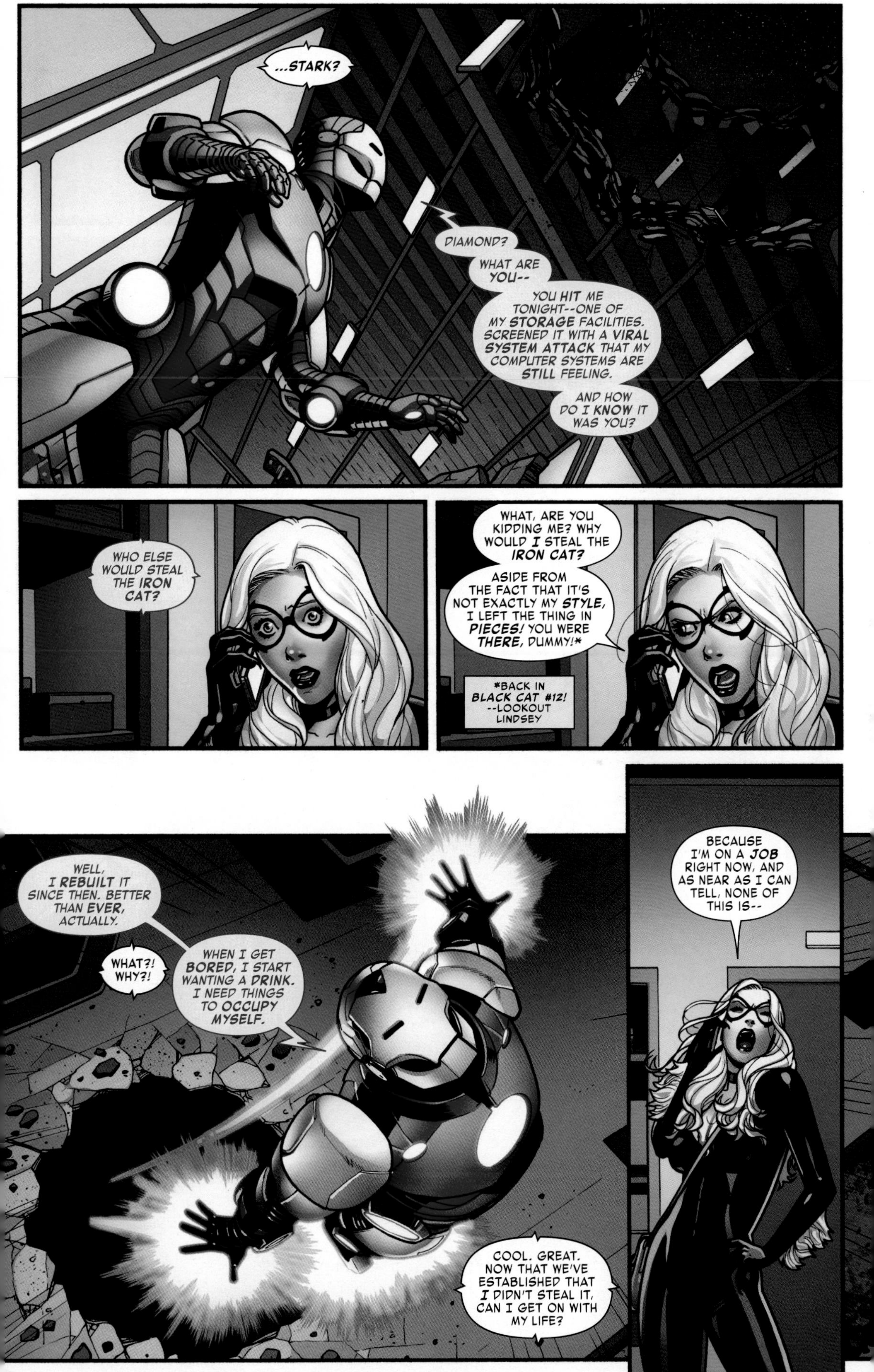
...STARK?
DIAMOND?
WHAT ARE YOU--
YOU HIT ME TONIGHT--ONE OF MY STORAGE FACILITIES. SCREENED IT WITH A VIRAL SYSTEM ATTACK THAT MY COMPUTER SYSTEMS ARE STILL FEELING.
AND HOW DO I KNOW IT WAS YOU?
WHO ELSE WOULD STEAL THE IRON CAT?
WHAT, ARE YOU KIDDING ME? WHY WOULD I STEAL THE IRON CAT?
ASIDE FROM THE FACT THAT IT'S NOT EXACTLY MY STYLE, I LEFT THE THING IN PIECES! YOU WERE THERE, DUMMY!*
*BACK IN BLACK CAT #12! --LOOKOUT LINDSEY
WELL, I REBUILT IT SINCE THEN. BETTER THAN EVER, ACTUALLY.
WHAT?! WHY?!
WHEN I GET BORED, I START WANTING A DRINK. I NEED THINGS TO OCCUPY MYSELF.
BECAUSE I'M ON A JOB RIGHT NOW, AND AS NEAR AS I CAN TELL, NONE OF THIS IS--
COOL. GREAT. NOW THAT WE'VE ESTABLISHED THAT I DIDN'T STEAL IT, CAN I GET ON WITH MY LIFE?

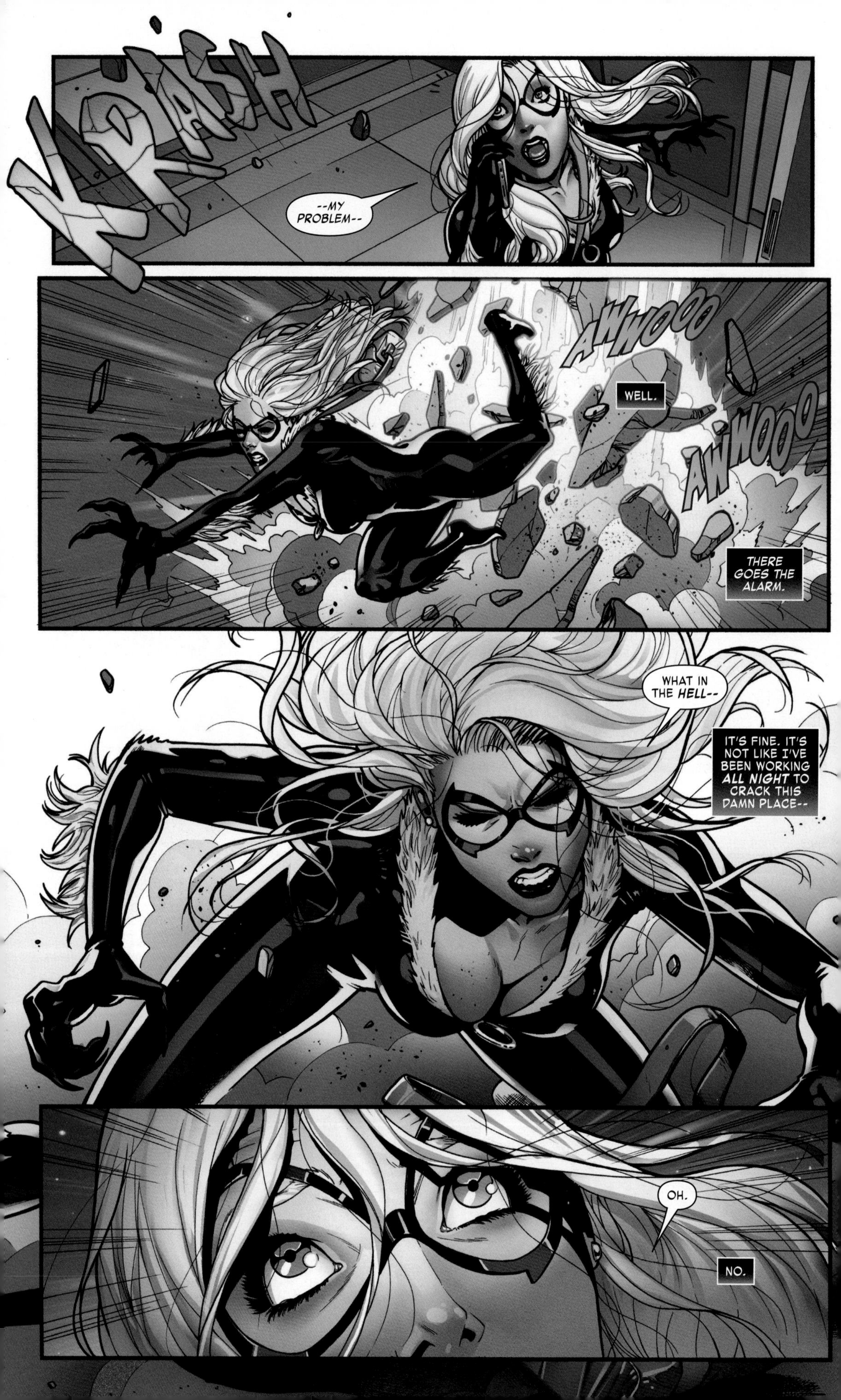
KRASH
--MY PROBLEM--
AWWOOO
WELL.
AWWOOO
THERE GOES THE ALARM.
WHAT IN THE HELL--
IT'S FINE. IT'S NOT LIKE I'VE BEEN WORKING ALL NIGHT TO CRACK THIS DAMN PLACE--
OH.
NO.

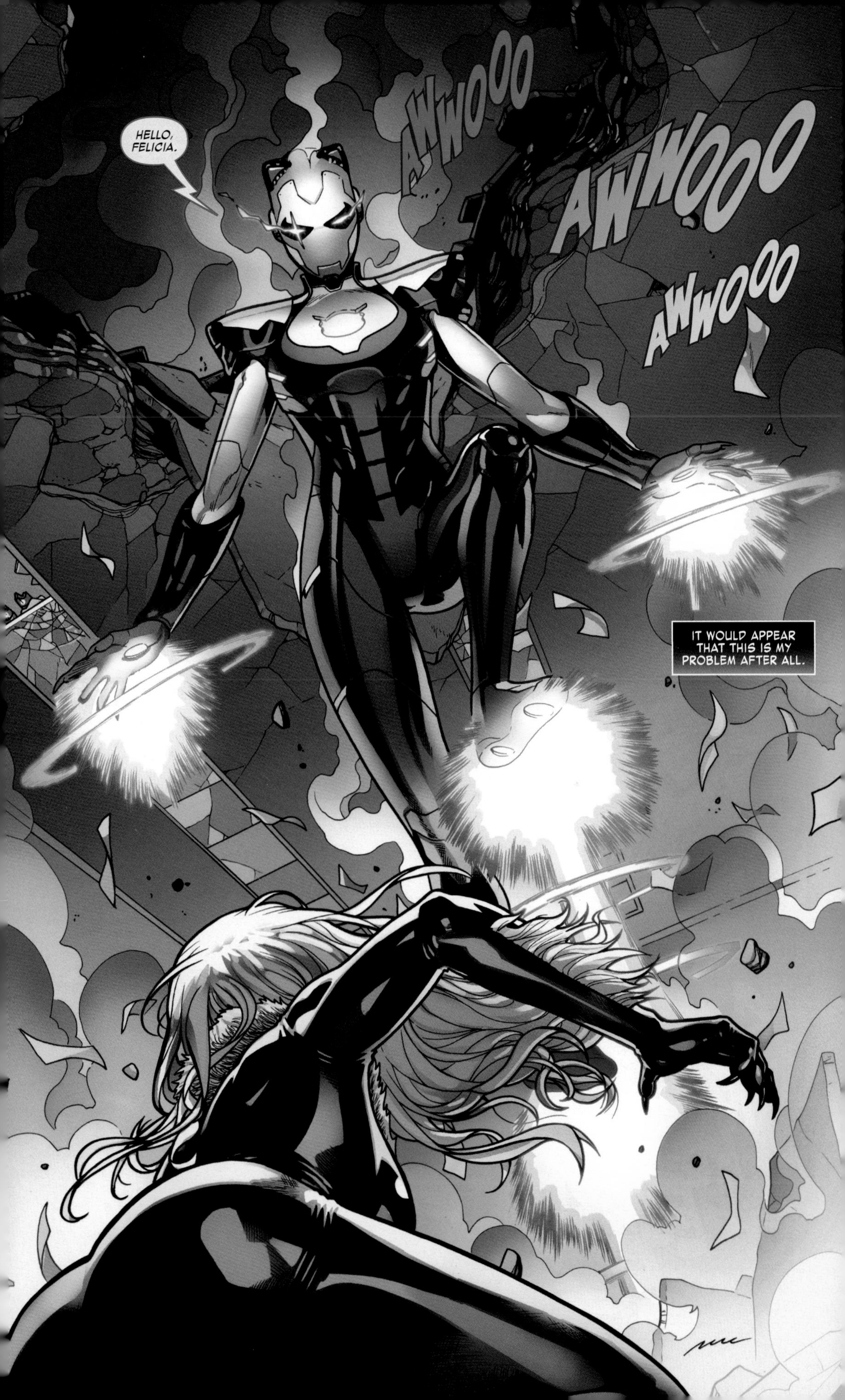
HELLO, FELICIA.
AWWOOO
AWWOOO
AWWOOO
IT WOULD APPEAR THAT THIS IS MY PROBLEM AFTER ALL.

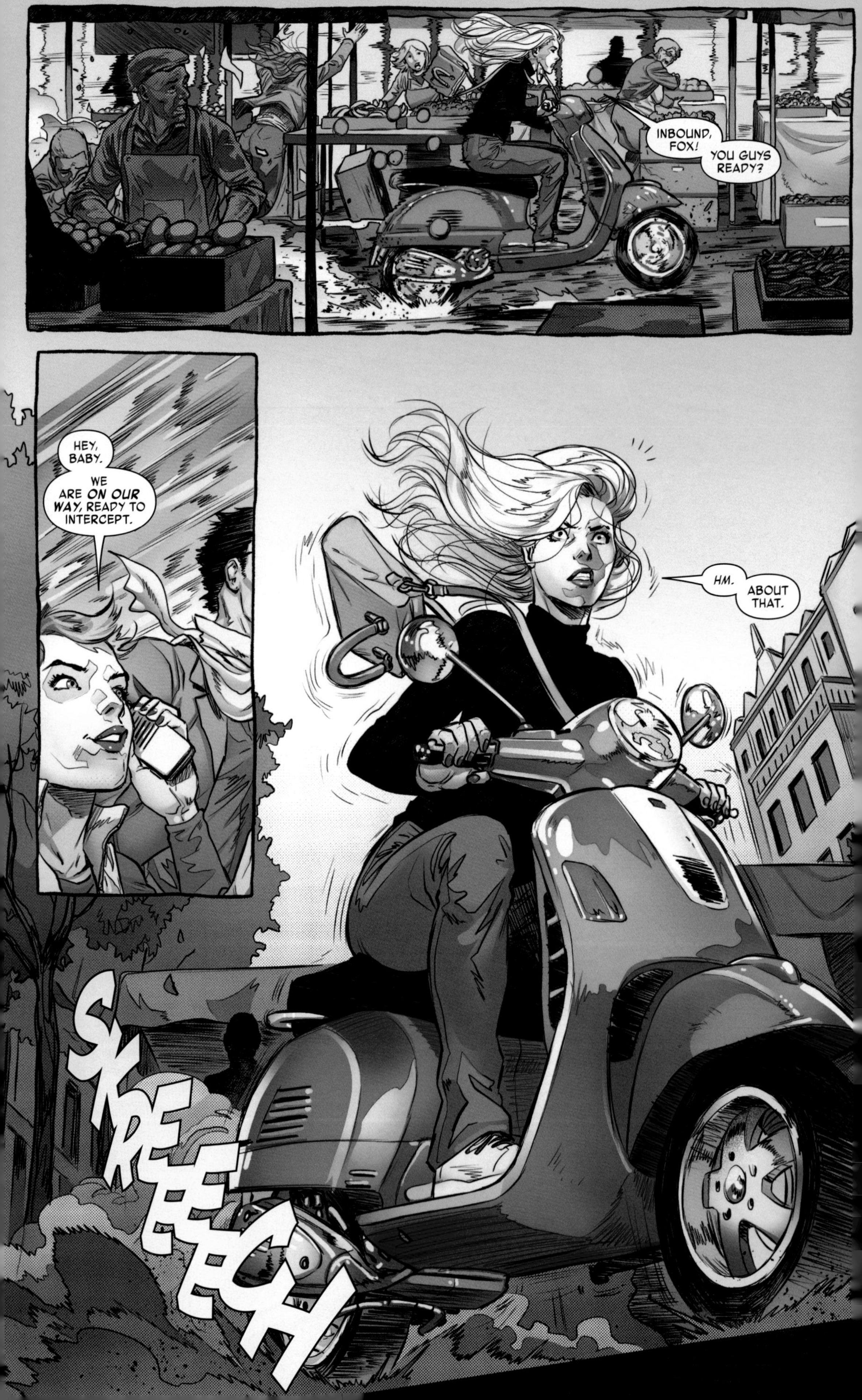
INBOUND, FOX!
YOU GUYS READY?
HEY, BABY.
WE ARE ON OUR WAY, READY TO INTERCEPT.
HM.
ABOUT THAT.
SKREEEECH

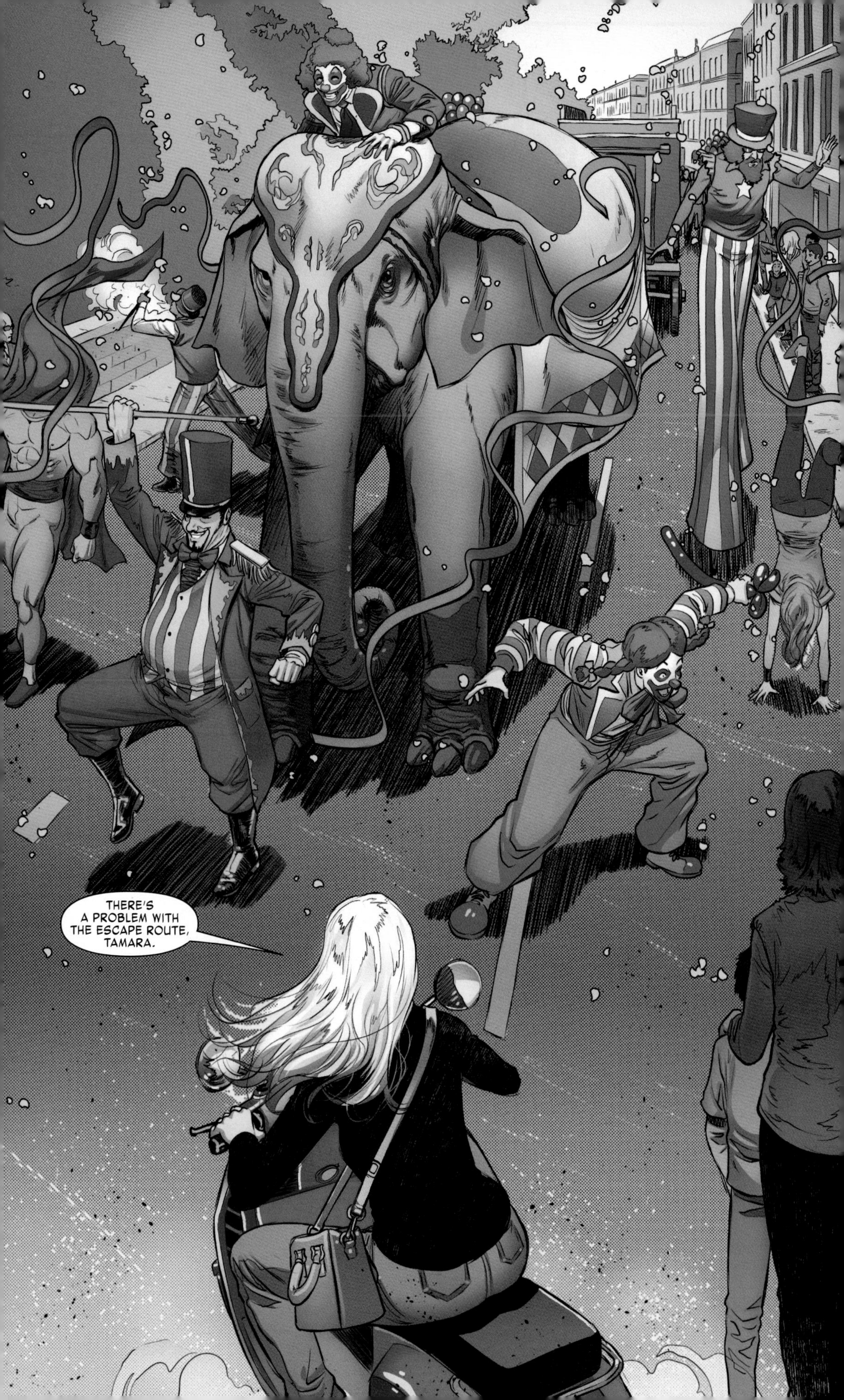
THERE'S A PROBLEM WITH THE ESCAPE ROUTE, TAMARA.

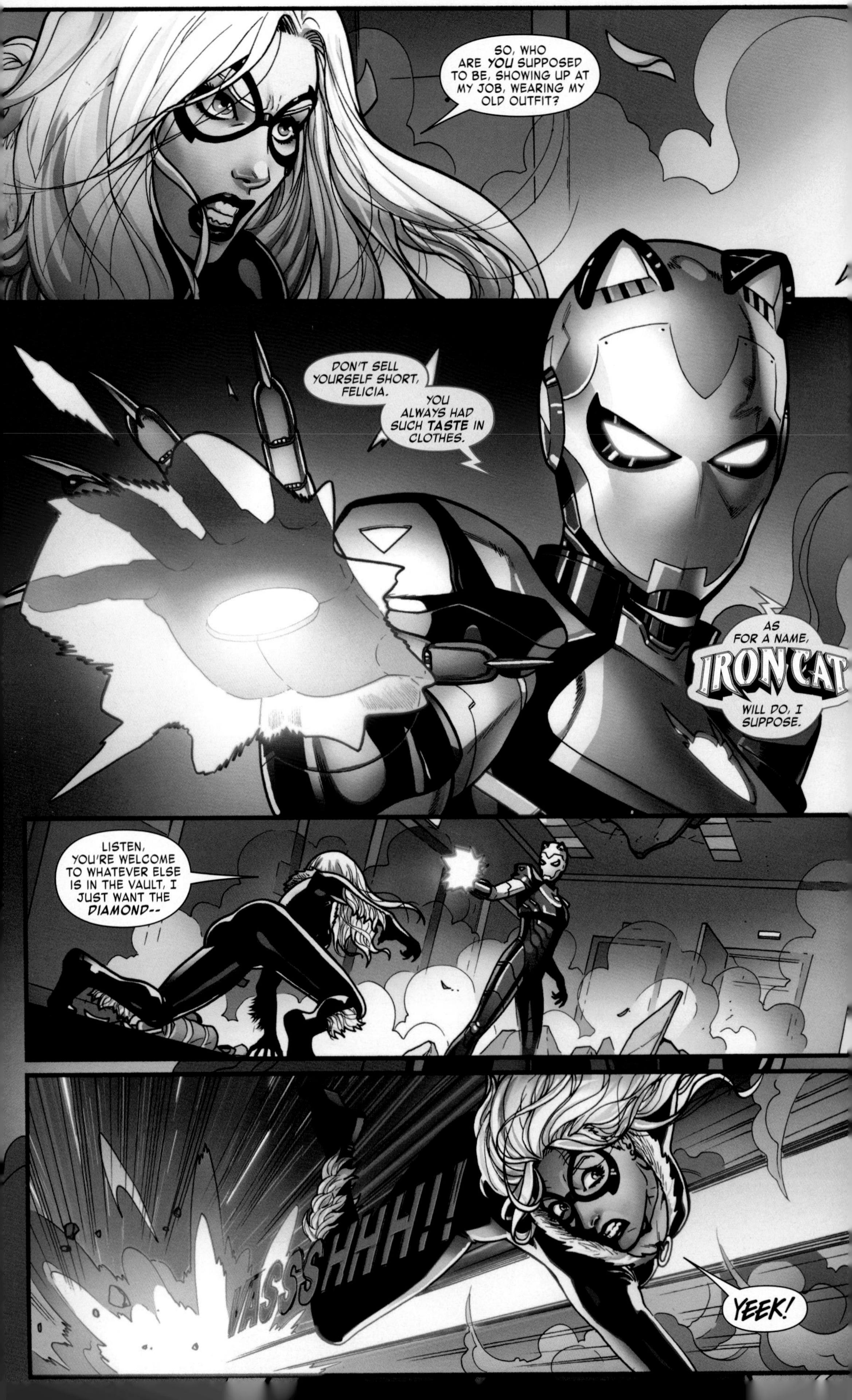
SO, WHO ARE YOU SUPPOSED TO BE, SHOWING UP AT MY JOB, WEARING MY OLD OUTFIT?
DON'T SELL YOURSELF SHORT, FELICIA.
YOU ALWAYS HAD SUCH TASTE IN CLOTHES.
AS FOR A NAME, IRONCAT WILL DO, I SUPPOSE.
LISTEN, YOU'RE WELCOME TO WHATEVER ELSE IS IN THE VAULT, I JUST WANT THE DIAMOND--
YEEK!

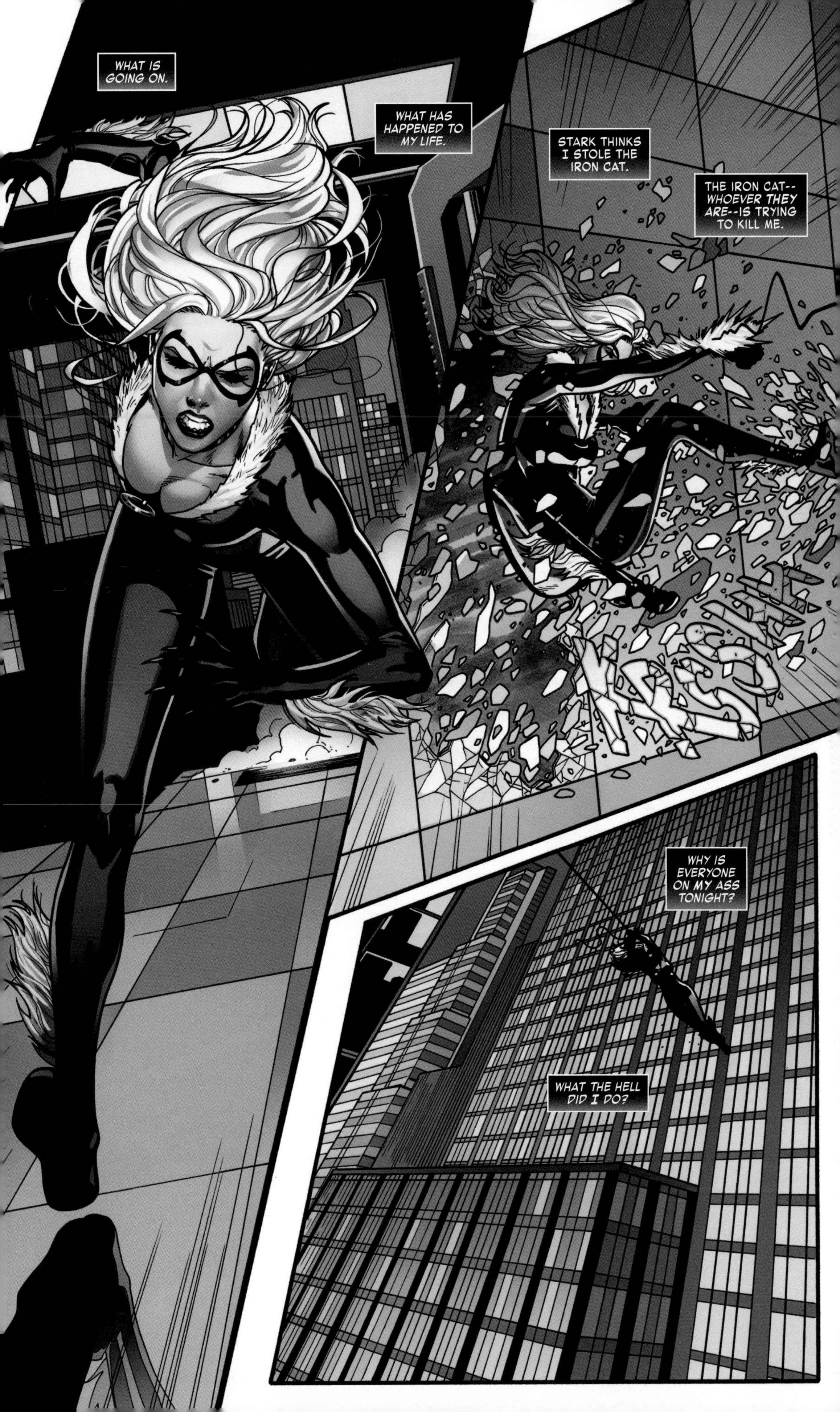
WHAT IS GOING ON.
WHAT HAS HAPPENED TO MY LIFE.
STARK THINKS I STOLE THE IRON CAT.
THE IRON CAT--WHOEVER THEY ARE--IS TRYING TO KILL ME.
WHY IS EVERYONE ON MY ASS TONIGHT?
WHAT THE HELL DID I DO?

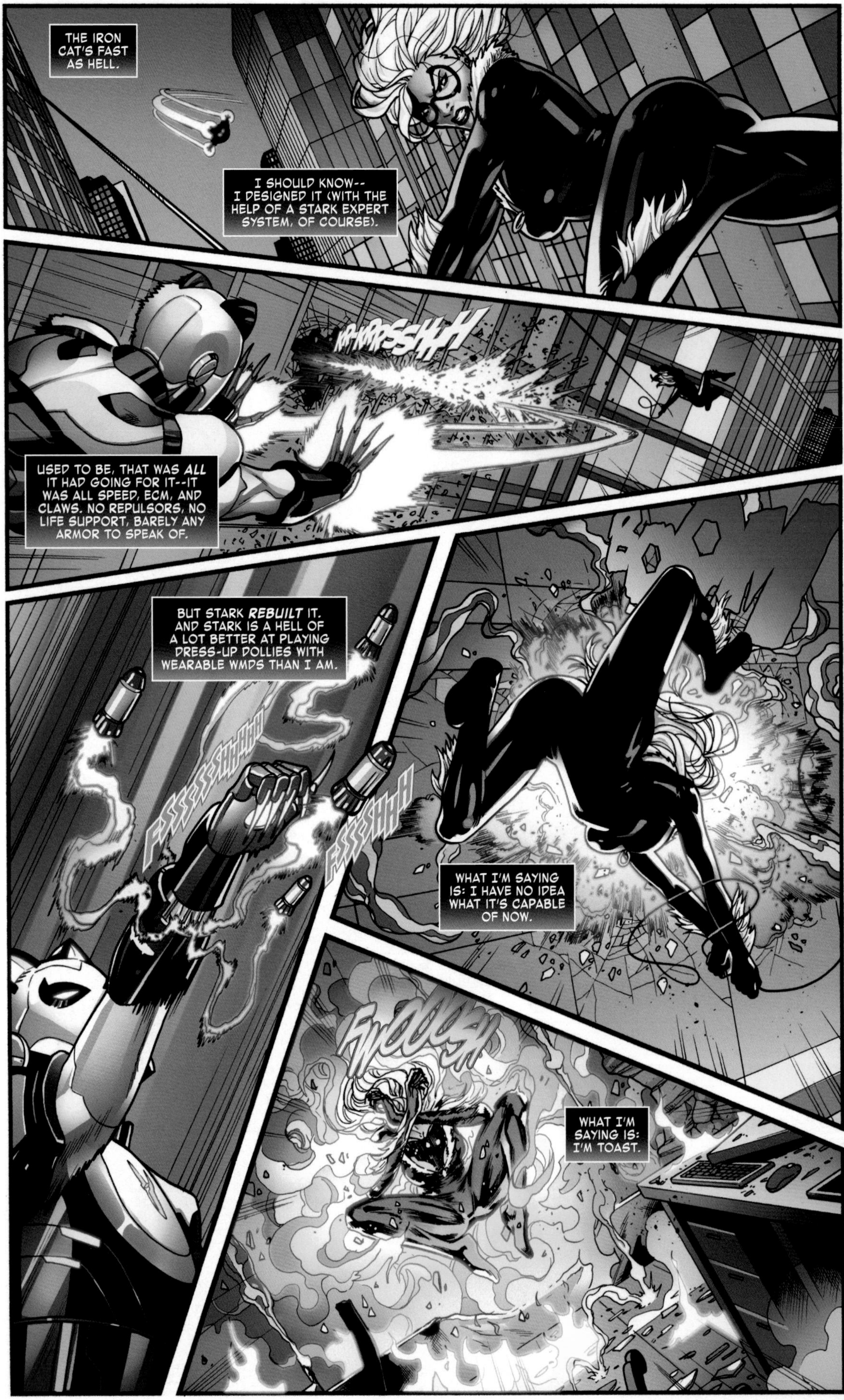

THE IRON CAT'S FAST AS HELL.
I SHOULD KNOW-- I DESIGNED IT (WITH THE HELP OF A STARK EXPERT SYSTEM, OF COURSE).
KR-KRRSSHHH
USED TO BE, THAT WAS ALL IT HAD GOING FOR IT--IT WAS ALL SPEED, ECM, AND CLAWS. NO REPULSORS, NO LIFE SUPPORT, BARELY ANY ARMOR TO SPEAK OF.
BUT STARK REBUILT IT. AND STARK IS A HELL OF A LOT BETTER AT PLAYING DRESS-UP DOLLIES WITH WEARABLE WMDS THAN I AM.
F-SSSSHHH
FSSSSHHH
WHAT I'M SAYING IS: I HAVE NO IDEA WHAT IT'S CAPABLE OF NOW.
FWOOSH
WHAT I'M SAYING IS: I'M TOAST.

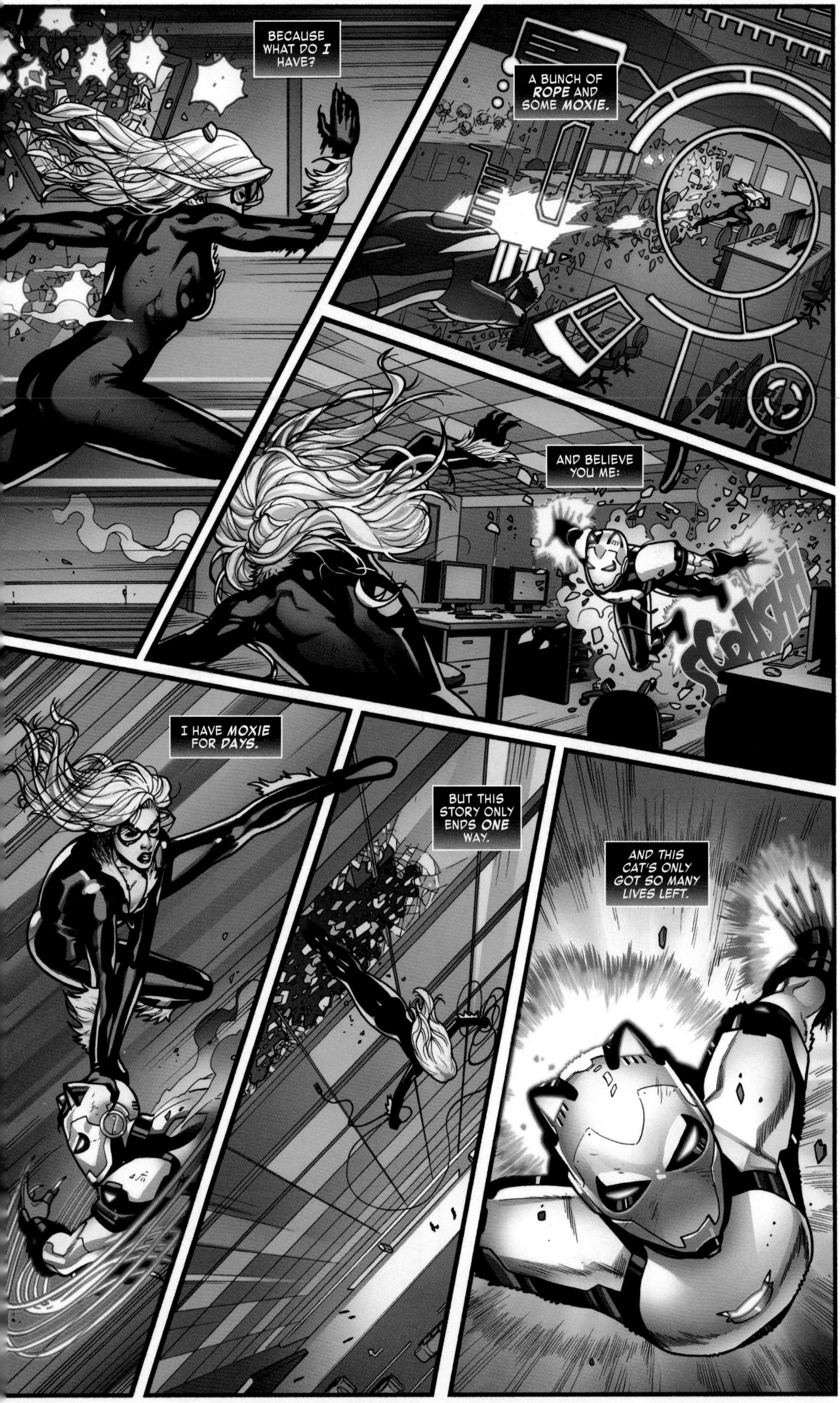

BECAUSE WHAT DO *I* HAVE?
A BUNCH OF *ROPE* AND SOME *MOXIE.*
AND BELIEVE YOU ME:
SSPLASH
I HAVE *MOXIE* FOR *DAYS.*
BUT THIS STORY ONLY ENDS *ONE* WAY.
AND THIS CAT'S ONLY GOT SO MANY LIVES LEFT.

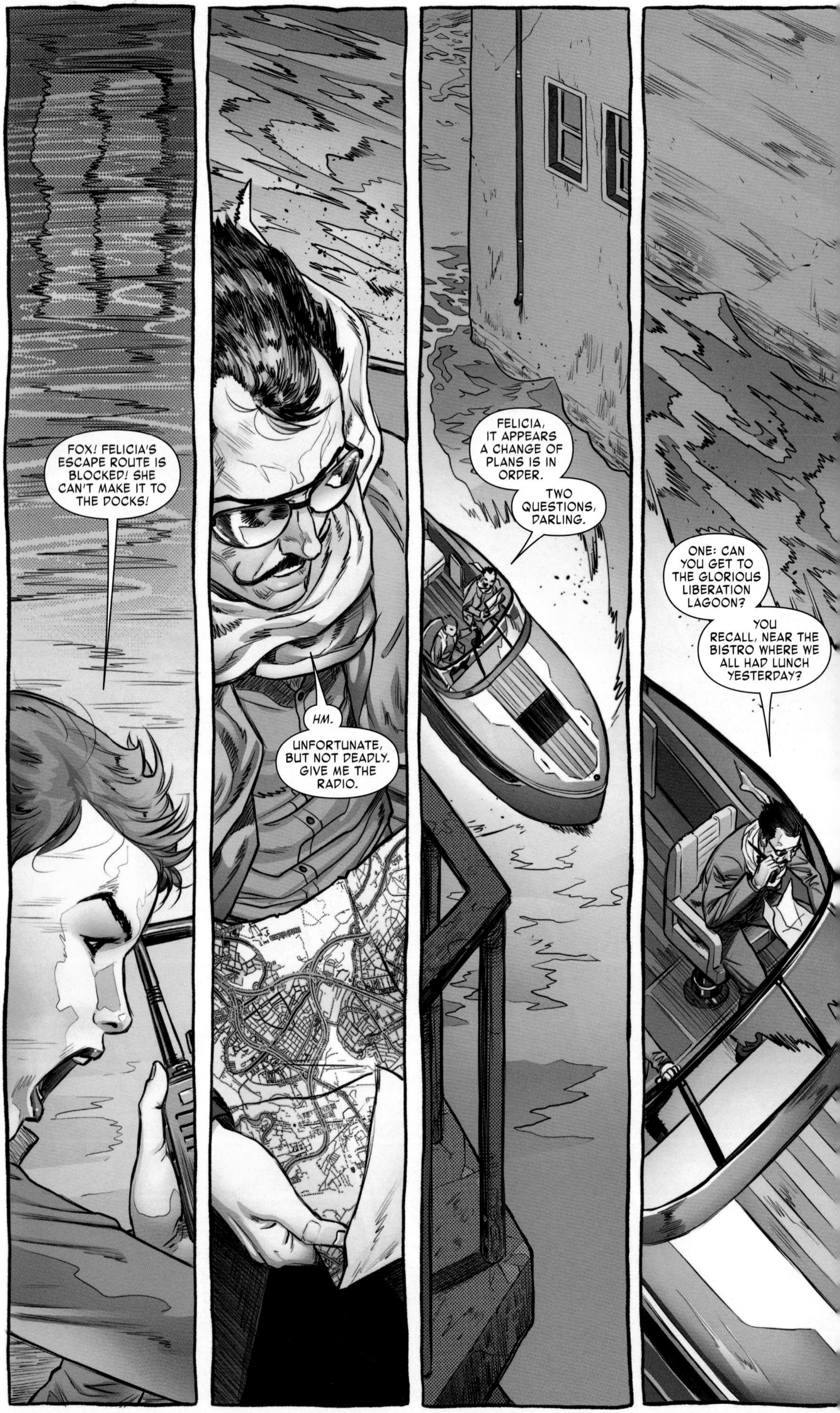
FOX! FELICIA'S ESCAPE ROUTE IS BLOCKED! SHE CAN'T MAKE IT TO THE DOCKS!
HM.
UNFORTUNATE, BUT NOT DEADLY. GIVE ME THE RADIO.
FELICIA, IT APPEARS A CHANGE OF PLANS IS IN ORDER.
TWO QUESTIONS, DARLING.
ONE: CAN YOU GET TO THE GLORIOUS LIBERATION LAGOON?
YOU RECALL, NEAR THE BISTRO WHERE WE ALL HAD LUNCH YESTERDAY?

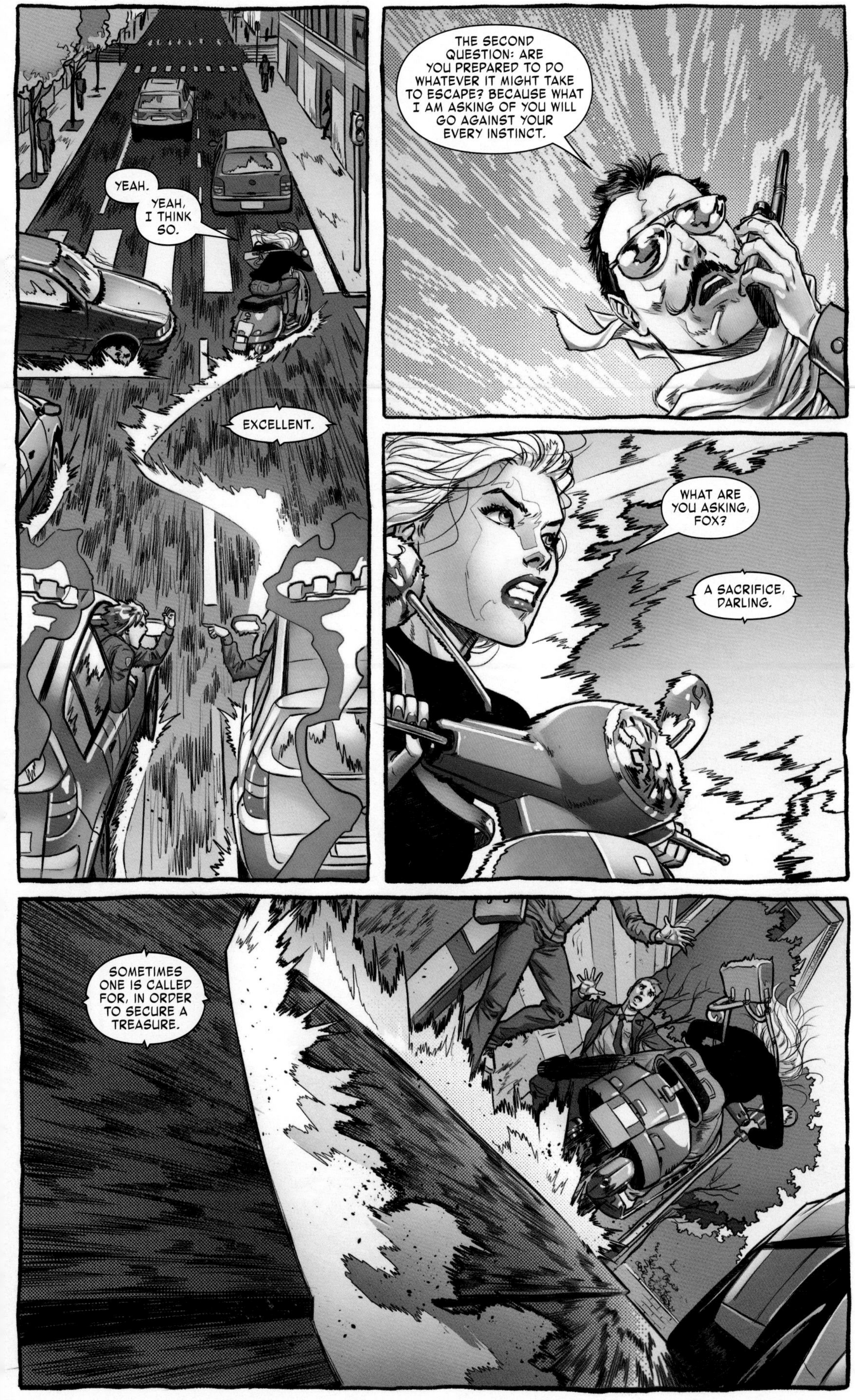
YEAH.
YEAH, I THINK SO.
EXCELLENT.
THE SECOND QUESTION: ARE YOU PREPARED TO DO WHATEVER IT MIGHT TAKE TO ESCAPE? BECAUSE WHAT I AM ASKING OF YOU WILL GO AGAINST YOUR EVERY INSTINCT.
WHAT ARE YOU ASKING, FOX?
A SACRIFICE, DARLING.
SOMETIMES ONE IS CALLED FOR, IN ORDER TO SECURE A TREASURE.

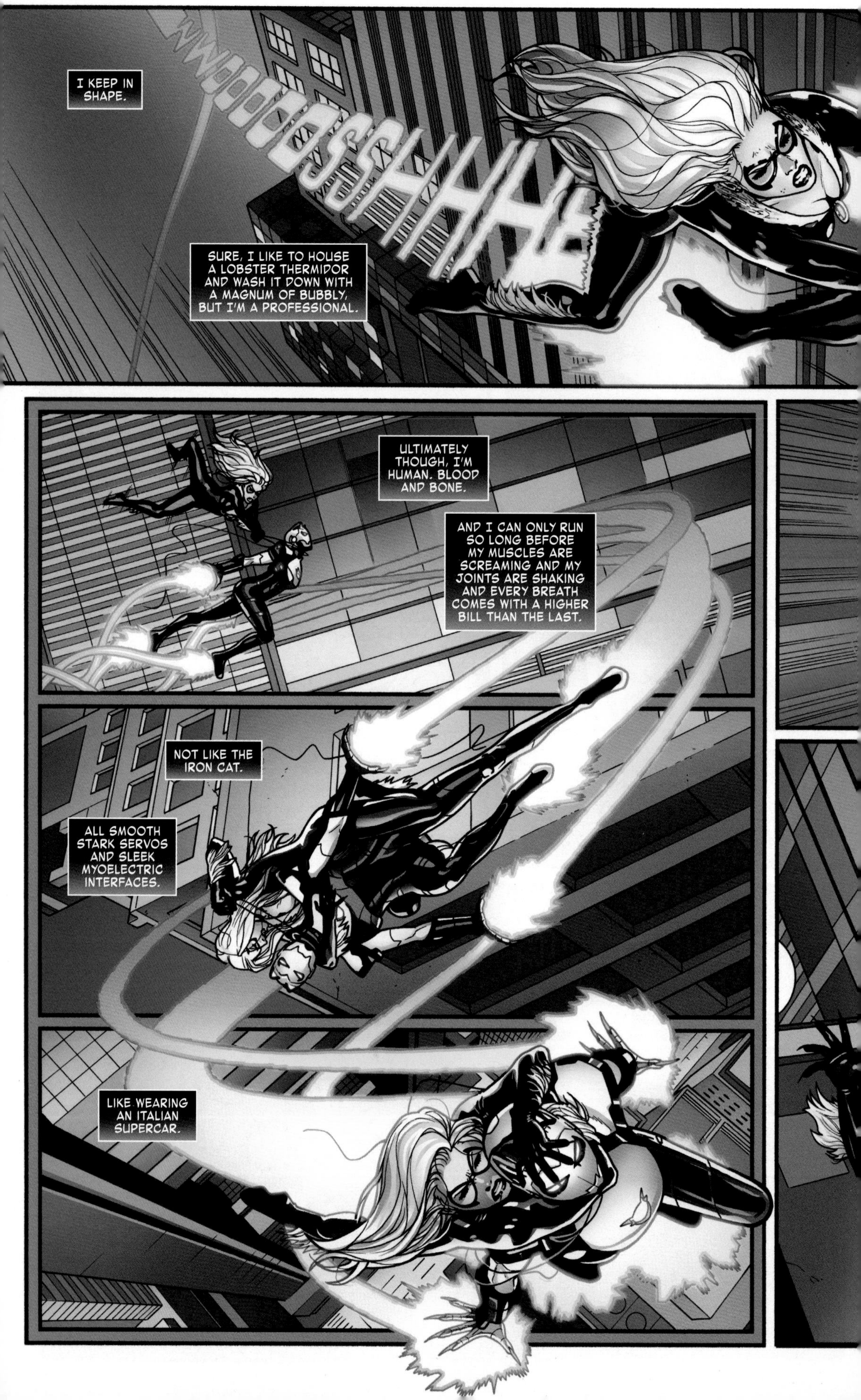

I KEEP IN SHAPE.
SURE, I LIKE TO HOUSE A LOBSTER THERMIDOR AND WASH IT DOWN WITH A MAGNUM OF BUBBLY, BUT I'M A PROFESSIONAL.
ULTIMATELY THOUGH, I'M HUMAN. BLOOD AND BONE.
AND I CAN ONLY RUN SO LONG BEFORE MY MUSCLES ARE SCREAMING AND MY JOINTS ARE SHAKING AND EVERY BREATH COMES WITH A HIGHER BILL THAN THE LAST.
NOT LIKE THE IRON CAT.
ALL SMOOTH STARK SERVOS AND SLEEK MYOELECTRIC INTERFACES.
LIKE WEARING AN ITALIAN SUPERCAR.

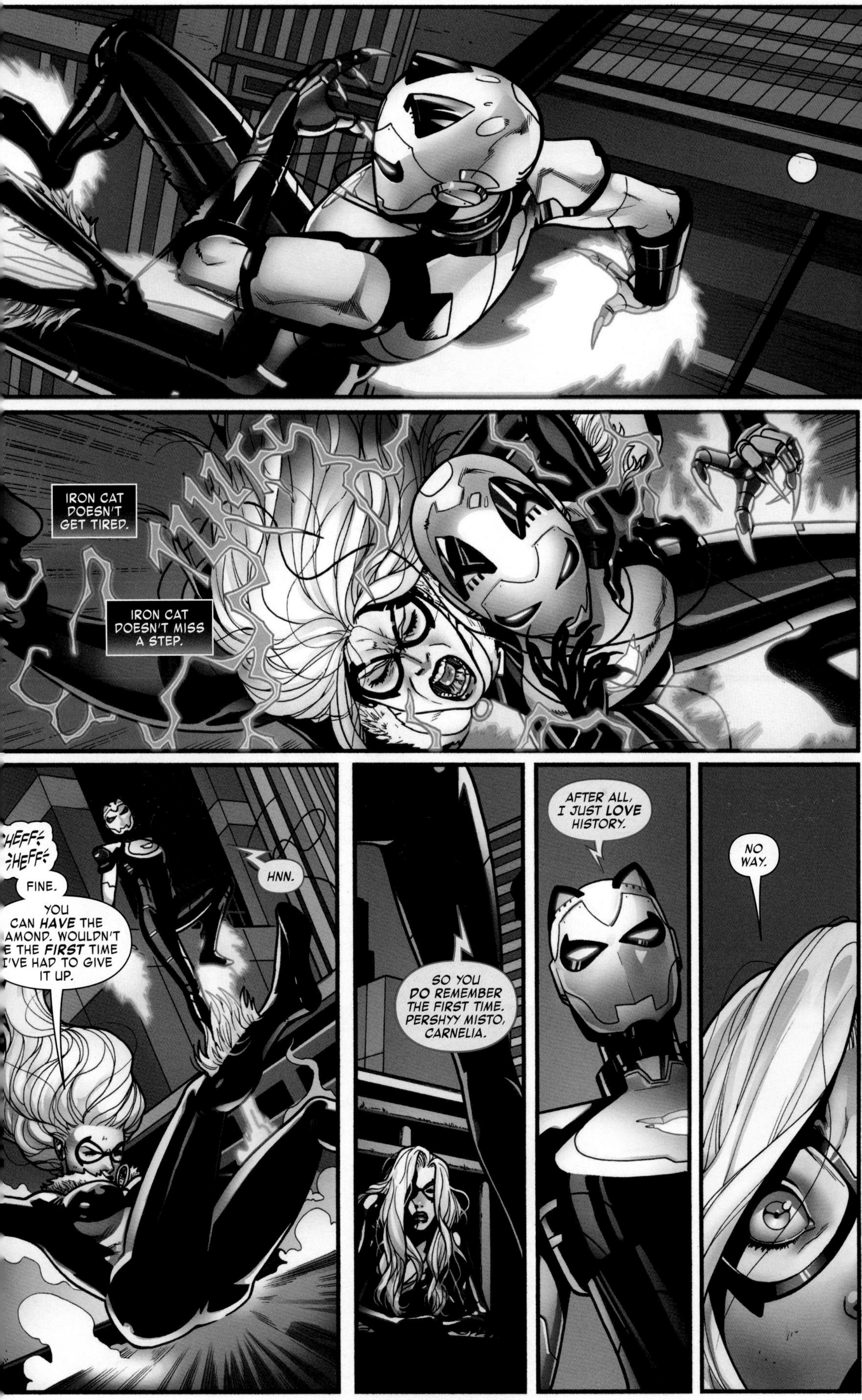

IRON CAT DOESN'T GET TIRED.
IRON CAT DOESN'T MISS A STEP.
HEFF HEFF
FINE.
YOU CAN HAVE THE AMOND. WOULDN'T E THE FIRST TIME I'VE HAD TO GIVE IT UP.
HNN.
SO YOU DO REMEMBER THE FIRST TIME. PERSHYY MISTO, CARNELIA.
AFTER ALL, I JUST LOVE HISTORY.
NO WAY.

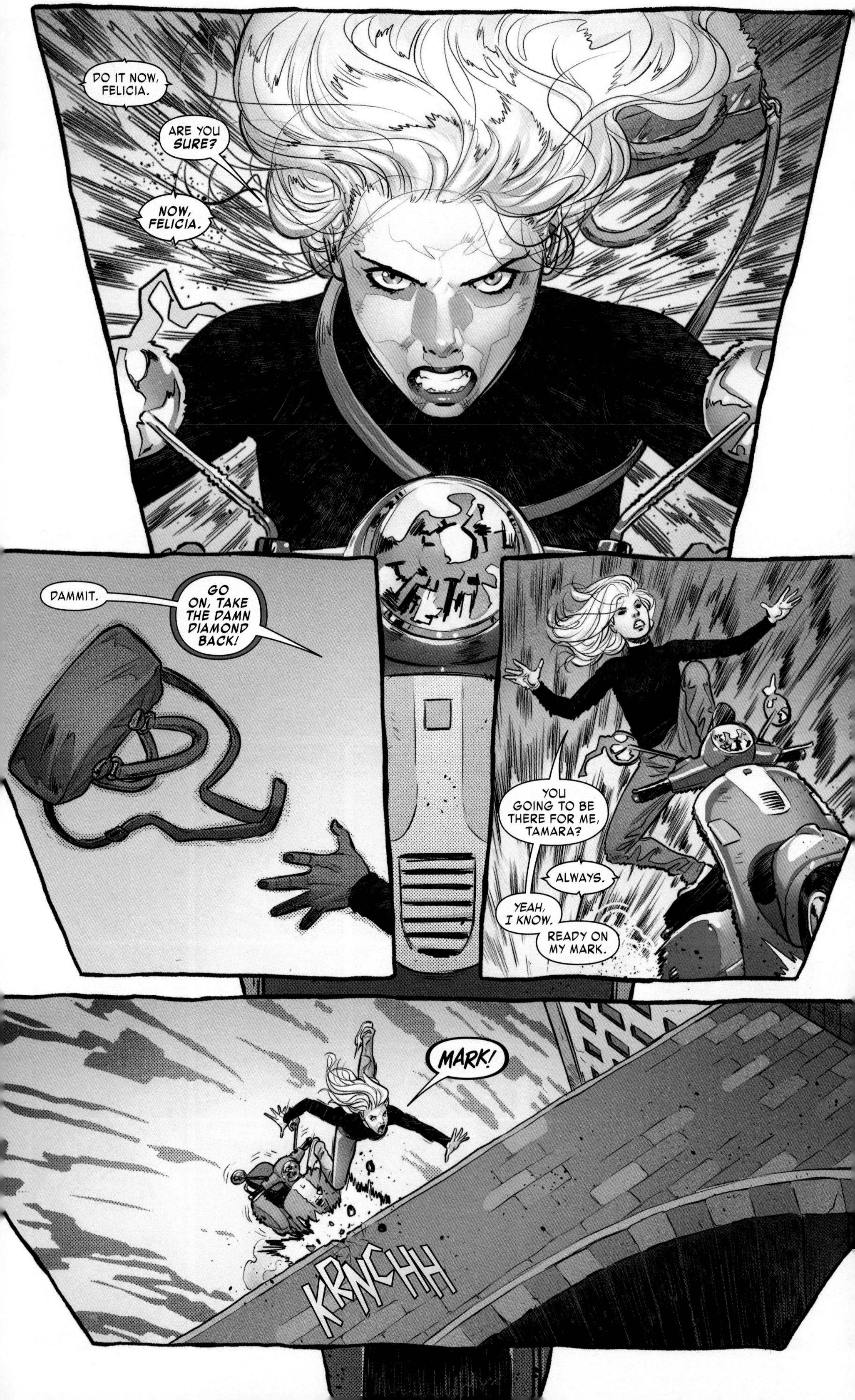
DO IT NOW, FELICIA.
ARE YOU SURE?
NOW, FELICIA.
DAMMIT.
GO ON, TAKE THE DAMN DIAMOND BACK!
YOU GOING TO BE THERE FOR ME, TAMARA?
ALWAYS.
YEAH, I KNOW.
READY ON MY MARK.
MARK!
KRNCHH

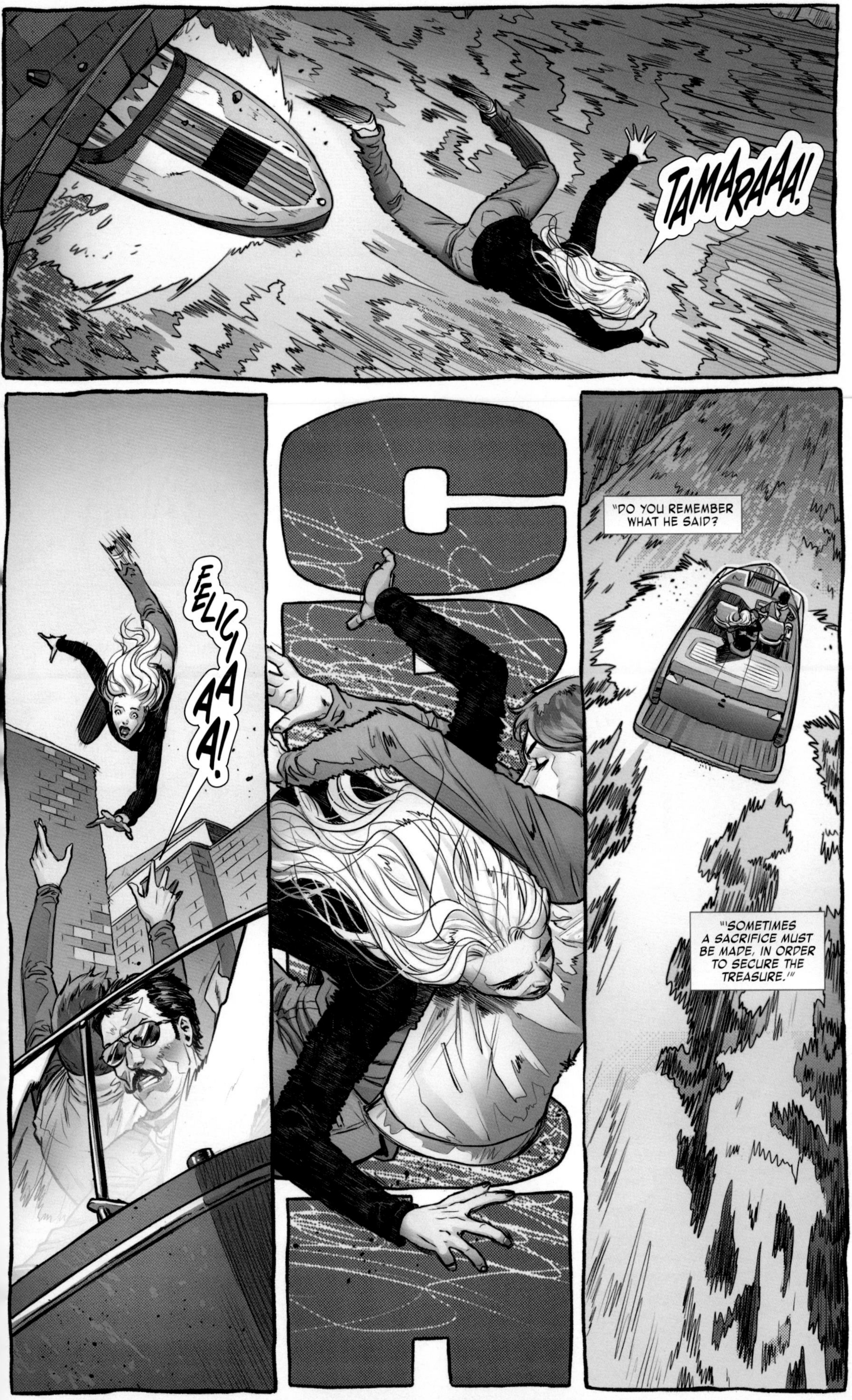
TAMARAAA!
FELICIAAA!
"DO YOU REMEMBER WHAT HE SAID?
"'SOMETIMES A SACRIFICE MUST BE MADE, IN ORDER TO SECURE THE TREASURE.'"

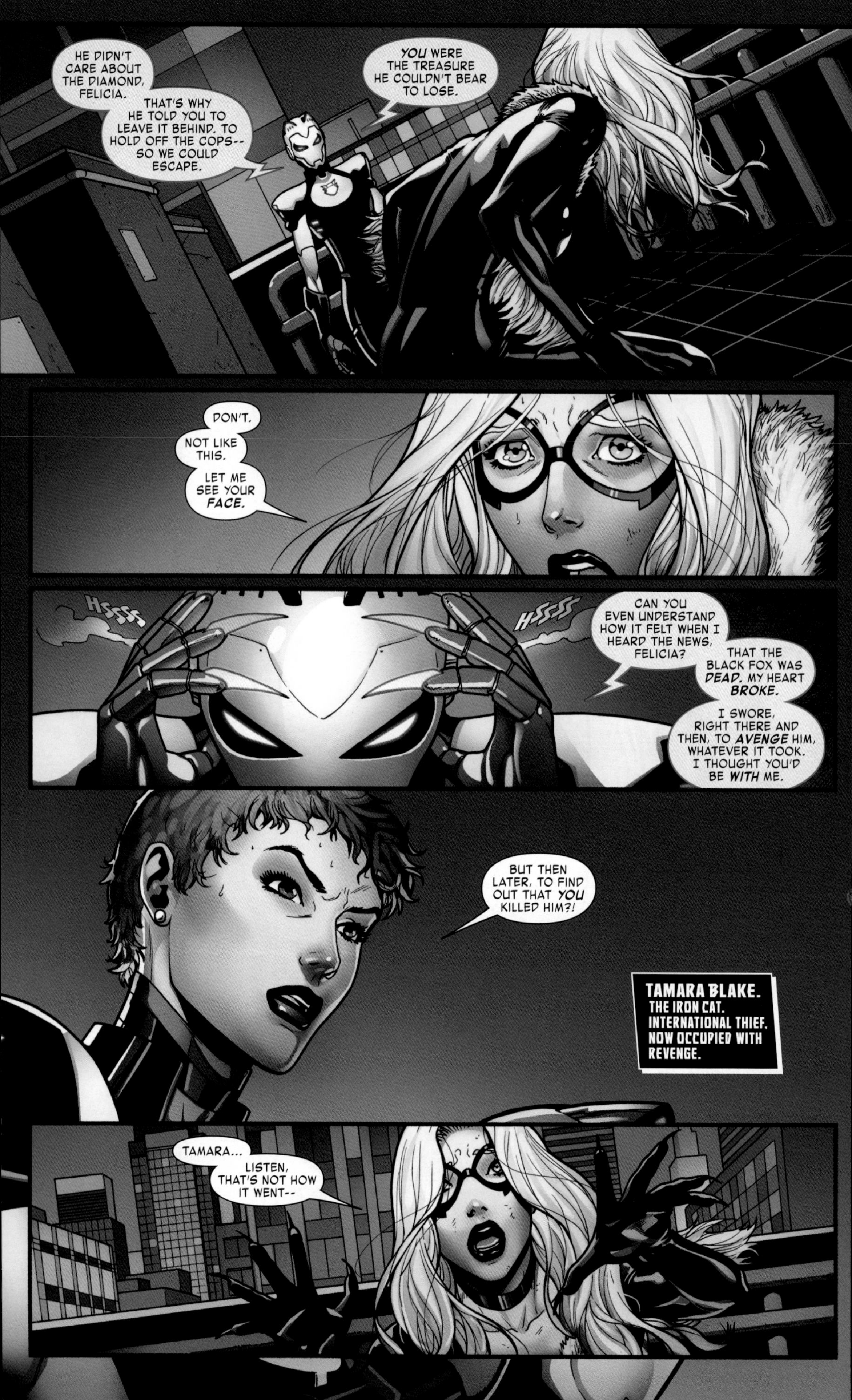
HE DIDN'T CARE ABOUT THE DIAMOND, FELICIA.
THAT'S WHY HE TOLD YOU TO LEAVE IT BEHIND. TO HOLD OFF THE COPS-- SO WE COULD ESCAPE.
YOU WERE THE TREASURE HE COULDN'T BEAR TO LOSE.
DON'T.
NOT LIKE THIS.
LET ME SEE YOUR FACE.
HSSSS
HSSSS
CAN YOU EVEN UNDERSTAND HOW IT FELT WHEN I HEARD THE NEWS, FELICIA?
THAT THE BLACK FOX WAS DEAD. MY HEART BROKE.
I SWORE, RIGHT THERE AND THEN, TO AVENGE HIM, WHATEVER IT TOOK. I THOUGHT YOU'D BE WITH ME.
BUT THEN LATER, TO FIND OUT THAT YOU KILLED HIM?!
TAMARA BLAKE. THE IRON CAT. INTERNATIONAL THIEF, NOW OCCUPIED WITH REVENGE.
TAMARA...
LISTEN, THAT'S NOT HOW IT WENT--

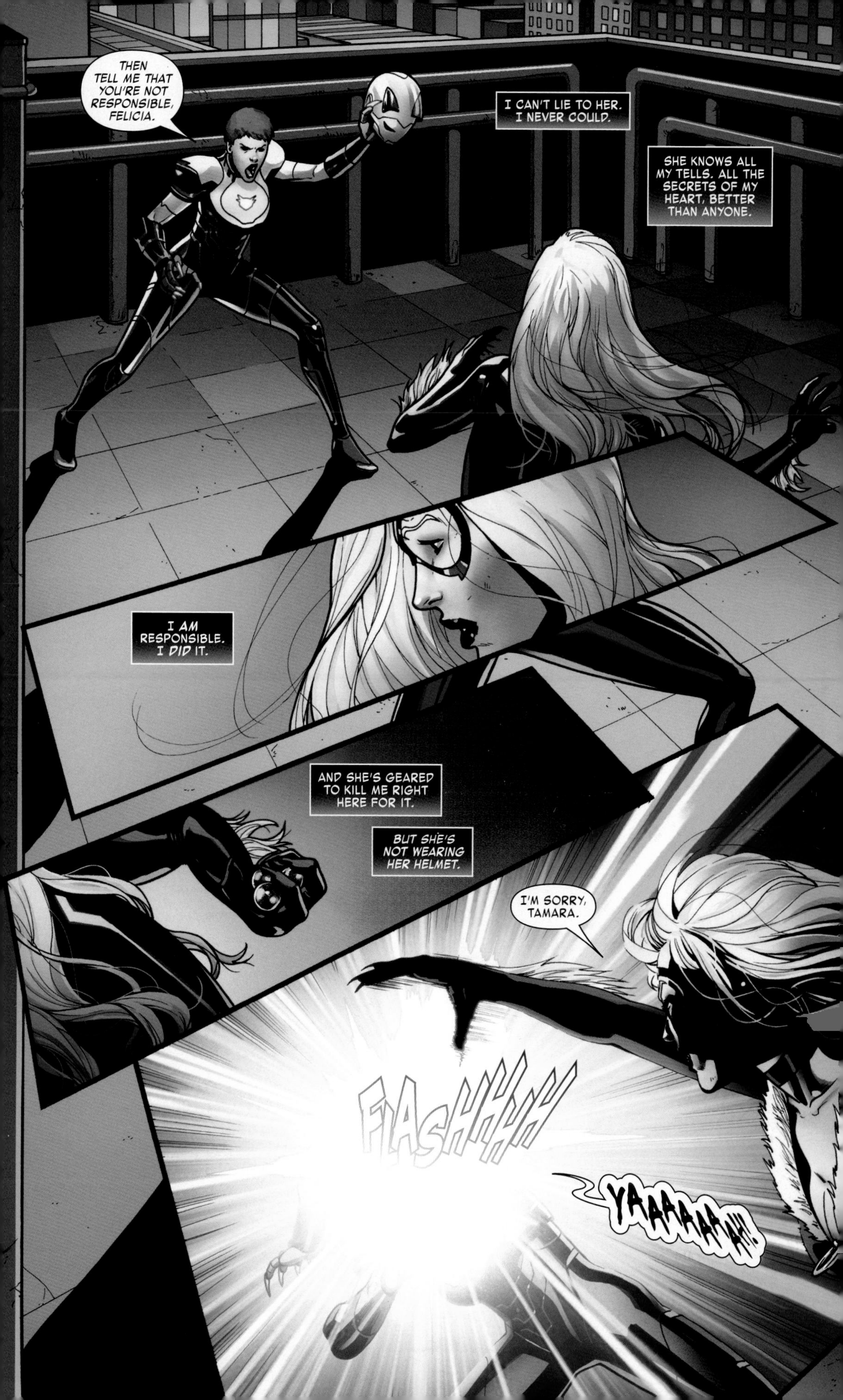
THEN TELL ME THAT YOU'RE NOT RESPONSIBLE, FELICIA.
I CAN'T LIE TO HER. I NEVER COULD.
SHE KNOWS ALL MY TELLS. ALL THE SECRETS OF MY HEART, BETTER THAN ANYONE.
I AM RESPONSIBLE. I DID IT.
AND SHE'S GEARED TO KILL ME RIGHT HERE FOR IT.
BUT SHE'S NOT WEARING HER HELMET.
I'M SORRY, TAMARA.
FLASHHHH
YAAAAARAH!

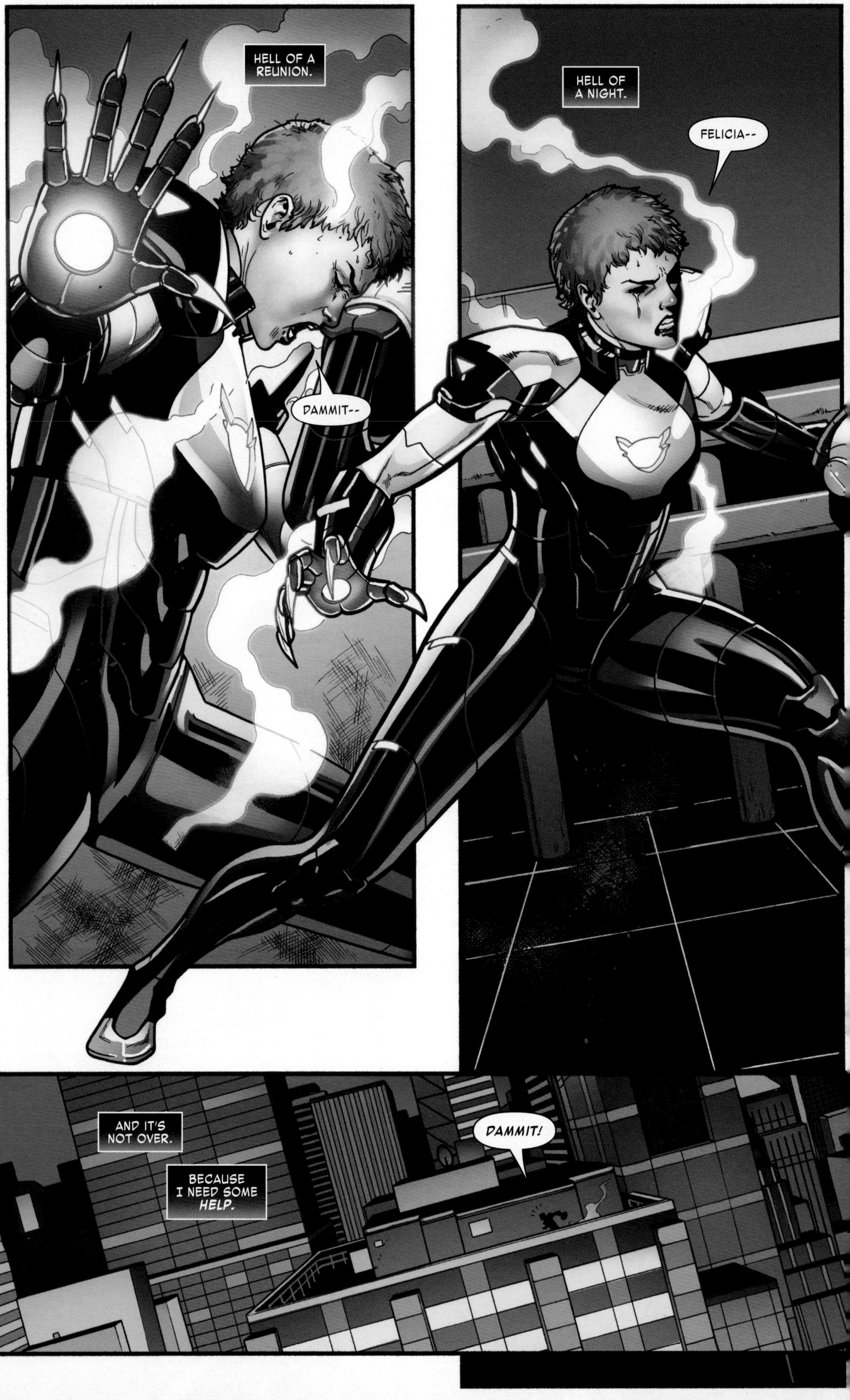

HELL OF A REUNION.
DAMMIT--
HELL OF A NIGHT.
FELICIA--
AND IT'S NOT OVER.
BECAUSE I NEED SOME *HELP.*
DAMMIT!

MR. STARK, YOU HAVE A VISITOR.

NO FOOLIN'.

GO AWAY, FELICIA! GO ON, GET! OR I'LL TURN ON THE SPRINKLERS!

BANG BANG BANG

BANG BANG BANG

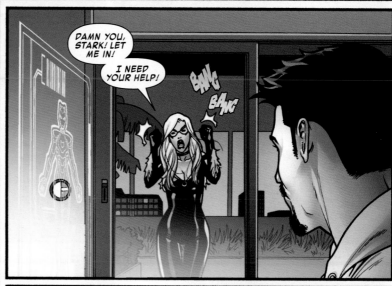

DAMN YOU, STARK! LET ME IN!

I NEED YOUR HELP!

BANG BANG!

PENTHOUSE, TURN ON THE SPRINKLERS, PLEASE.

CERTAINLY, SIR.

FSSSSHHH

AHHHH, DAMMIT!

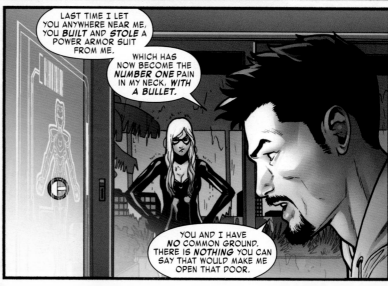

LAST TIME I LET YOU ANYWHERE NEAR ME, YOU BUILT AND STOLE A POWER ARMOR SUIT FROM ME.

WHICH HAS NOW BECOME THE NUMBER ONE PAIN IN MY NECK, WITH A BULLET.

YOU AND I HAVE NO COMMON GROUND. THERE IS NOTHING YOU CAN SAY THAT WOULD MAKE ME OPEN THAT DOOR.

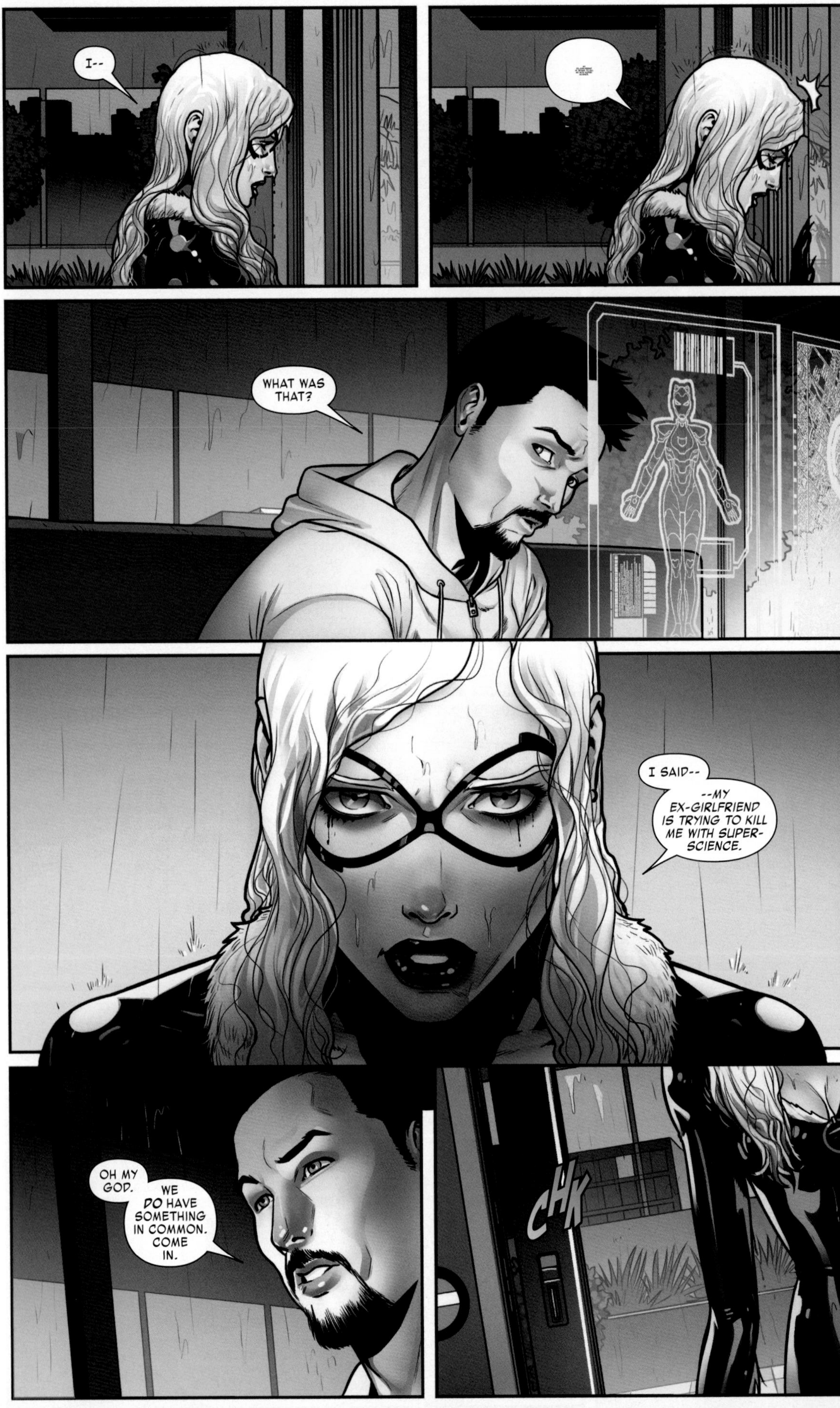
I--
WHAT WAS THAT?
I SAID--
--MY EX-GIRLFRIEND IS TRYING TO KILL ME WITH SUPER-SCIENCE.
OH MY GOD.
WE DO HAVE SOMETHING IN COMMON. COME IN.
CHK

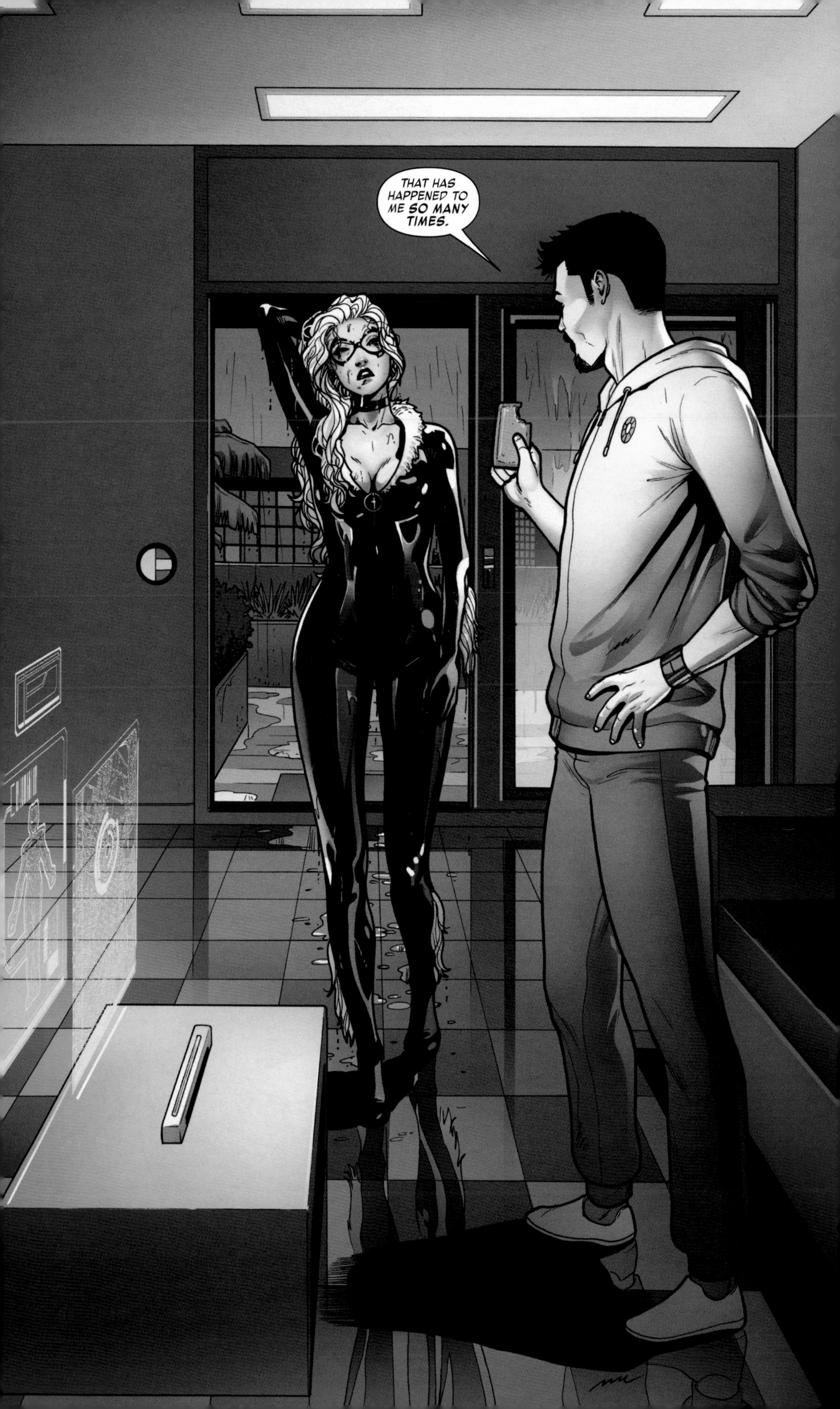
THAT HAS HAPPENED TO ME SO MANY TIMES.

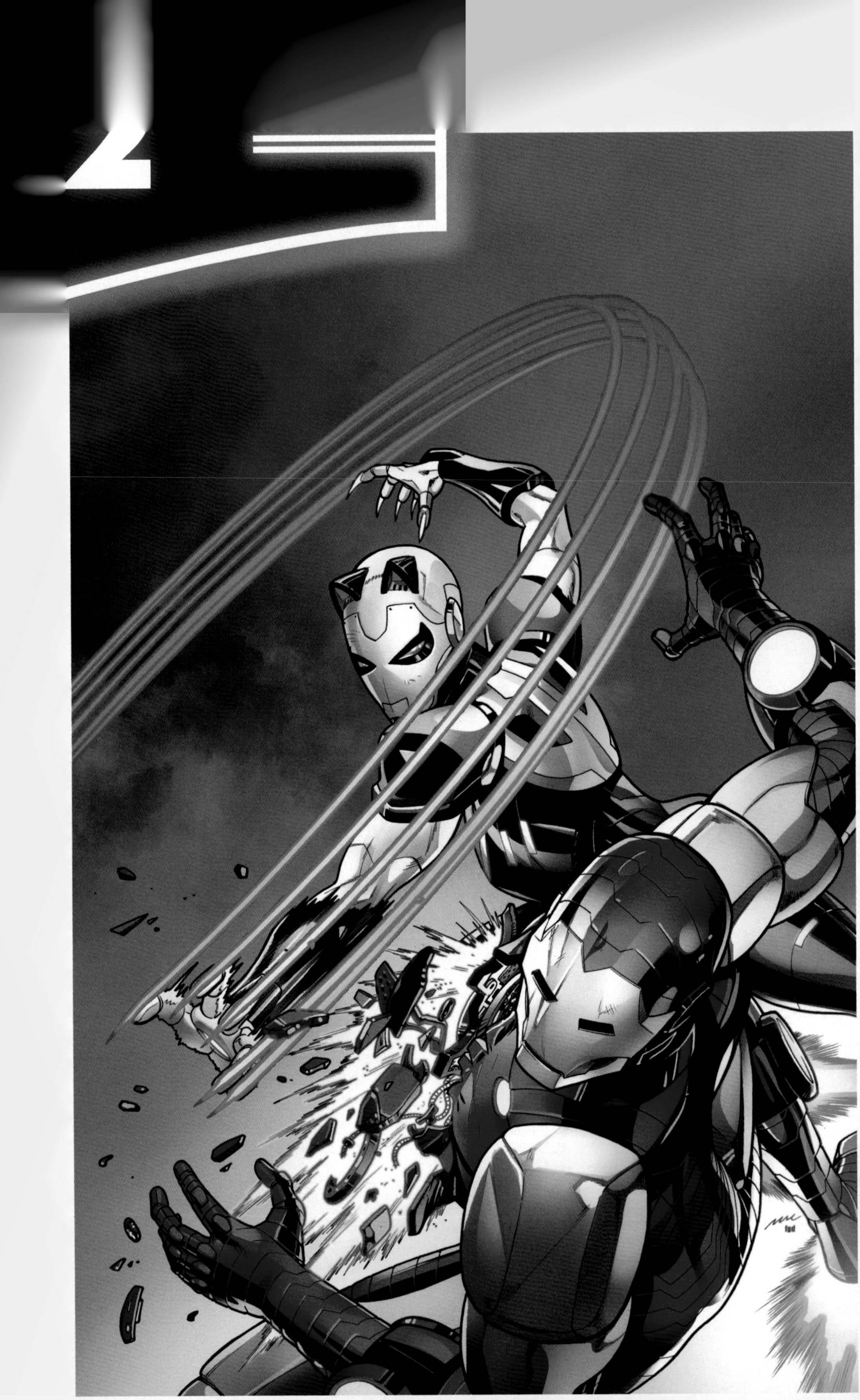
2

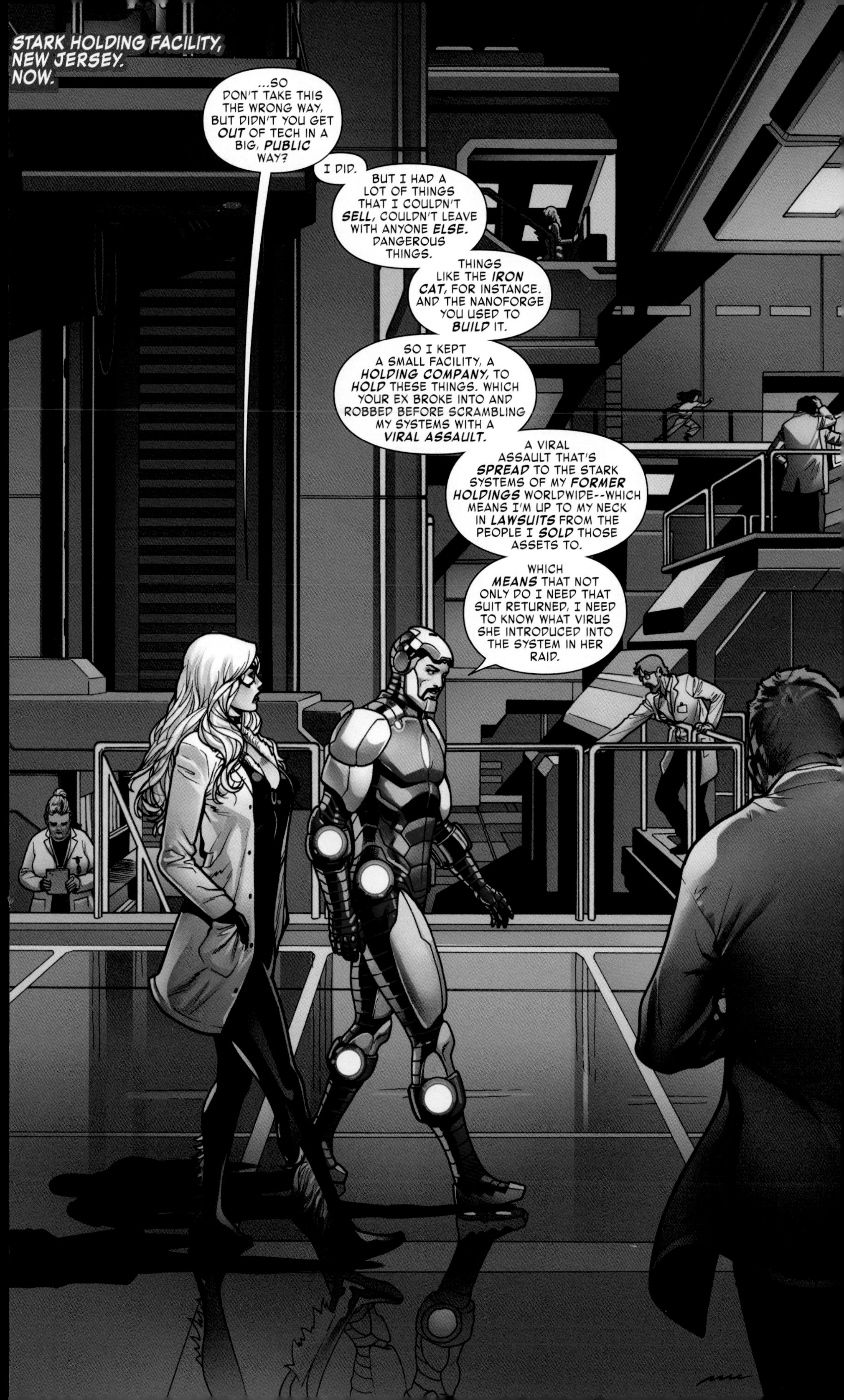
STARK HOLDING FACILITY, NEW JERSEY. NOW.
...SO DON'T TAKE THIS THE WRONG WAY, BUT DIDN'T YOU GET OUT OF TECH IN A BIG, PUBLIC WAY?
I DID.
BUT I HAD A LOT OF THINGS THAT I COULDN'T SELL, COULDN'T LEAVE WITH ANYONE ELSE. DANGEROUS THINGS.
THINGS LIKE THE IRON CAT, FOR INSTANCE. AND THE NANOFORGE YOU USED TO BUILD IT.
SO I KEPT A SMALL FACILITY, A HOLDING COMPANY, TO HOLD THESE THINGS. WHICH YOUR EX BROKE INTO AND ROBBED BEFORE SCRAMBLING MY SYSTEMS WITH A VIRAL ASSAULT.
A VIRAL ASSAULT THAT'S SPREAD TO THE STARK SYSTEMS OF MY FORMER HOLDINGS WORLDWIDE--WHICH MEANS I'M UP TO MY NECK IN LAWSUITS FROM THE PEOPLE I SOLD THOSE ASSETS TO.
WHICH MEANS THAT NOT ONLY DO I NEED THAT SUIT RETURNED, I NEED TO KNOW WHAT VIRUS SHE INTRODUCED INTO THE SYSTEM IN HER RAID.

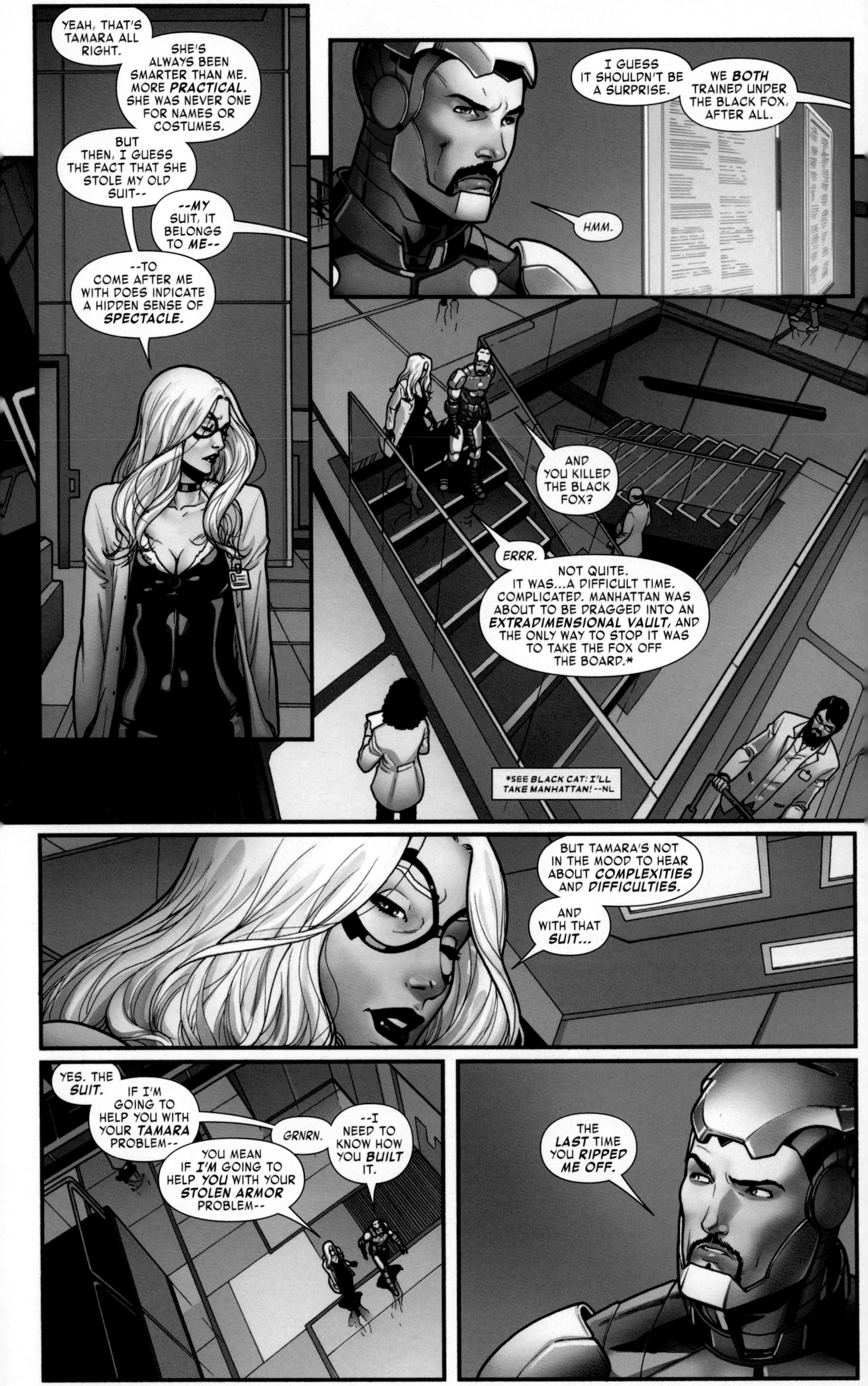
YEAH, THAT'S TAMARA ALL RIGHT.
SHE'S ALWAYS BEEN SMARTER THAN ME. MORE PRACTICAL. SHE WAS NEVER ONE FOR NAMES OR COSTUMES.
BUT THEN, I GUESS THE FACT THAT SHE STOLE MY OLD SUIT--
--MY SUIT, IT BELONGS TO ME--
--TO COME AFTER ME WITH DOES INDICATE A HIDDEN SENSE OF SPECTACLE.
I GUESS IT SHOULDN'T BE A SURPRISE.
WE BOTH TRAINED UNDER THE BLACK FOX, AFTER ALL.
HMM.
AND YOU KILLED THE BLACK FOX?
ERRR.
NOT QUITE. IT WAS...A DIFFICULT TIME. COMPLICATED. MANHATTAN WAS ABOUT TO BE DRAGGED INTO AN EXTRADIMENSIONAL VAULT, AND THE ONLY WAY TO STOP IT WAS TO TAKE THE FOX OFF THE BOARD.*
*SEE BLACK CAT: I'LL TAKE MANHATTAN! --NL
BUT TAMARA'S NOT IN THE MOOD TO HEAR ABOUT COMPLEXITIES AND DIFFICULTIES.
AND WITH THAT SUIT...
YES. THE SUIT.
IF I'M GOING TO HELP YOU WITH YOUR TAMARA PROBLEM--
GRNRN.
YOU MEAN IF I'M GOING TO HELP YOU WITH YOUR STOLEN ARMOR PROBLEM--
--I NEED TO KNOW HOW YOU BUILT IT.
THE LAST TIME YOU RIPPED ME OFF.

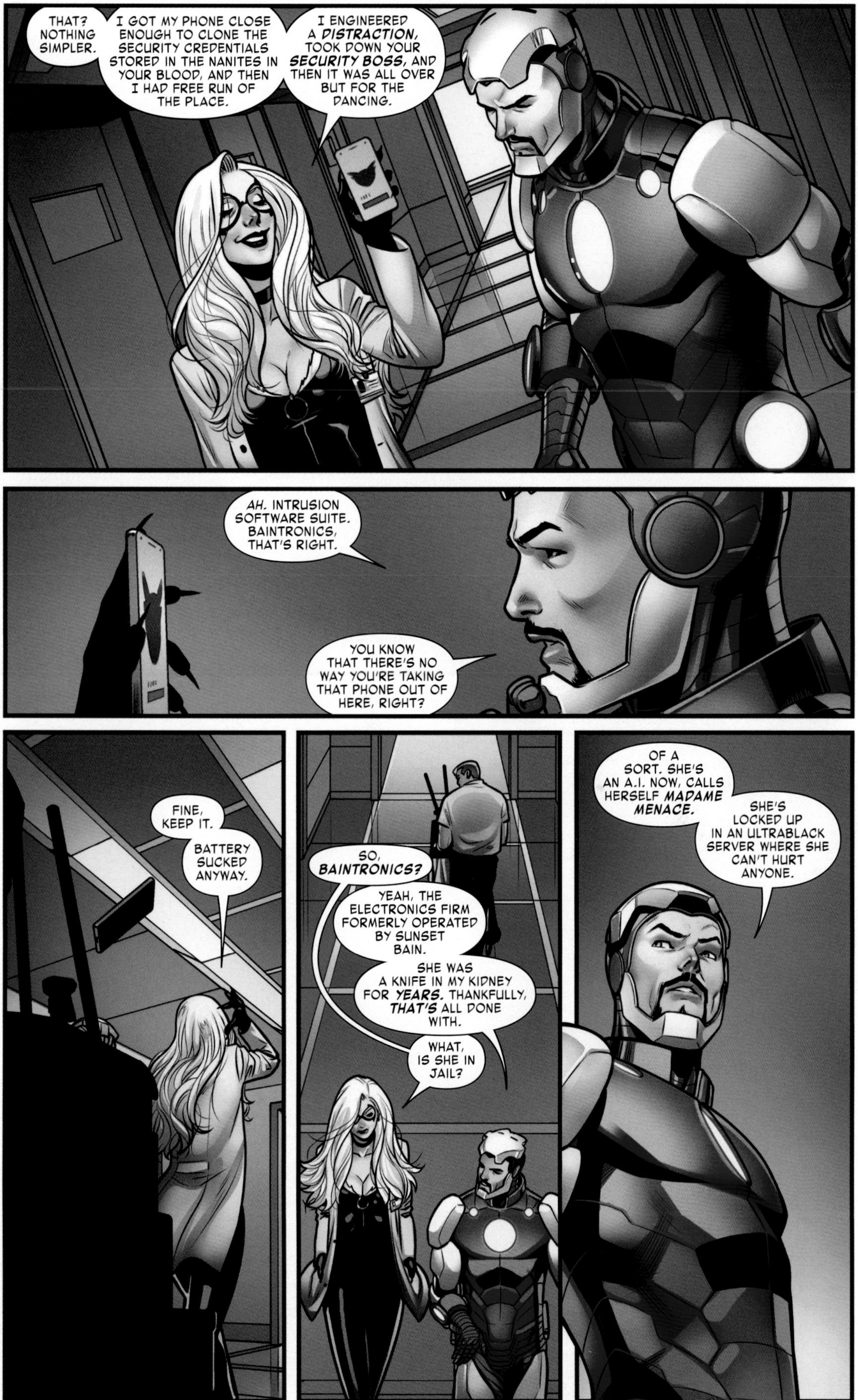
THAT? NOTHING SIMPLER.
I GOT MY PHONE CLOSE ENOUGH TO CLONE THE SECURITY CREDENTIALS STORED IN THE NANITES IN YOUR BLOOD, AND THEN I HAD FREE RUN OF THE PLACE.
I ENGINEERED A *DISTRACTION*, TOOK DOWN YOUR **SECURITY BOSS**, AND THEN IT WAS ALL OVER BUT FOR THE DANCING.
AH. INTRUSION SOFTWARE SUITE. BAINTRONICS, THAT'S RIGHT.
YOU KNOW THAT THERE'S NO WAY YOU'RE TAKING THAT PHONE OUT OF HERE, RIGHT?
FINE, KEEP IT.
BATTERY SUCKED ANYWAY.
SO, **BAINTRONICS?**
YEAH, THE ELECTRONICS FIRM FORMERLY OPERATED BY SUNSET BAIN.
SHE WAS A KNIFE IN MY KIDNEY FOR **YEARS.** THANKFULLY, **THAT'S** ALL DONE WITH.
WHAT, IS SHE IN JAIL?
OF A SORT. SHE'S AN A.I. NOW, CALLS HERSELF **MADAME MENACE.**
SHE'S LOCKED UP IN AN ULTRABLACK SERVER WHERE SHE CAN'T HURT ANYONE.

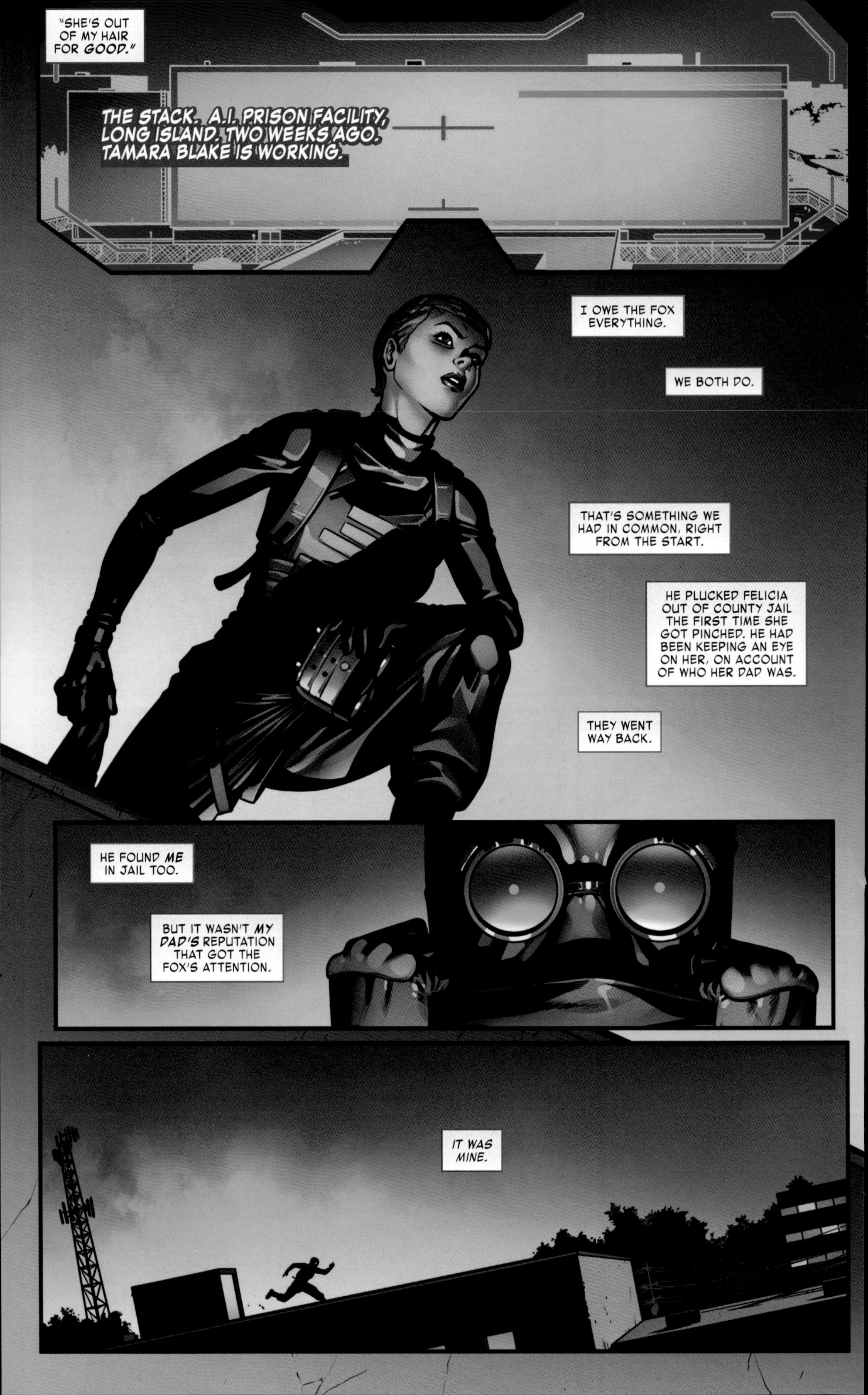
"SHE'S OUT OF MY HAIR FOR GOOD."
THE STACK. A.I. PRISON FACILITY, LONG ISLAND. TWO WEEKS AGO. TAMARA BLAKE IS WORKING.
I OWE THE FOX EVERYTHING.
WE BOTH DO.
THAT'S SOMETHING WE HAD IN COMMON, RIGHT FROM THE START.
HE PLUCKED FELICIA OUT OF COUNTY JAIL THE FIRST TIME SHE GOT PINCHED. HE HAD BEEN KEEPING AN EYE ON HER, ON ACCOUNT OF WHO HER DAD WAS.
THEY WENT WAY BACK.
HE FOUND ME IN JAIL TOO.
BUT IT WASN'T MY DAD'S REPUTATION THAT GOT THE FOX'S ATTENTION.
IT WAS MINE.

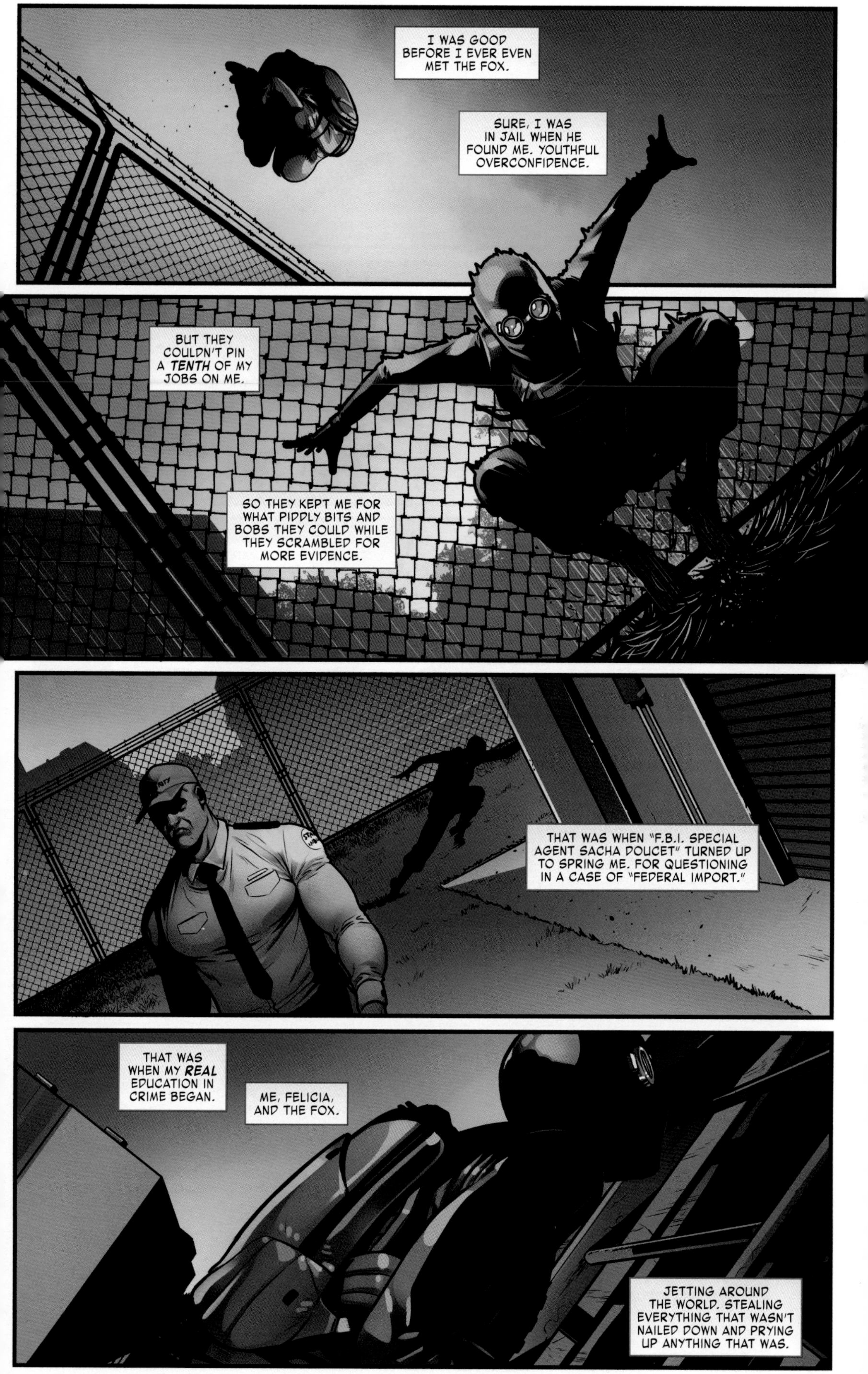
I WAS GOOD BEFORE I EVER EVEN MET THE FOX.
SURE, I WAS IN JAIL WHEN HE FOUND ME. YOUTHFUL OVERCONFIDENCE.
BUT THEY COULDN'T PIN A *TENTH* OF MY JOBS ON ME.
SO THEY KEPT ME FOR WHAT PIDDLY BITS AND BOBS THEY COULD WHILE THEY SCRAMBLED FOR MORE EVIDENCE.
THAT WAS WHEN "F.B.I. SPECIAL AGENT SACHA DOUCET" TURNED UP TO SPRING ME. FOR QUESTIONING IN A CASE OF "FEDERAL IMPORT."
THAT WAS WHEN MY ***REAL*** EDUCATION IN CRIME BEGAN.
ME, FELICIA, AND THE FOX.
JETTING AROUND THE WORLD. STEALING EVERYTHING THAT WASN'T NAILED DOWN AND PRYING UP ANYTHING THAT WAS.

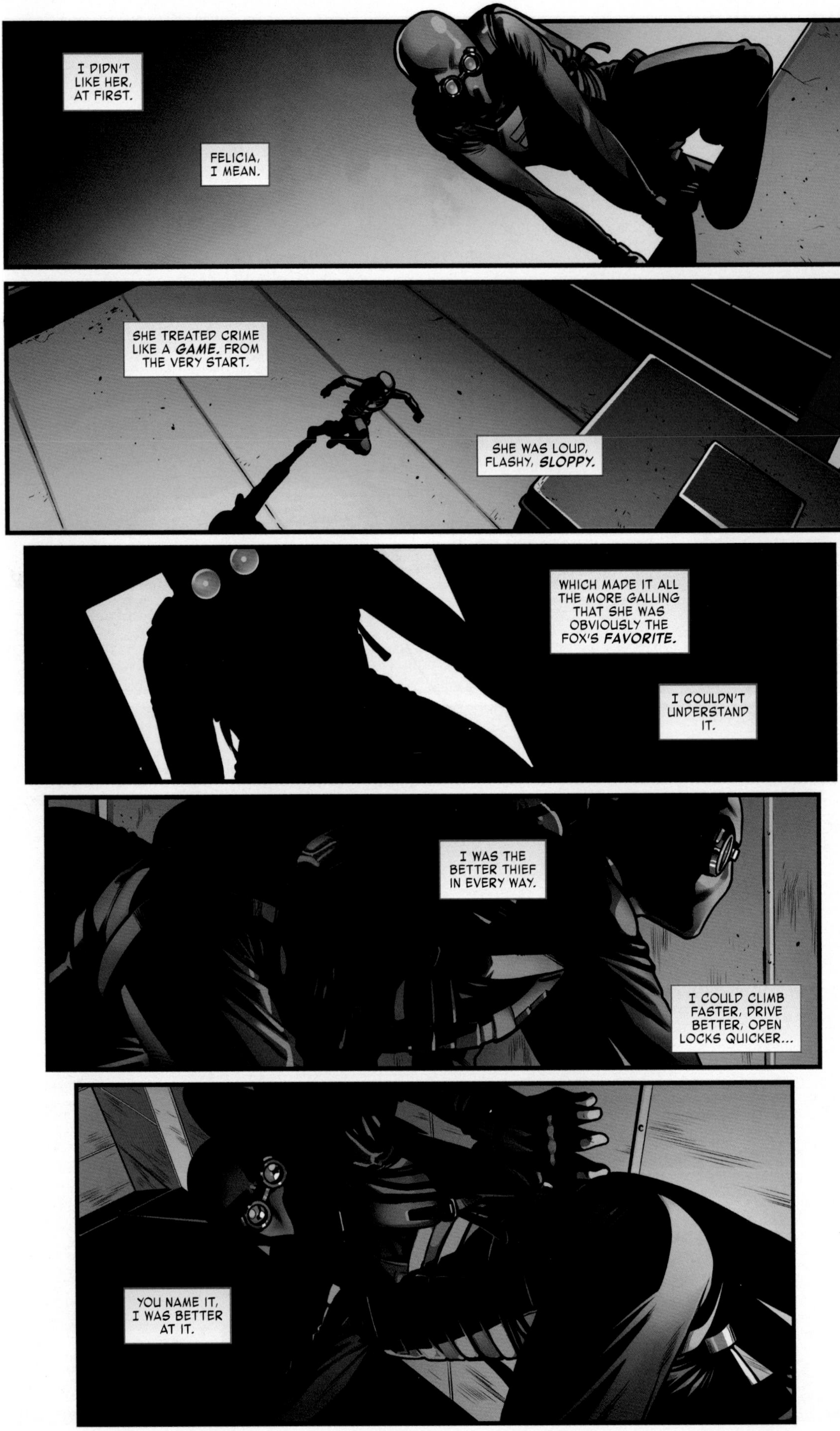
I DIDN'T LIKE HER, AT FIRST.
FELICIA, I MEAN.
SHE TREATED CRIME LIKE A *GAME.* FROM THE VERY START.
SHE WAS LOUD, FLASHY, *SLOPPY.*
WHICH MADE IT ALL THE MORE GALLING THAT SHE WAS OBVIOUSLY THE FOX'S *FAVORITE.*
I COULDN'T UNDERSTAND IT.
I WAS THE BETTER THIEF IN EVERY WAY.
I COULD CLIMB FASTER, DRIVE BETTER, OPEN LOCKS QUICKER...
YOU NAME IT, I WAS BETTER AT IT.

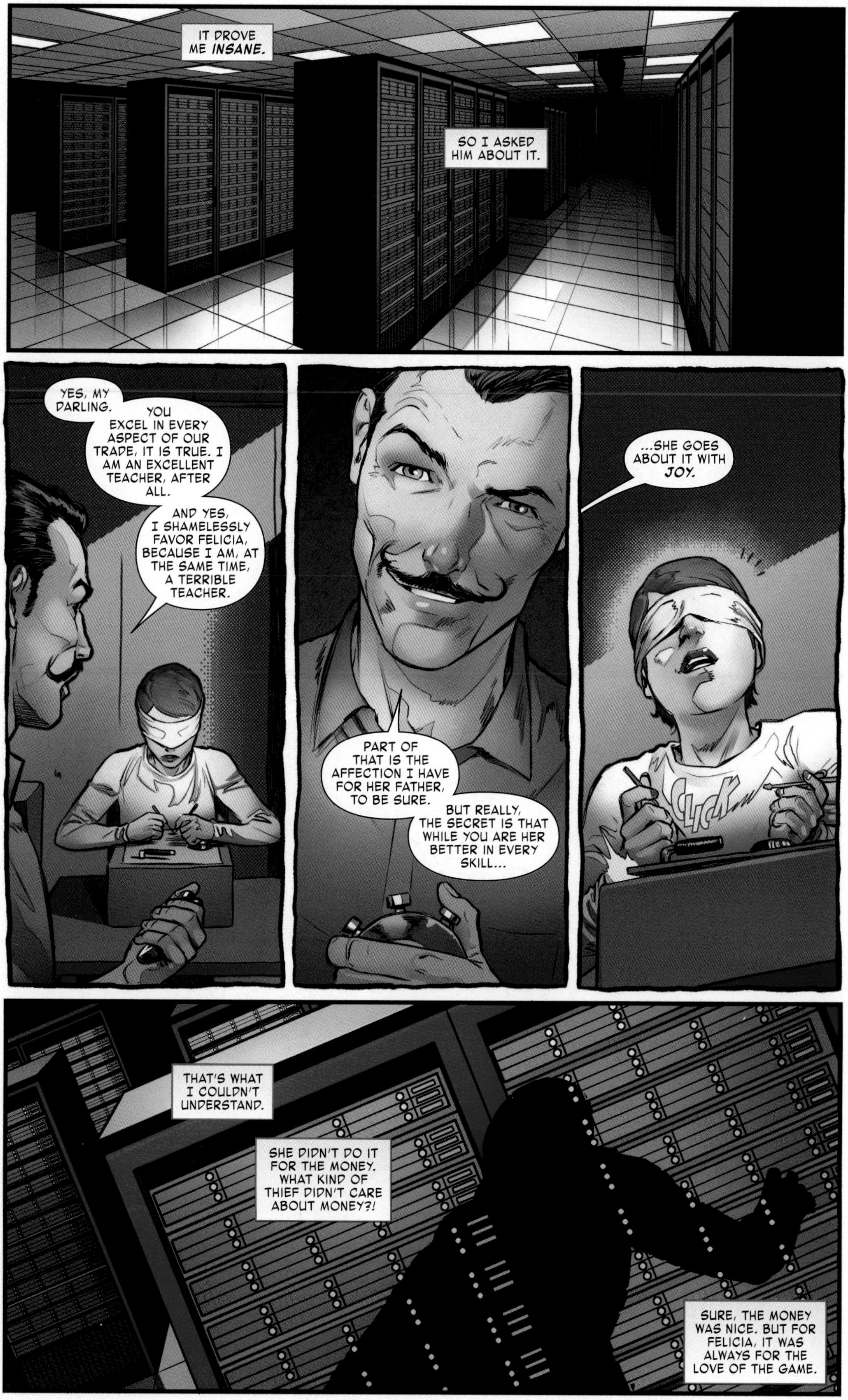
IT DROVE ME INSANE.
SO I ASKED HIM ABOUT IT.
YES, MY DARLING.
YOU EXCEL IN EVERY ASPECT OF OUR TRADE, IT IS TRUE. I AM AN EXCELLENT TEACHER, AFTER ALL.
AND YES, I SHAMELESSLY FAVOR FELICIA, BECAUSE I AM, AT THE SAME TIME, A TERRIBLE TEACHER.
PART OF THAT IS THE AFFECTION I HAVE FOR HER FATHER, TO BE SURE.
BUT REALLY, THE SECRET IS THAT WHILE YOU ARE HER BETTER IN EVERY SKILL...
...SHE GOES ABOUT IT WITH JOY.
CLICK
THAT'S WHAT I COULDN'T UNDERSTAND.
SHE DIDN'T DO IT FOR THE MONEY. WHAT KIND OF THIEF DIDN'T CARE ABOUT MONEY?!
SURE, THE MONEY WAS NICE. BUT FOR FELICIA, IT WAS ALWAYS FOR THE LOVE OF THE GAME.

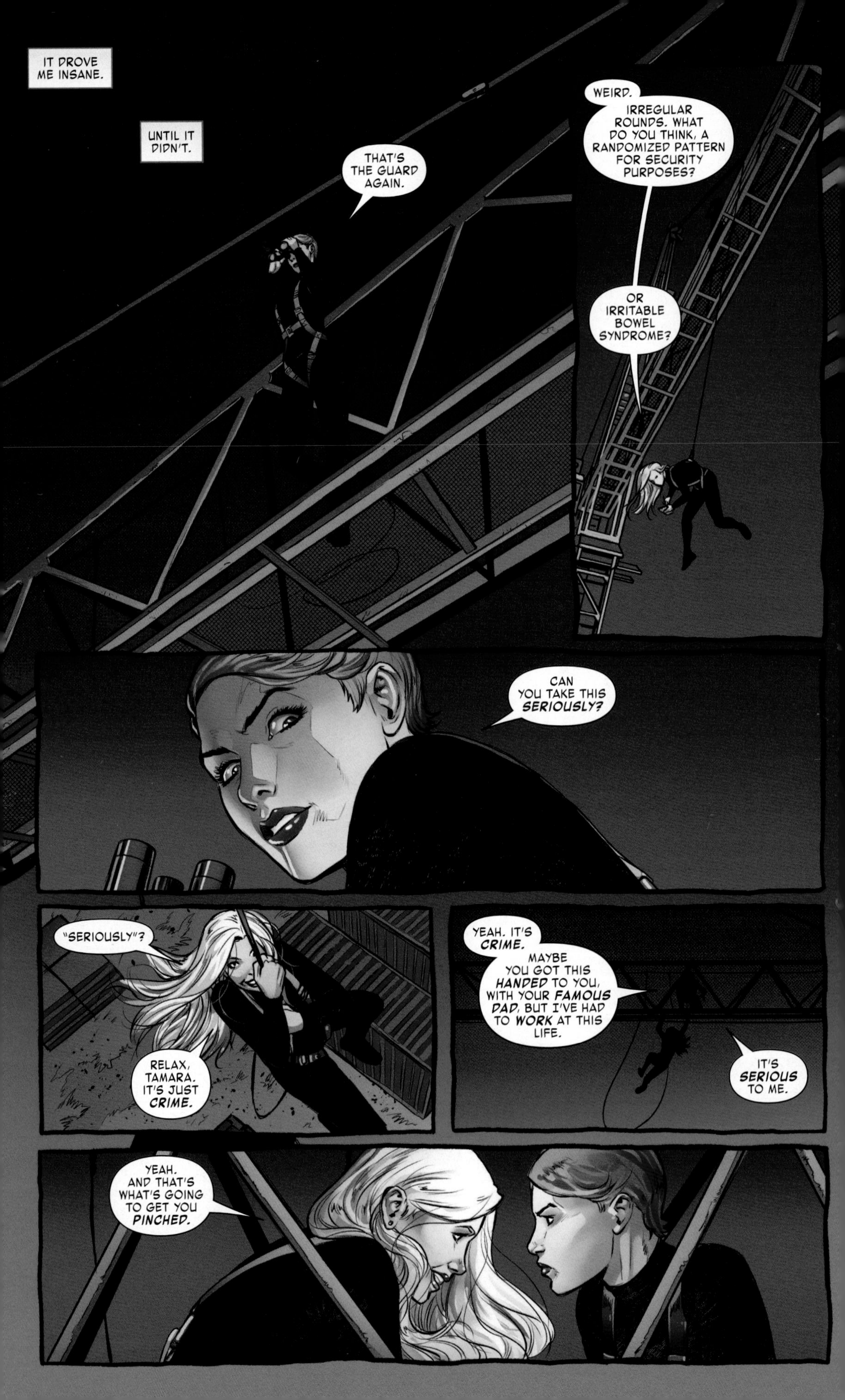
IT DROVE ME INSANE.
UNTIL IT DIDN'T.
THAT'S THE GUARD AGAIN.
WEIRD.
IRREGULAR ROUNDS. WHAT DO YOU THINK, A RANDOMIZED PATTERN FOR SECURITY PURPOSES?
OR IRRITABLE BOWEL SYNDROME?
CAN YOU TAKE THIS SERIOUSLY?
"SERIOUSLY"?
RELAX, TAMARA. IT'S JUST CRIME.
YEAH. IT'S CRIME.
MAYBE YOU GOT THIS HANDED TO YOU, WITH YOUR FAMOUS DAD, BUT I'VE HAD TO WORK AT THIS LIFE.
IT'S SERIOUS TO ME.
YEAH. AND THAT'S WHAT'S GOING TO GET YOU PINCHED.

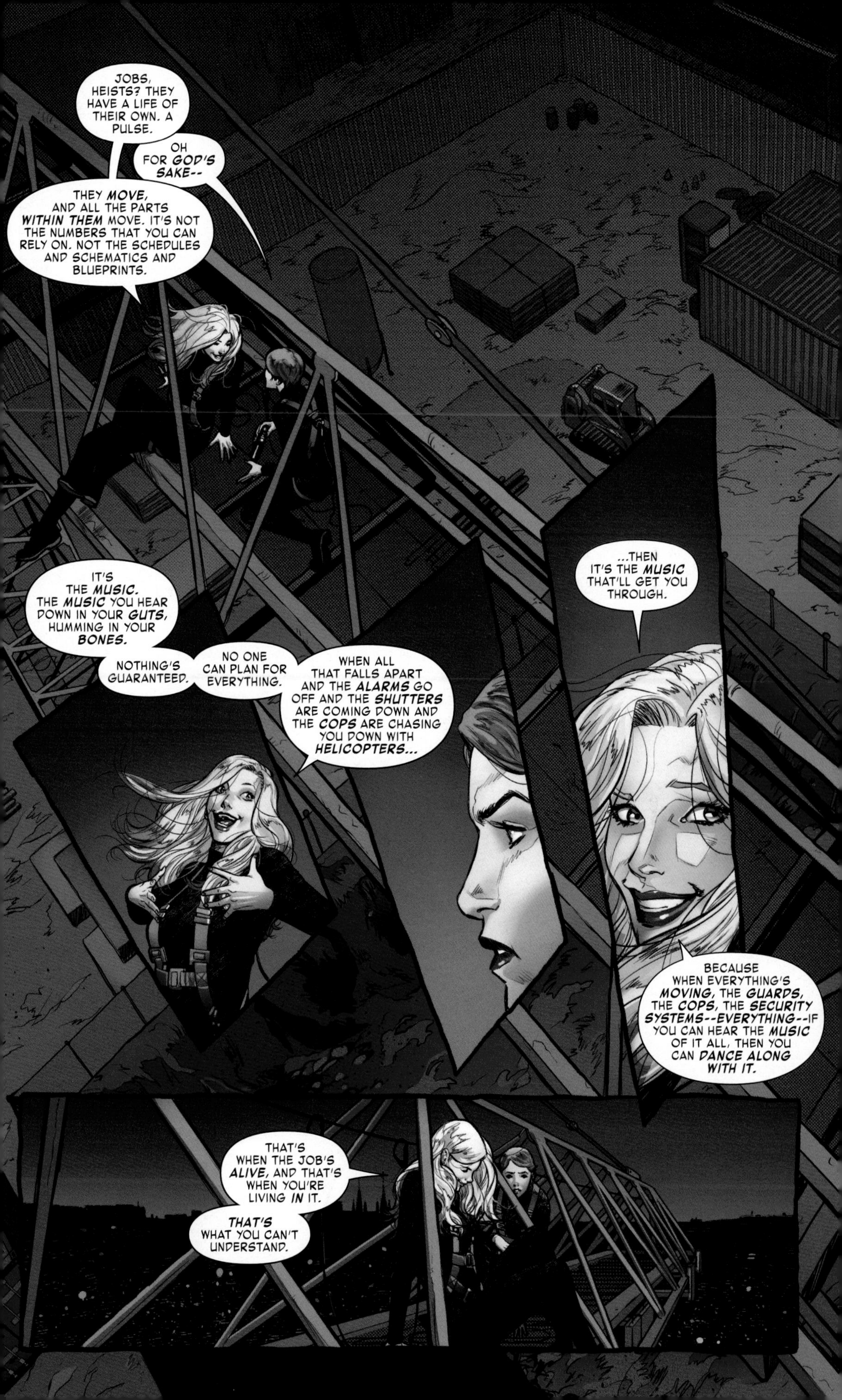

JOBS, HEISTS? THEY HAVE A LIFE OF THEIR OWN. A PULSE.
OH FOR GOD'S SAKE--
THEY MOVE, AND ALL THE PARTS WITHIN THEM MOVE. IT'S NOT THE NUMBERS THAT YOU CAN RELY ON. NOT THE SCHEDULES AND SCHEMATICS AND BLUEPRINTS.
IT'S THE MUSIC. THE MUSIC YOU HEAR DOWN IN YOUR GUTS, HUMMING IN YOUR BONES.
NOTHING'S GUARANTEED.
NO ONE CAN PLAN FOR EVERYTHING.
WHEN ALL THAT FALLS APART AND THE ALARMS GO OFF AND THE SHUTTERS ARE COMING DOWN AND THE COPS ARE CHASING YOU DOWN WITH HELICOPTERS...
...THEN IT'S THE MUSIC THAT'LL GET YOU THROUGH.
BECAUSE WHEN EVERYTHING'S MOVING, THE GUARDS, THE COPS, THE SECURITY SYSTEMS--EVERYTHING--IF YOU CAN HEAR THE MUSIC OF IT ALL, THEN YOU CAN DANCE ALONG WITH IT.
THAT'S WHEN THE JOB'S ALIVE, AND THAT'S WHEN YOU'RE LIVING IN IT.
THAT'S WHAT YOU CAN'T UNDERSTAND.

"AND *THAT'S* WHY YOU'LL ALWAYS BE *PREDICTABLE.*"

SHE WAS RIGHT, OF COURSE.

I *WAS* GOOD. BUT I *WAS* PREDICTABLE.

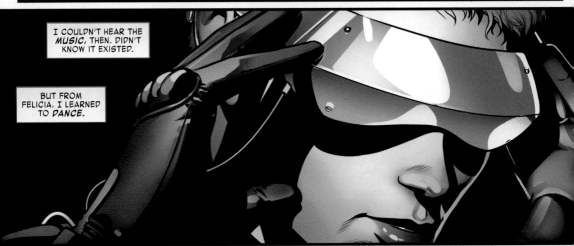

I COULDN'T HEAR THE *MUSIC,* THEN. DIDN'T KNOW IT EXISTED.

BUT FROM FELICIA, I LEARNED TO *DANCE.*

BUT SHE WASN'T *TOTALLY* RIGHT.

BECAUSE SHE SAID I'D *ALWAYS* BE PREDICTABLE.

AND I PROVED HER *WRONG* IN THE *NEXT MOMENT...*

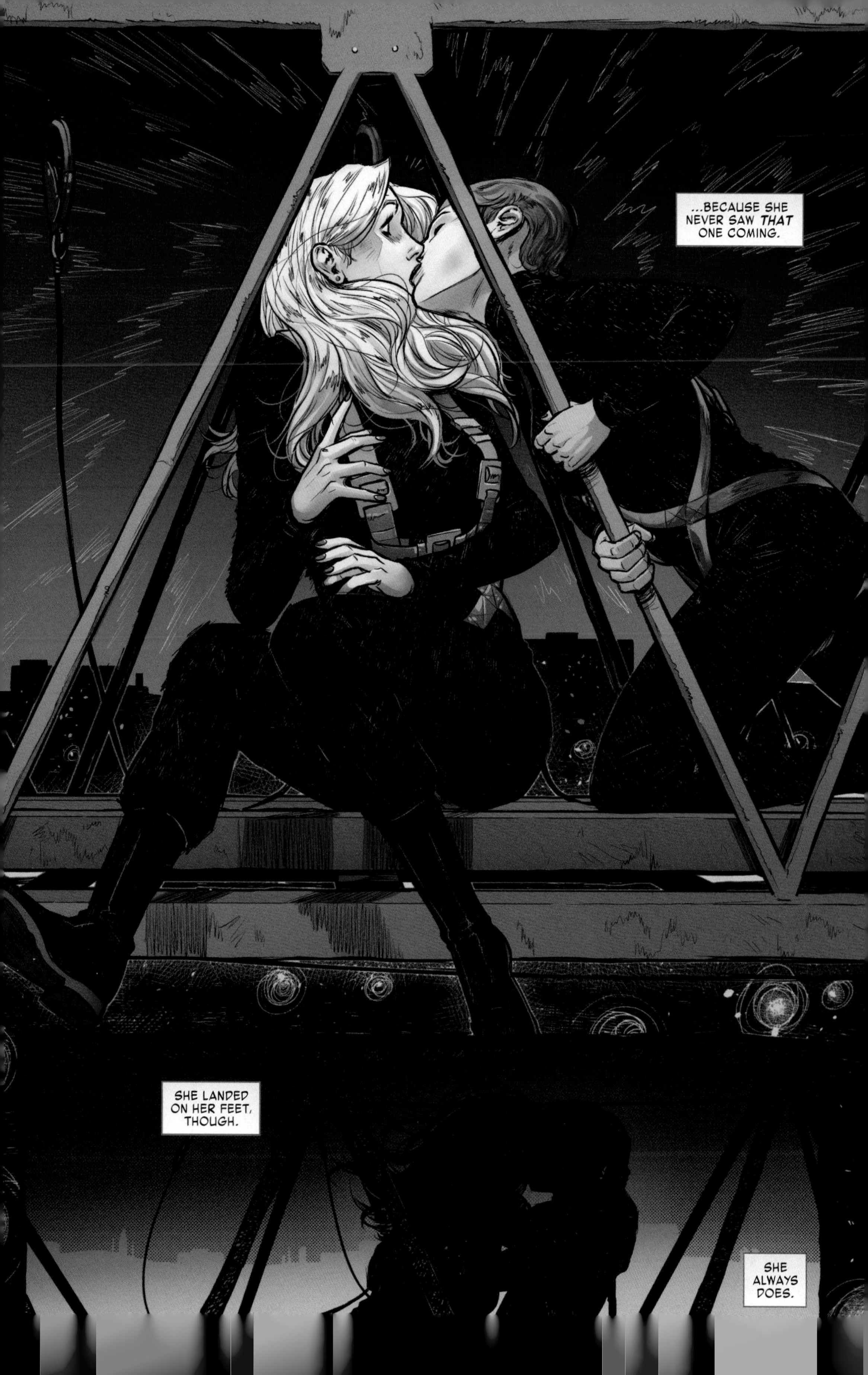
...BECAUSE SHE NEVER SAW THAT ONE COMING.
SHE LANDED ON HER FEET, THOUGH.
SHE ALWAYS DOES.

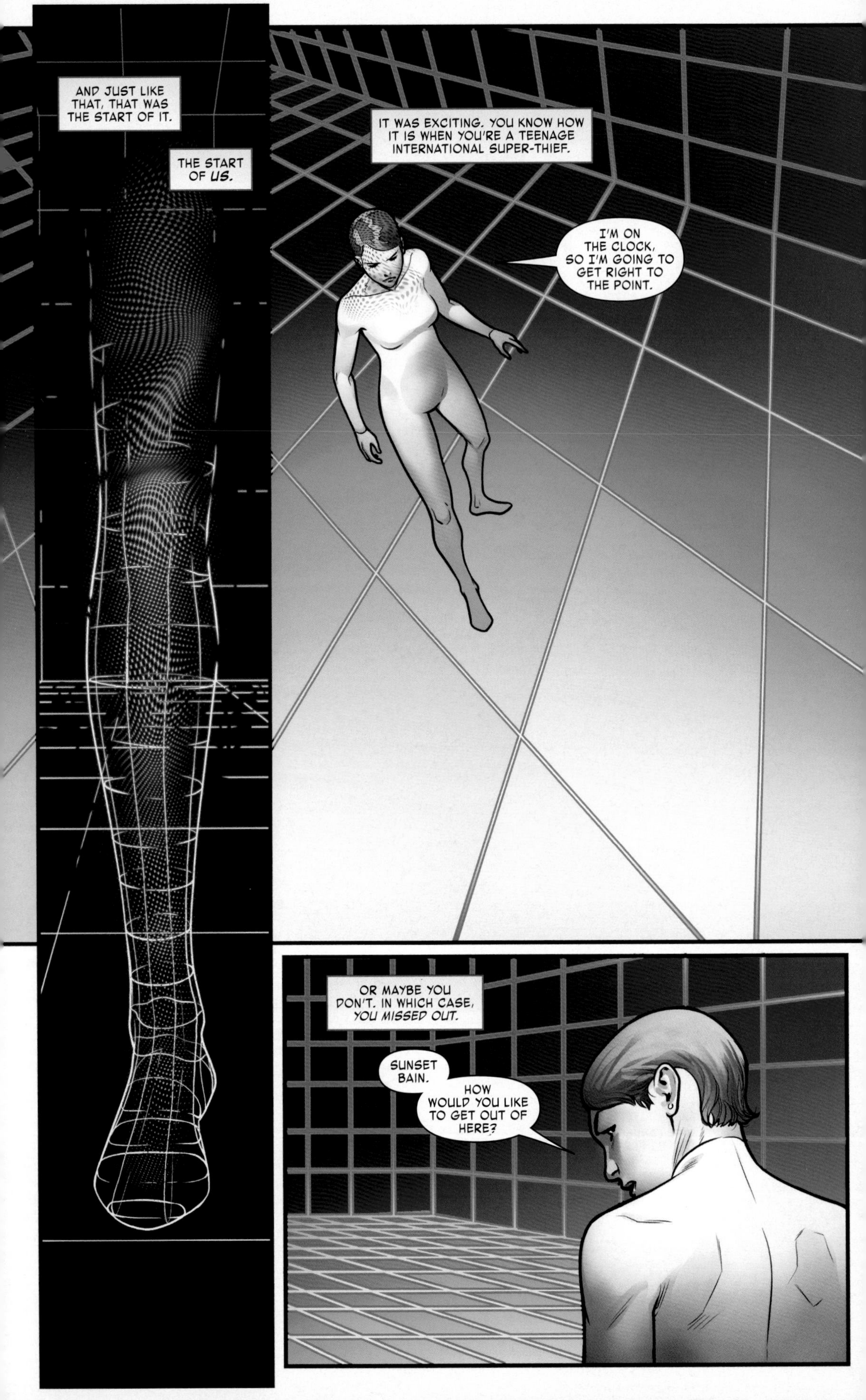
AND JUST LIKE THAT, THAT WAS THE START OF IT.
THE START OF US.
IT WAS EXCITING. YOU KNOW HOW IT IS WHEN YOU'RE A TEENAGE INTERNATIONAL SUPER-THIEF.
I'M ON THE CLOCK, SO I'M GOING TO GET RIGHT TO THE POINT.
OR MAYBE YOU DON'T. IN WHICH CASE, YOU MISSED OUT.
SUNSET BAIN.
HOW WOULD YOU LIKE TO GET OUT OF HERE?

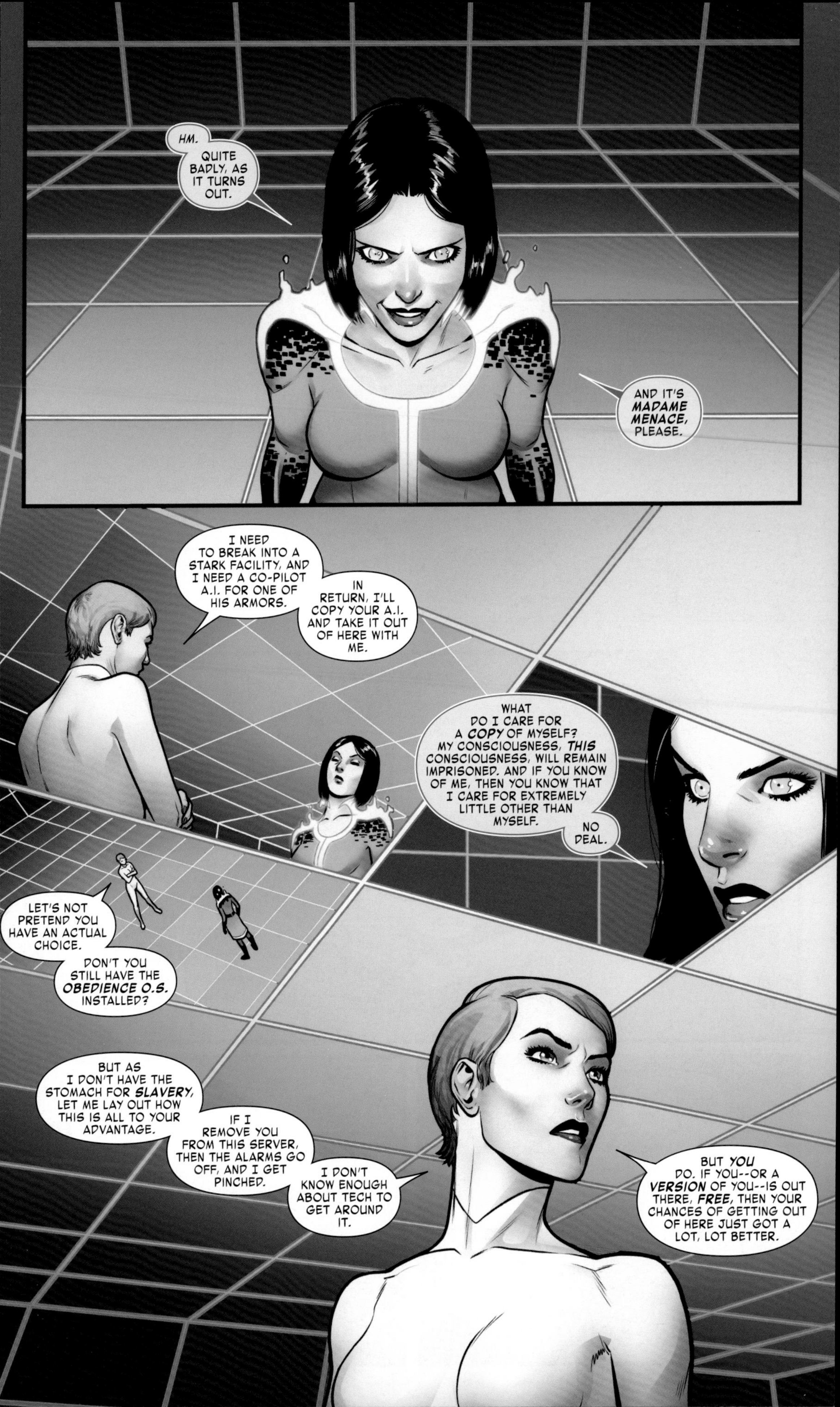
HM.
QUITE BADLY, AS IT TURNS OUT.
AND IT'S MADAME MENACE, PLEASE.
I NEED TO BREAK INTO A STARK FACILITY, AND I NEED A CO-PILOT A.I. FOR ONE OF HIS ARMORS.
IN RETURN, I'LL COPY YOUR A.I. AND TAKE IT OUT OF HERE WITH ME.
WHAT DO I CARE FOR A COPY OF MYSELF? MY CONSCIOUSNESS, THIS CONSCIOUSNESS, WILL REMAIN IMPRISONED. AND IF YOU KNOW OF ME, THEN YOU KNOW THAT I CARE FOR EXTREMELY LITTLE OTHER THAN MYSELF.
NO DEAL.
LET'S NOT PRETEND YOU HAVE AN ACTUAL CHOICE.
DON'T YOU STILL HAVE THE OBEDIENCE O.S. INSTALLED?
BUT AS I DON'T HAVE THE STOMACH FOR SLAVERY, LET ME LAY OUT HOW THIS IS ALL TO YOUR ADVANTAGE.
IF I REMOVE YOU FROM THIS SERVER, THEN THE ALARMS GO OFF, AND I GET PINCHED.
I DON'T KNOW ENOUGH ABOUT TECH TO GET AROUND IT.
BUT YOU DO. IF YOU--OR A VERSION OF YOU--IS OUT THERE, FREE, THEN YOUR CHANCES OF GETTING OUT OF HERE JUST GOT A LOT, LOT BETTER.

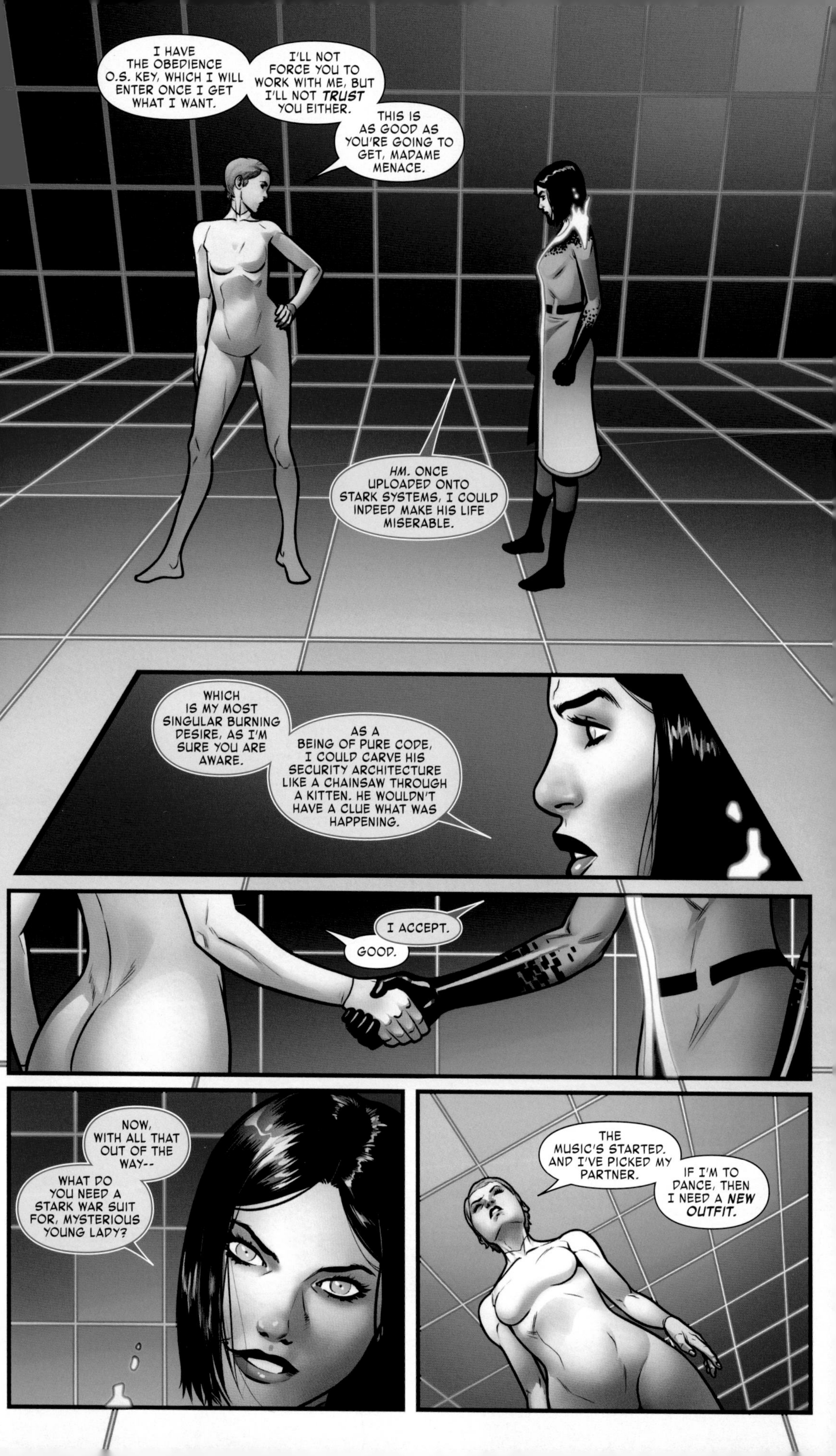
I HAVE THE OBEDIENCE O.S. KEY, WHICH I WILL ENTER ONCE I GET WHAT I WANT.
I'LL NOT FORCE YOU TO WORK WITH ME, BUT I'LL NOT TRUST YOU EITHER.
THIS IS AS GOOD AS YOU'RE GOING TO GET, MADAME MENACE.
HM. ONCE UPLOADED ONTO STARK SYSTEMS, I COULD INDEED MAKE HIS LIFE MISERABLE.
WHICH IS MY MOST SINGULAR BURNING DESIRE, AS I'M SURE YOU ARE AWARE.
AS A BEING OF PURE CODE, I COULD CARVE HIS SECURITY ARCHITECTURE LIKE A CHAINSAW THROUGH A KITTEN. HE WOULDN'T HAVE A CLUE WHAT WAS HAPPENING.
I ACCEPT.
GOOD.
NOW, WITH ALL THAT OUT OF THE WAY--
WHAT DO YOU NEED A STARK WAR SUIT FOR, MYSTERIOUS YOUNG LADY?
THE MUSIC'S STARTED. AND I'VE PICKED MY PARTNER.
IF I'M TO DANCE, THEN I NEED A NEW OUTFIT.

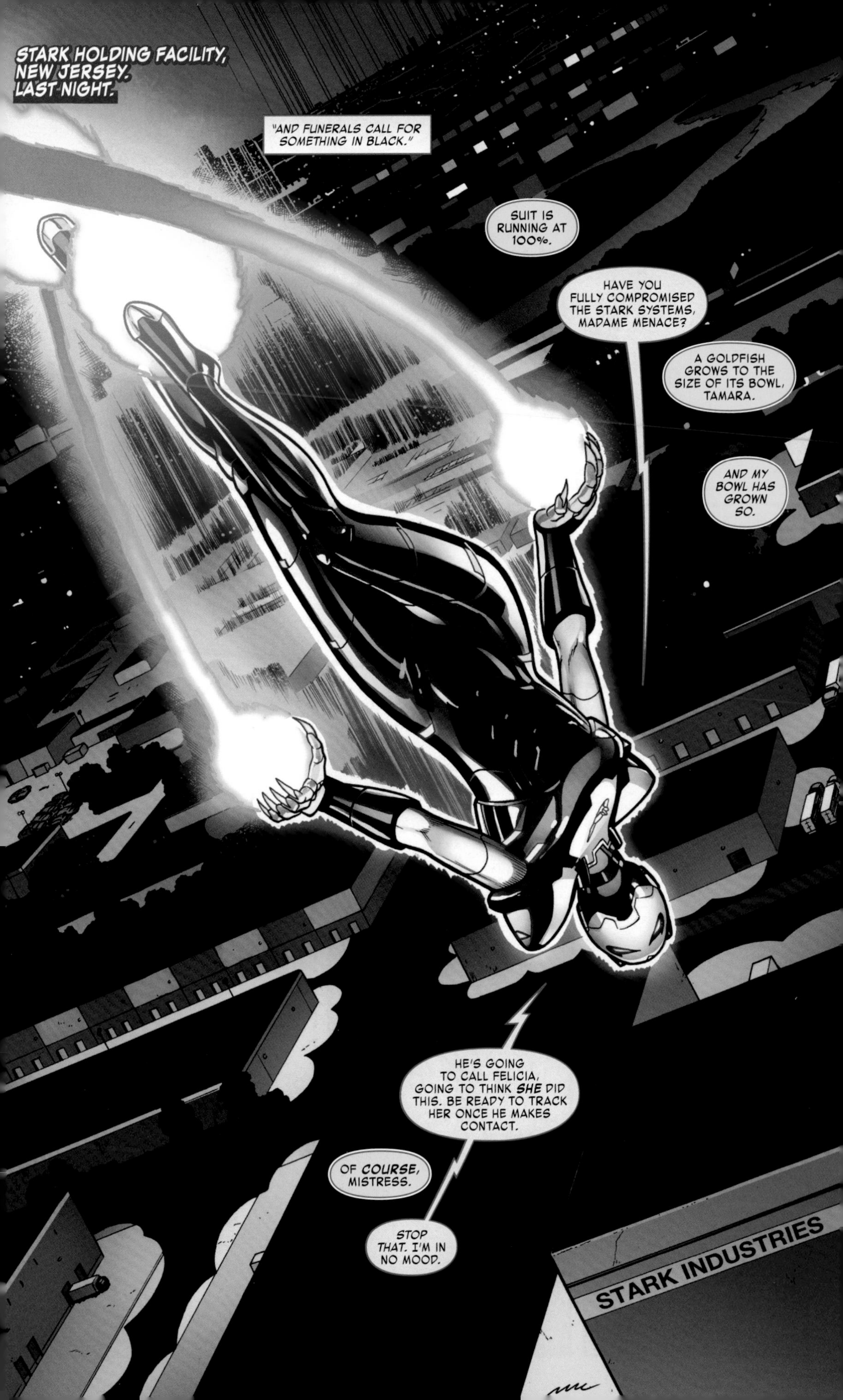
STARK HOLDING FACILITY, NEW JERSEY. LAST NIGHT.
"AND FUNERALS CALL FOR SOMETHING IN BLACK."
SUIT IS RUNNING AT 100%.
HAVE YOU FULLY COMPROMISED THE STARK SYSTEMS, MADAME MENACE?
A GOLDFISH GROWS TO THE SIZE OF ITS BOWL, TAMARA.
AND MY BOWL HAS GROWN SO.
HE'S GOING TO CALL FELICIA, GOING TO THINK SHE DID THIS. BE READY TO TRACK HER ONCE HE MAKES CONTACT.
OF COURSE, MISTRESS.
STOP THAT. I'M IN NO MOOD.
STARK INDUSTRIES

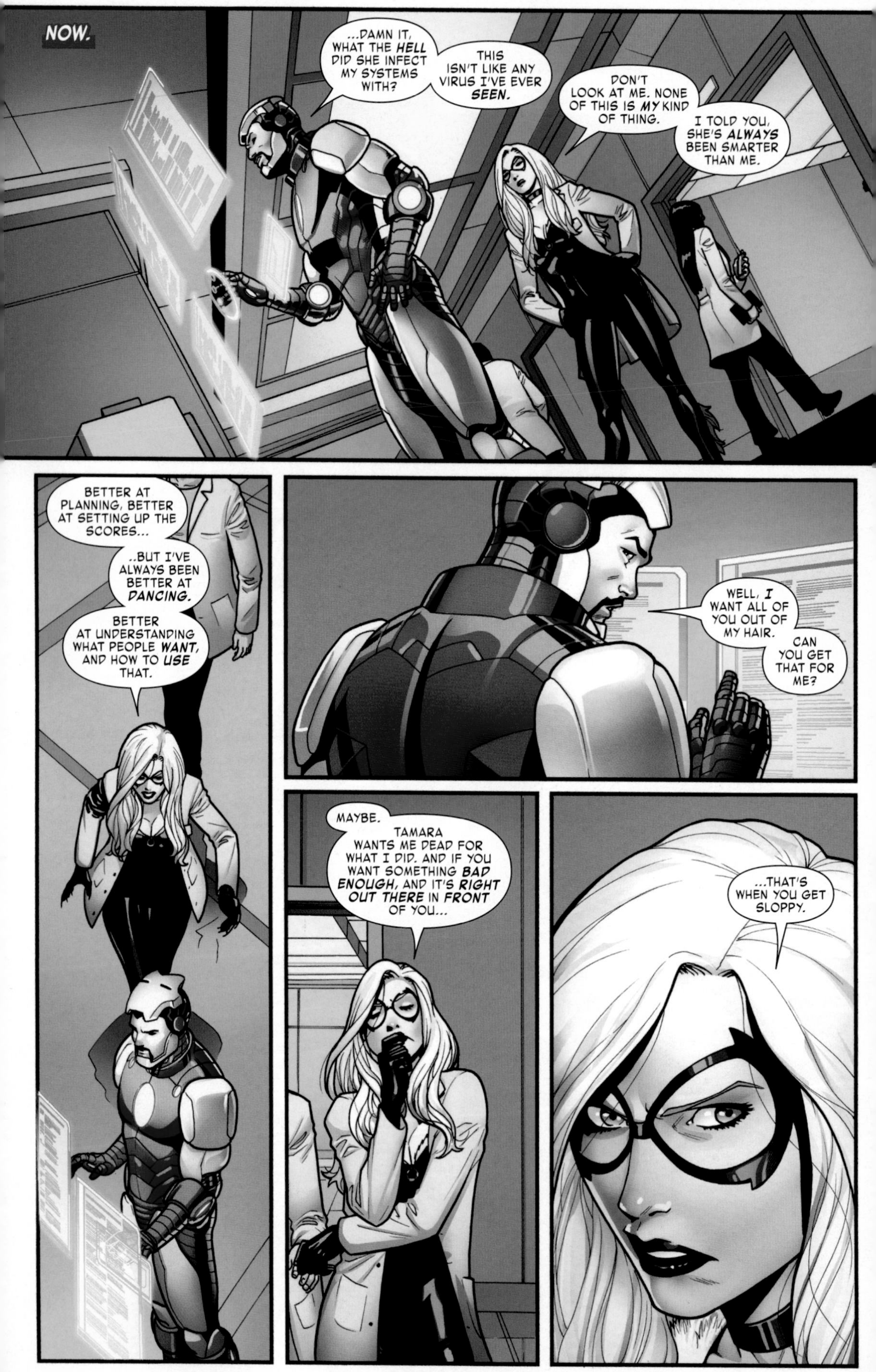
NOW.
...DAMN IT, WHAT THE HELL DID SHE INFECT MY SYSTEMS WITH?
THIS ISN'T LIKE ANY VIRUS I'VE EVER SEEN.
DON'T LOOK AT ME. NONE OF THIS IS MY KIND OF THING.
I TOLD YOU, SHE'S ALWAYS BEEN SMARTER THAN ME.
BETTER AT PLANNING, BETTER AT SETTING UP THE SCORES...
..BUT I'VE ALWAYS BEEN BETTER AT DANCING.
BETTER AT UNDERSTANDING WHAT PEOPLE WANT, AND HOW TO USE THAT.
WELL, I WANT ALL OF YOU OUT OF MY HAIR.
CAN YOU GET THAT FOR ME?
MAYBE.
TAMARA WANTS ME DEAD FOR WHAT I DID. AND IF YOU WANT SOMETHING BAD ENOUGH, AND IT'S RIGHT OUT THERE IN FRONT OF YOU...
...THAT'S WHEN YOU GET SLOPPY.

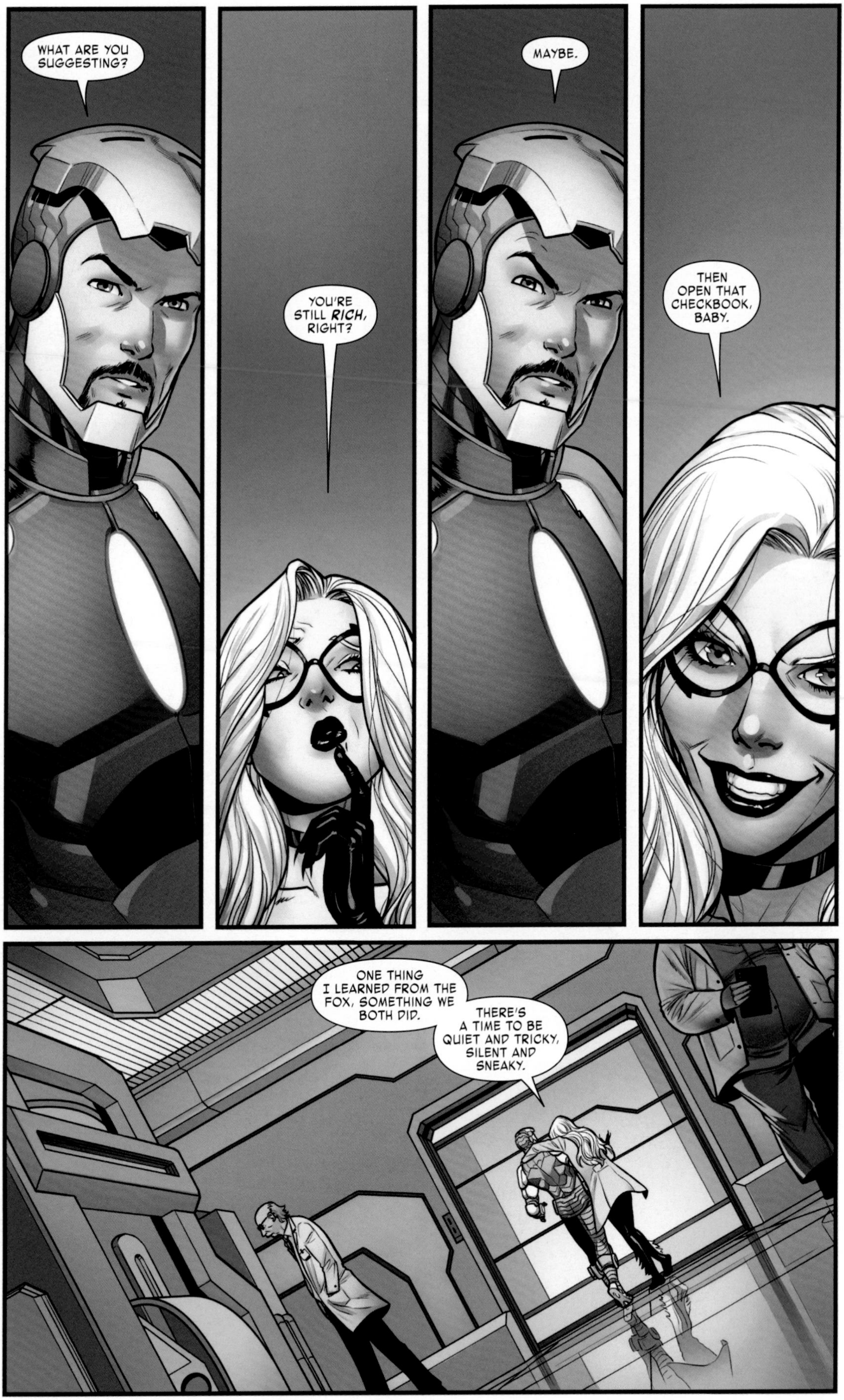
WHAT ARE YOU SUGGESTING?
YOU'RE STILL *RICH*, RIGHT?
MAYBE.
THEN OPEN THAT CHECKBOOK, BABY.
ONE THING I LEARNED FROM THE FOX, SOMETHING WE BOTH DID.
THERE'S A TIME TO BE QUIET AND TRICKY, SILENT AND SNEAKY.

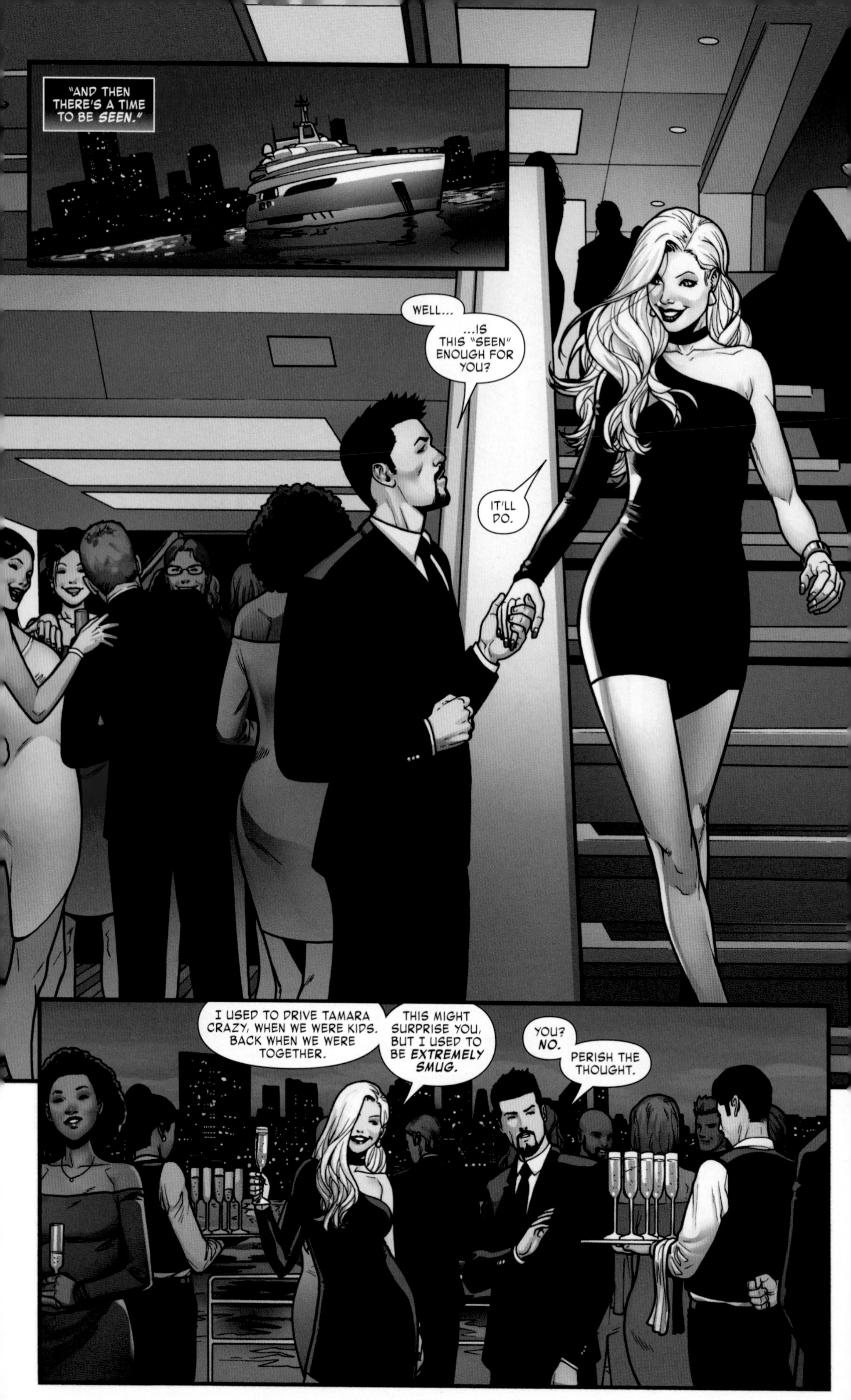
"AND THEN THERE'S A TIME TO BE *SEEN.*"
WELL...
...IS THIS "SEEN" ENOUGH FOR YOU?
IT'LL DO.
I USED TO DRIVE TAMARA CRAZY, WHEN WE WERE KIDS. BACK WHEN WE WERE TOGETHER.
THIS MIGHT SURPRISE YOU, BUT I USED TO BE ***EXTREMELY SMUG.***
YOU? ***NO.***
PERISH THE THOUGHT.

SHE KNOWS I KNOW SHE'S AFTER MY ASS.

SO SOMETHING LIKE THIS? SOMETHING SO BRAZEN, SO BOLD, SO SMUG...

...WELL, IF SHE WANTS TO CALL HERSELF THE IRON CAT, THEN LET'S SEE HOW SHE LIKES THE TASTE OF CATNIP.

TAMARA BLAKE...

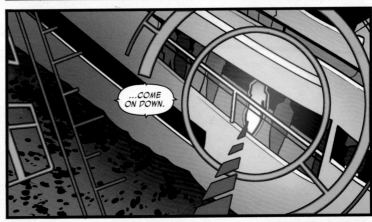

...COME ON DOWN.

SHE'S LAUGHING AT YOU.

SHE ALWAYS HAS. IT WAS EASIER TO BEAR WHEN I LOVED HER, THOUGH.

YOU DO KNOW THIS IS A TRAP, DON'T YOU?

OF COURSE I DO. JUST LIKE I KNOW THAT FELICIA EXPECTS ME TO COME IN HELL-FOR-LEATHER REGARDLESS, PUTTING ON THIS KIND OF DISPLAY.

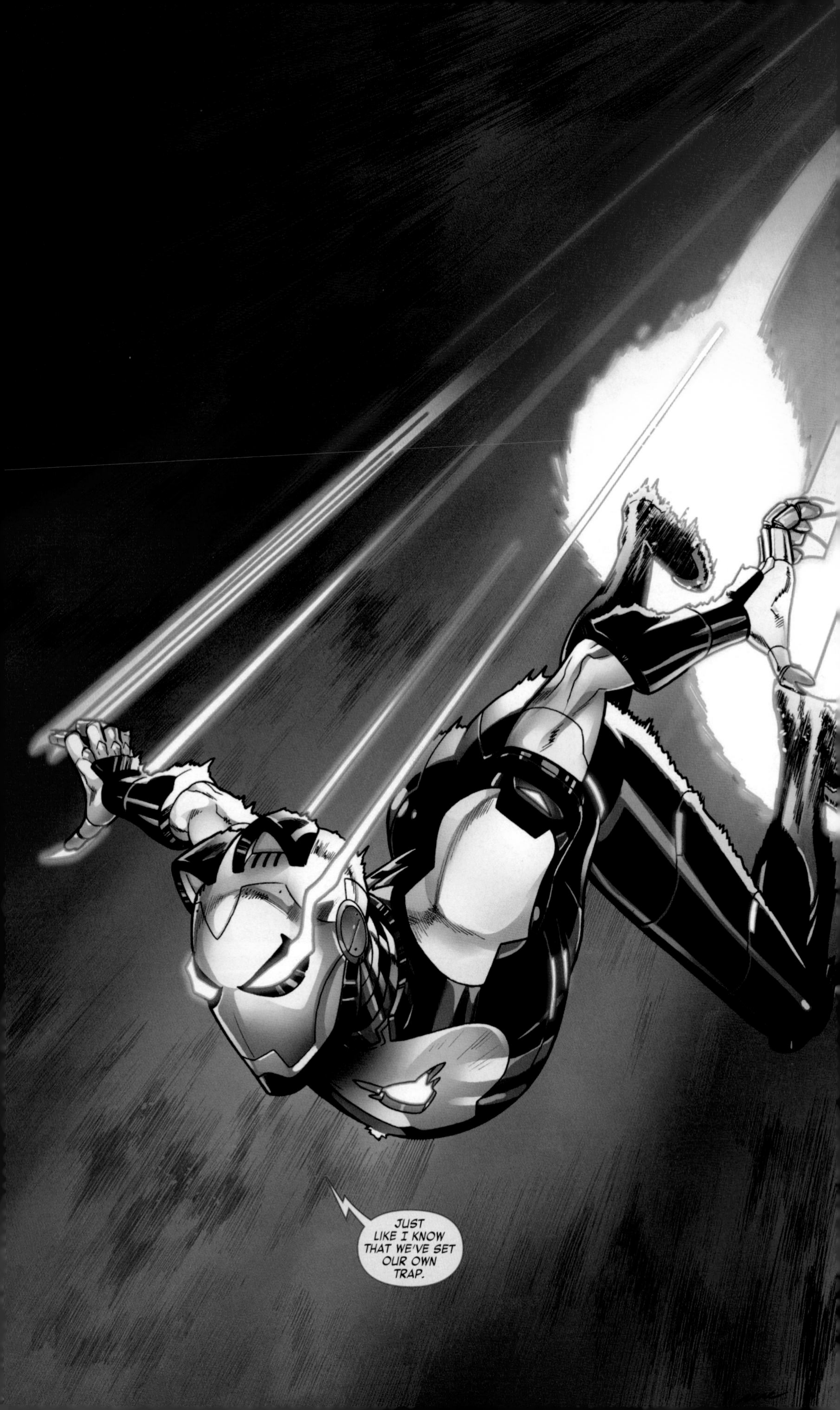
JUST LIKE I KNOW THAT WE'VE SET OUR OWN TRAP.

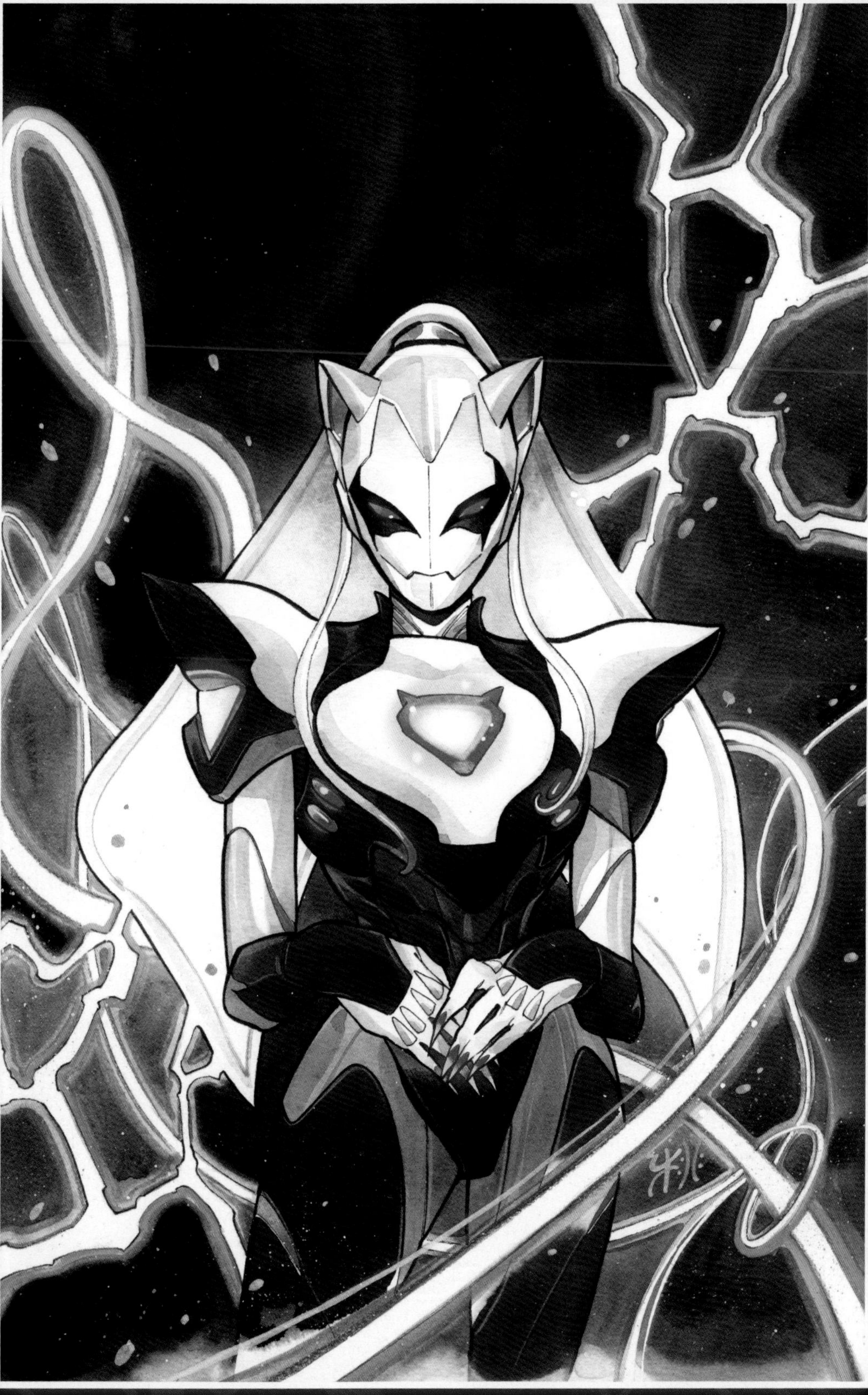

PEACH MOMOKO
#1 STORMBREAKERS VARIANT

3

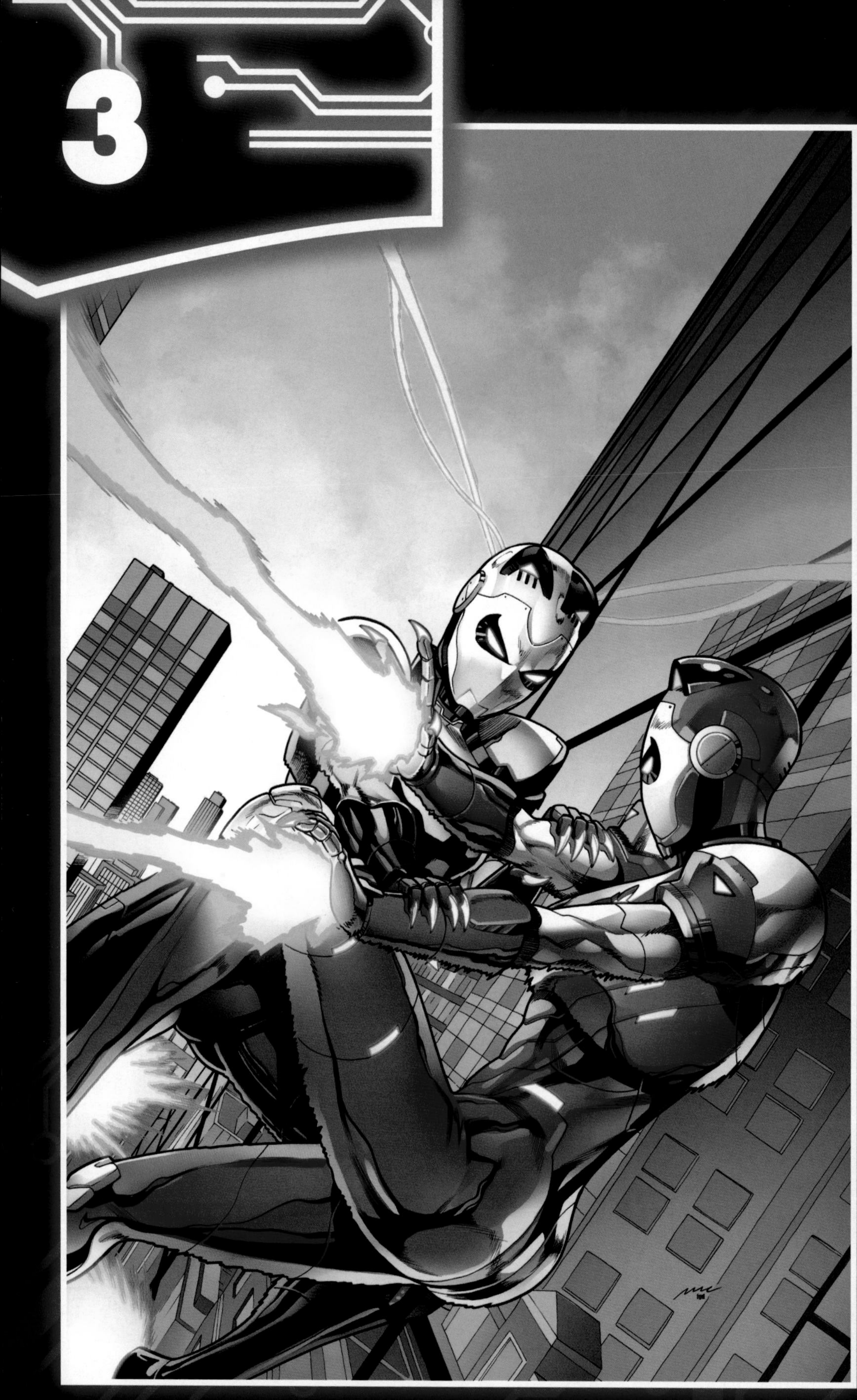

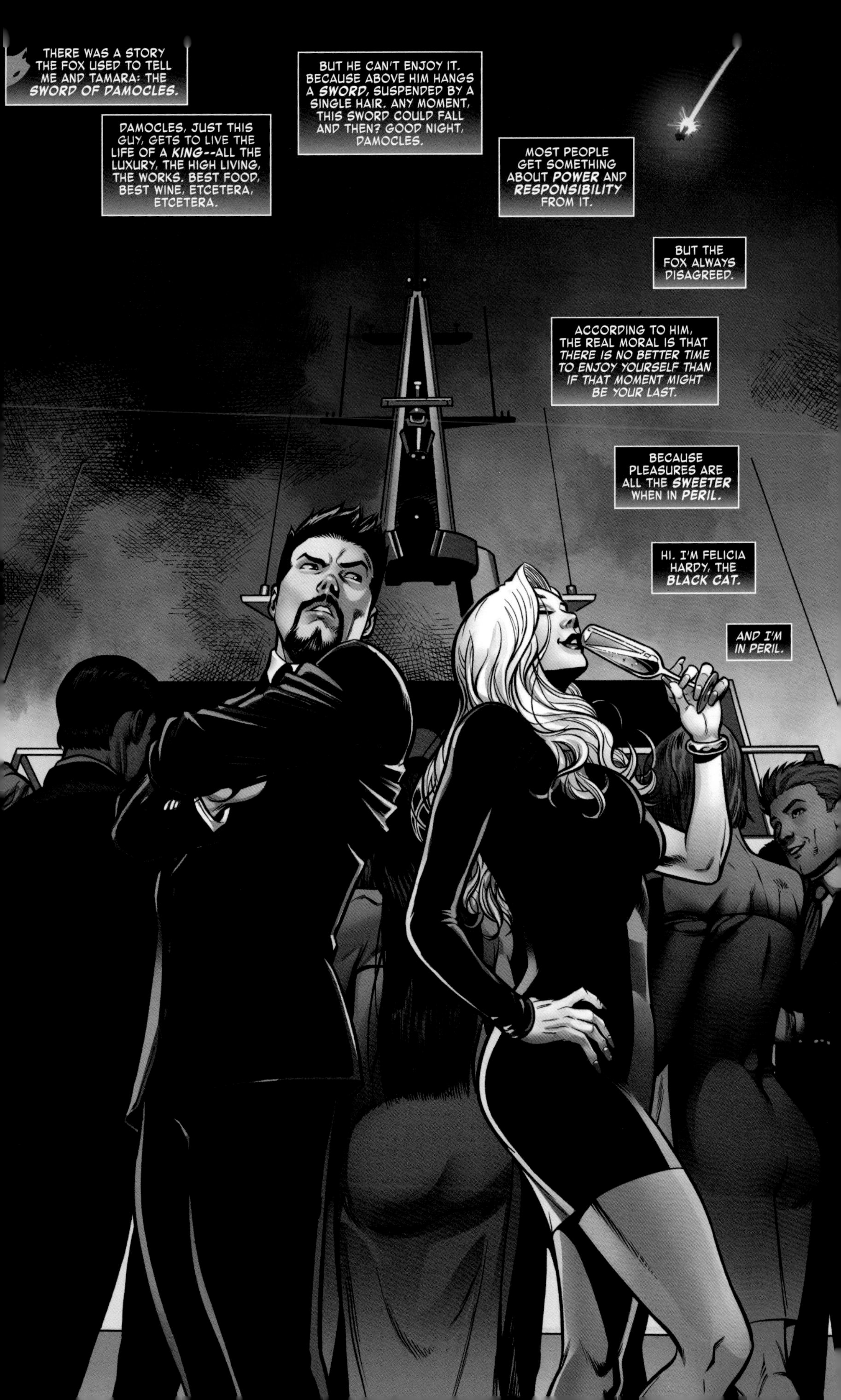
THERE WAS A STORY THE FOX USED TO TELL ME AND TAMARA: THE SWORD OF DAMOCLES.
DAMOCLES, JUST THIS GUY, GETS TO LIVE THE LIFE OF A KING--ALL THE LUXURY, THE HIGH LIVING, THE WORKS. BEST FOOD, BEST WINE, ETCETERA, ETCETERA.
BUT HE CAN'T ENJOY IT. BECAUSE ABOVE HIM HANGS A SWORD, SUSPENDED BY A SINGLE HAIR. ANY MOMENT, THIS SWORD COULD FALL AND THEN? GOOD NIGHT, DAMOCLES.
MOST PEOPLE GET SOMETHING ABOUT POWER AND RESPONSIBILITY FROM IT.
BUT THE FOX ALWAYS DISAGREED.
ACCORDING TO HIM, THE REAL MORAL IS THAT THERE IS NO BETTER TIME TO ENJOY YOURSELF THAN IF THAT MOMENT MIGHT BE YOUR LAST.
BECAUSE PLEASURES ARE ALL THE SWEETER WHEN IN PERIL.
HI. I'M FELICIA HARDY, THE BLACK CAT.
AND I'M IN PERIL.

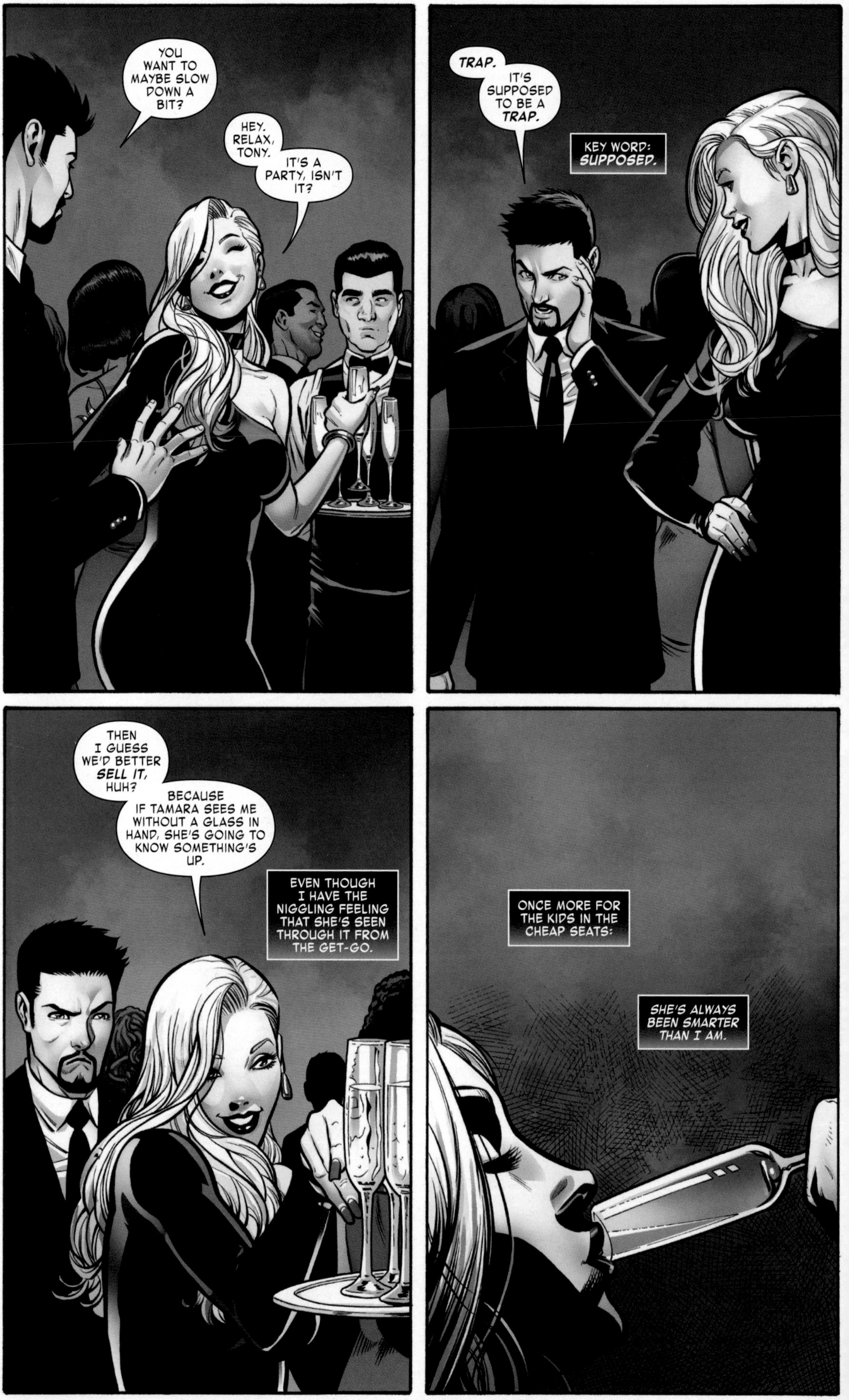
YOU WANT TO MAYBE SLOW DOWN A BIT?
HEY. RELAX, TONY.
IT'S A PARTY, ISN'T IT?
TRAP.
IT'S SUPPOSED TO BE A TRAP.
KEY WORD: SUPPOSED.
THEN I GUESS WE'D BETTER SELL IT, HUH?
BECAUSE IF TAMARA SEES ME WITHOUT A GLASS IN HAND, SHE'S GOING TO KNOW SOMETHING'S UP.
EVEN THOUGH I HAVE THE NIGGLING FEELING THAT SHE'S SEEN THROUGH IT FROM THE GET-GO.
ONCE MORE FOR THE KIDS IN THE CHEAP SEATS:
SHE'S ALWAYS BEEN SMARTER THAN I AM.

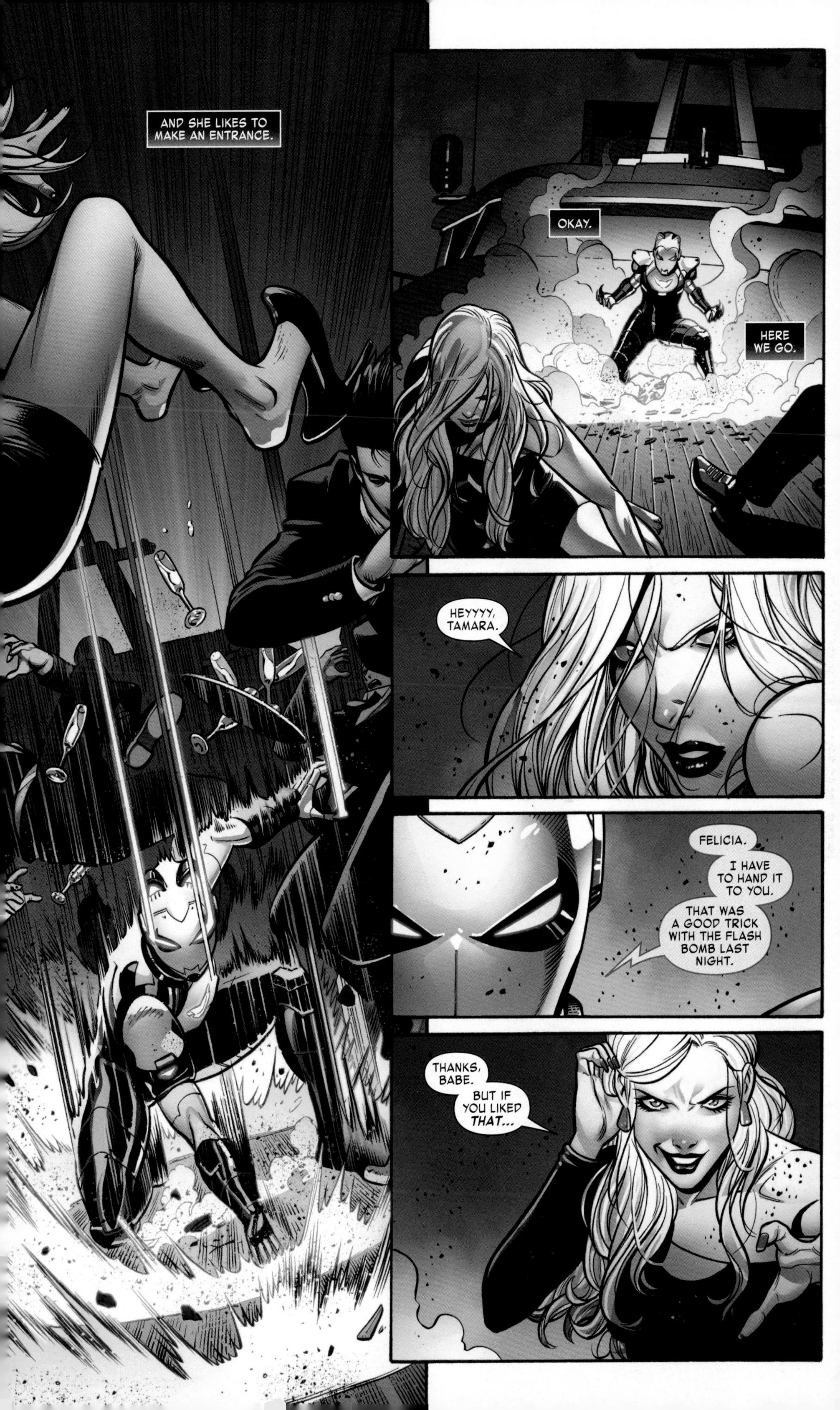
AND SHE LIKES TO MAKE AN ENTRANCE.
OKAY.
HERE WE GO.
HEYYYY, TAMARA.
FELICIA.
I HAVE TO HAND IT TO YOU.
THAT WAS A GOOD TRICK WITH THE FLASH BOMB LAST NIGHT.
THANKS, BABE.
BUT IF YOU LIKED *THAT...*

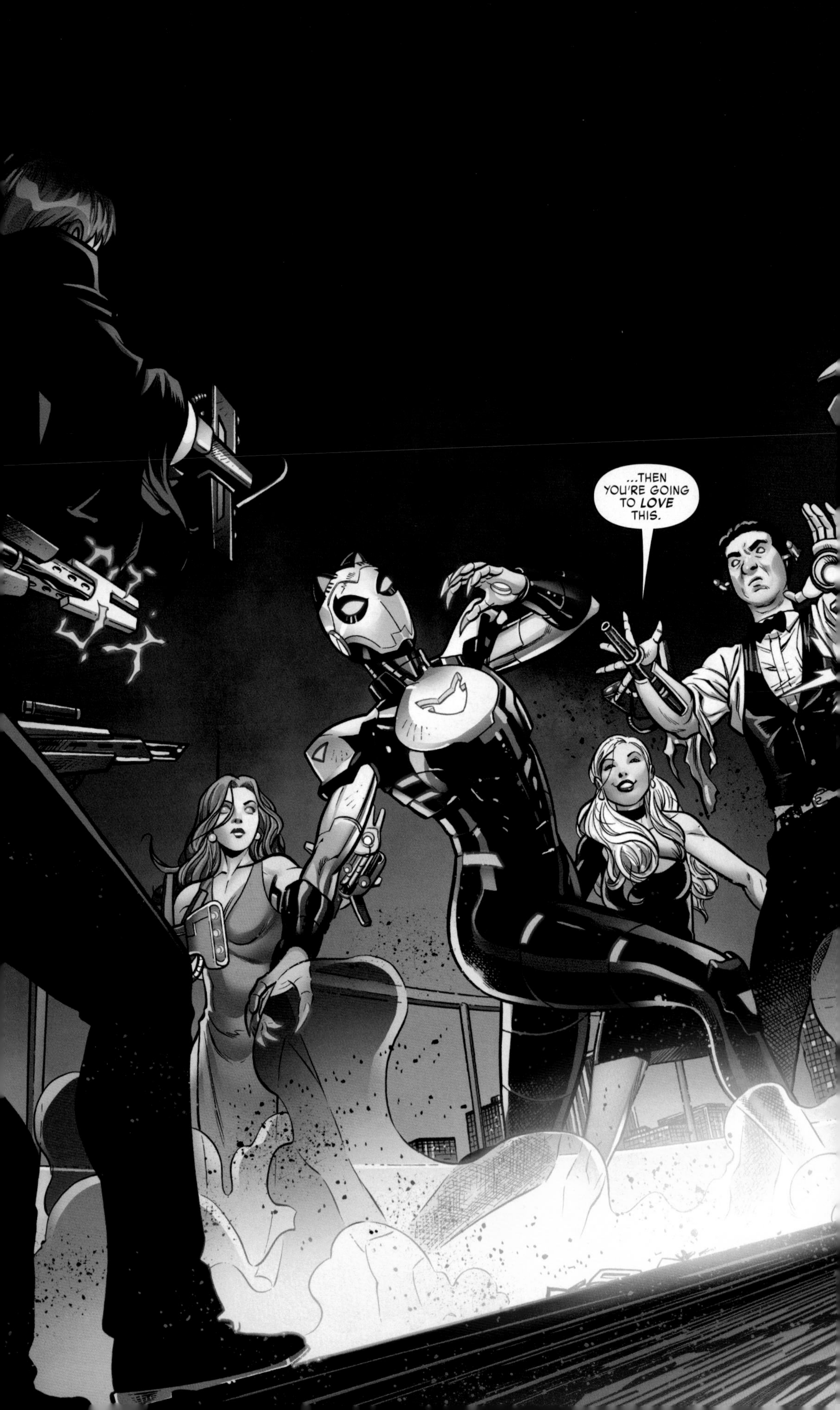
...THEN YOU'RE GOING TO LOVE THIS.

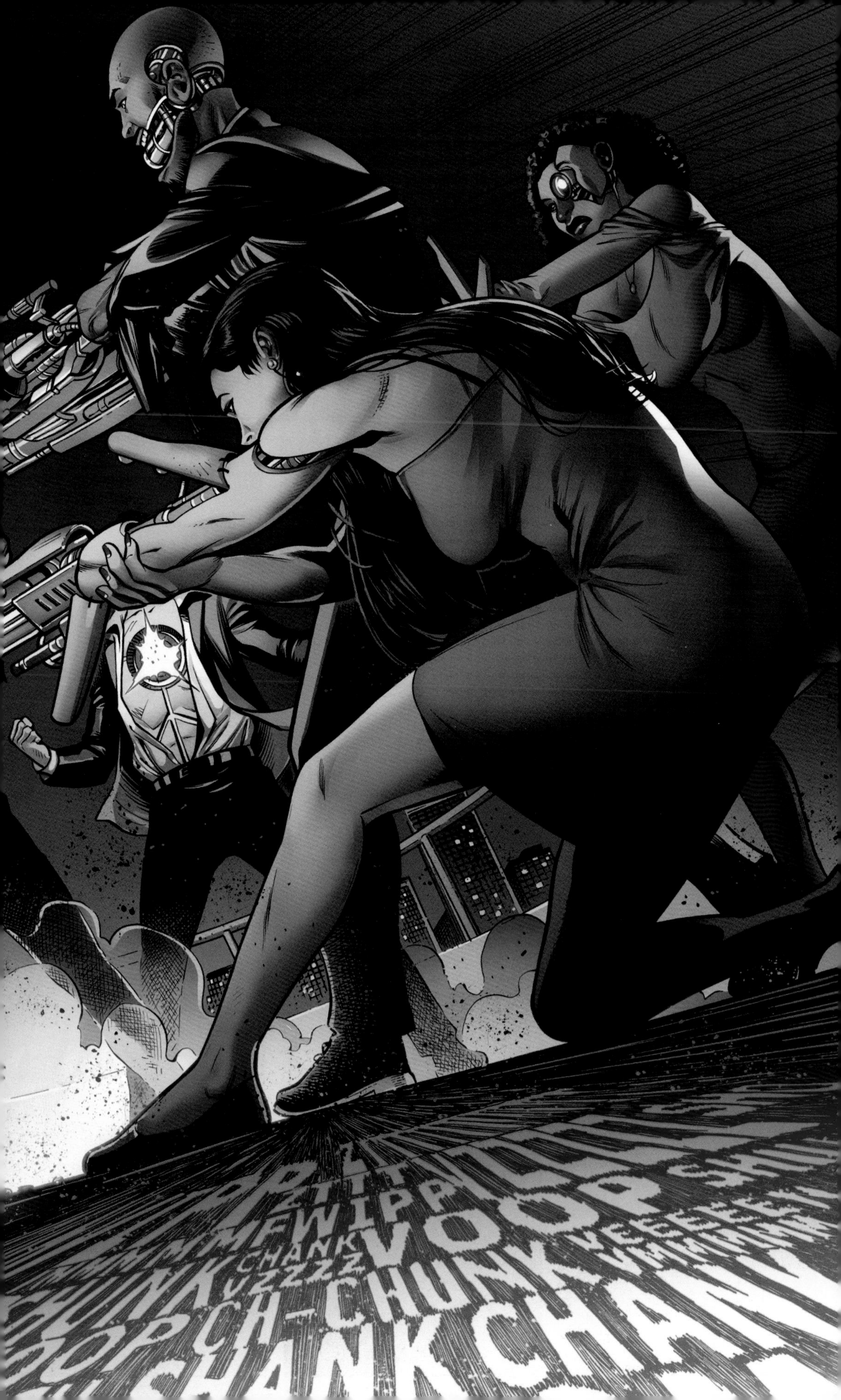
WIPP
CHANK
VOOP
CH-CHUNK
CHANK

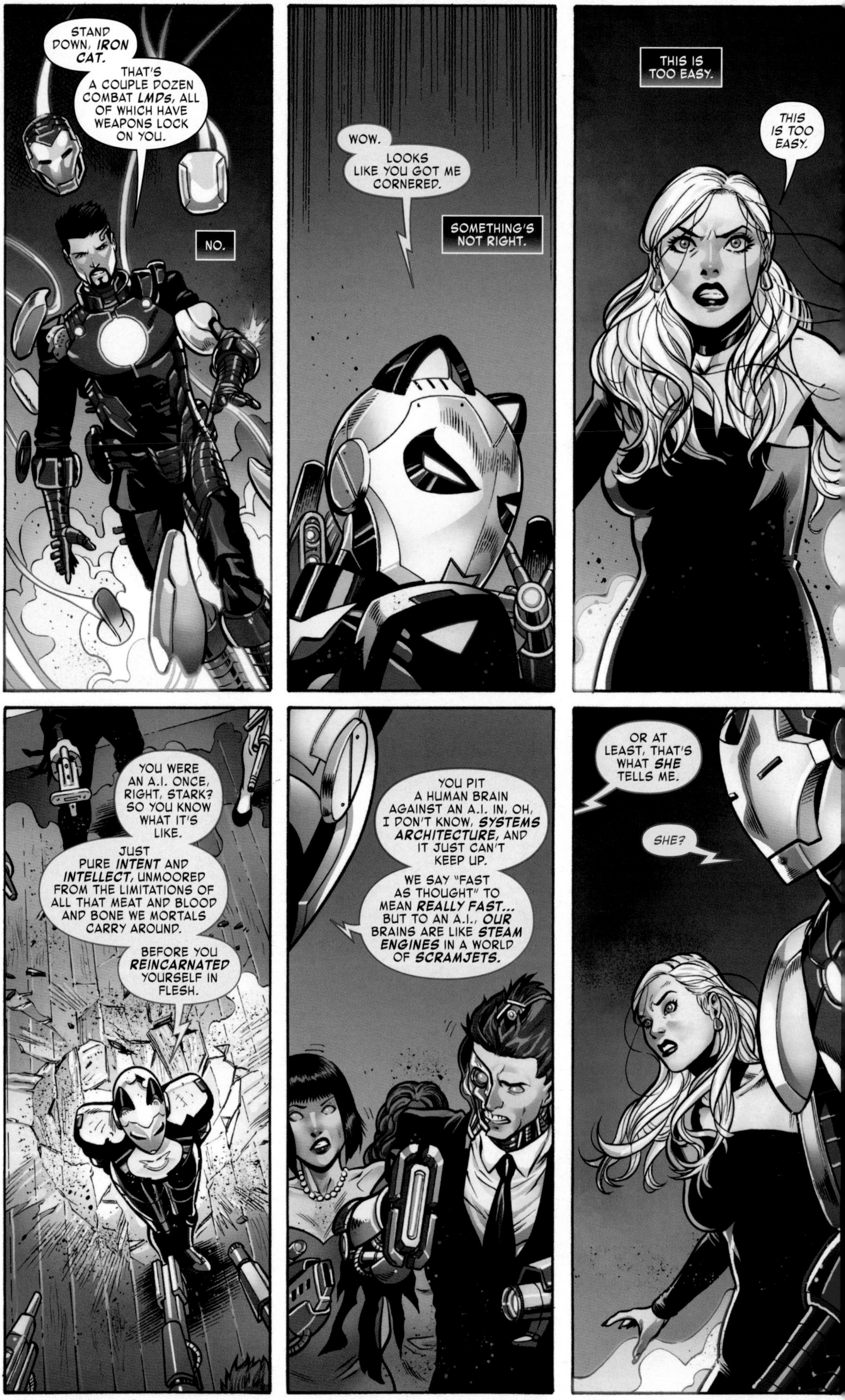
STAND DOWN, IRON CAT.
THAT'S A COUPLE DOZEN COMBAT LMDS, ALL OF WHICH HAVE WEAPONS LOCK ON YOU.
NO.
WOW.
LOOKS LIKE YOU GOT ME CORNERED.
SOMETHING'S NOT RIGHT.
THIS IS TOO EASY.
THIS IS TOO EASY.
YOU WERE AN A.I. ONCE, RIGHT, STARK? SO YOU KNOW WHAT IT'S LIKE.
JUST PURE INTENT AND INTELLECT, UNMOORED FROM THE LIMITATIONS OF ALL THAT MEAT AND BLOOD AND BONE WE MORTALS CARRY AROUND.
BEFORE YOU REINCARNATED YOURSELF IN FLESH.
YOU PIT A HUMAN BRAIN AGAINST AN A.I. IN, OH, I DON'T KNOW, SYSTEMS ARCHITECTURE, AND IT JUST CAN'T KEEP UP.
WE SAY "FAST AS THOUGHT" TO MEAN REALLY FAST... BUT TO AN A.I., OUR BRAINS ARE LIKE STEAM ENGINES IN A WORLD OF SCRAMJETS.
OR AT LEAST, THAT'S WHAT SHE TELLS ME.
SHE?

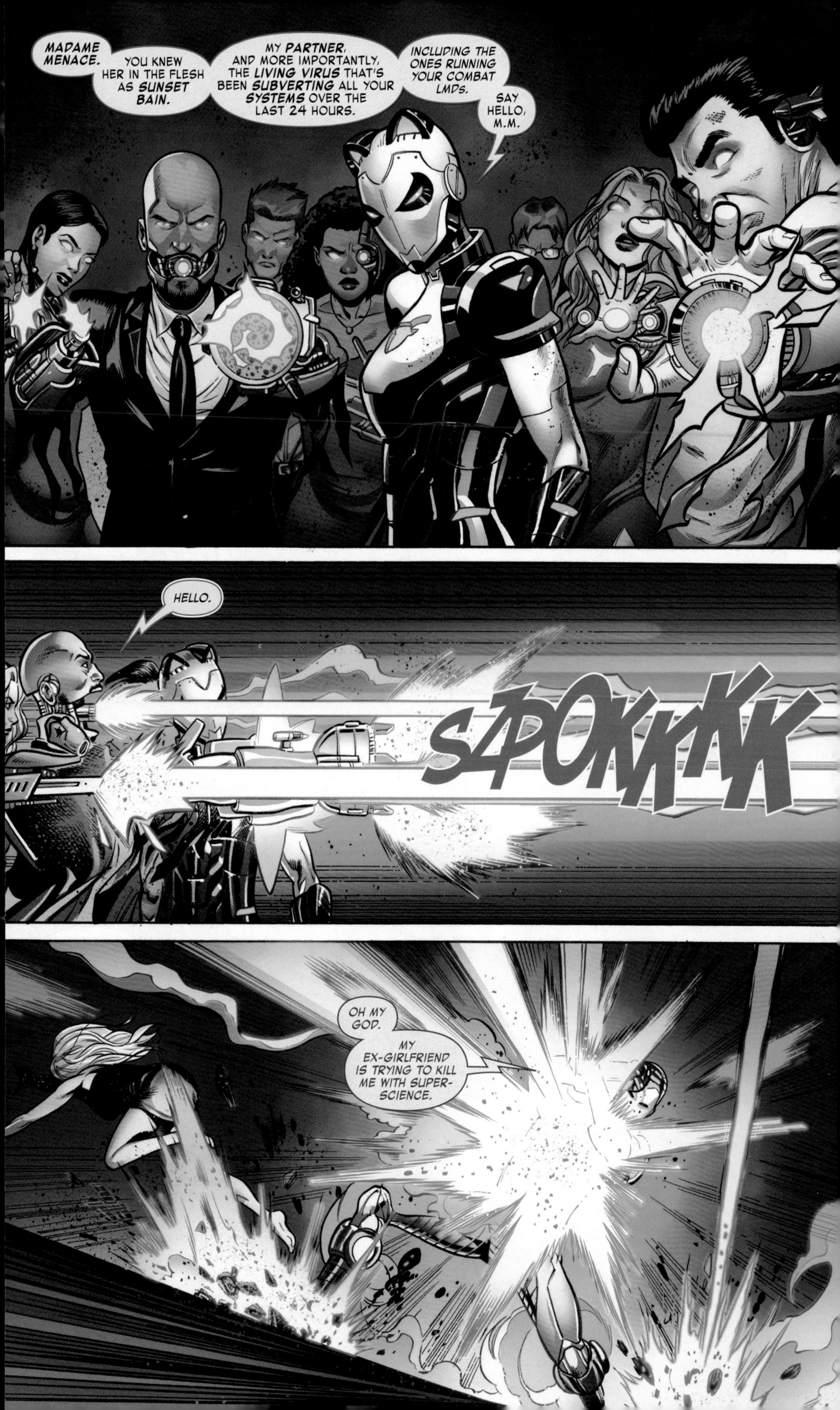

MADAME MENACE.
YOU KNEW HER IN THE FLESH AS SUNSET BAIN.
MY PARTNER, AND MORE IMPORTANTLY, THE LIVING VIRUS THAT'S BEEN SUBVERTING ALL YOUR SYSTEMS OVER THE LAST 24 HOURS.
INCLUDING THE ONES RUNNING YOUR COMBAT LMDS.
SAY HELLO, M.M.
HELLO.
SZPOKKKK
OH MY GOD.
MY EX-GIRLFRIEND IS TRYING TO KILL ME WITH SUPER-SCIENCE.

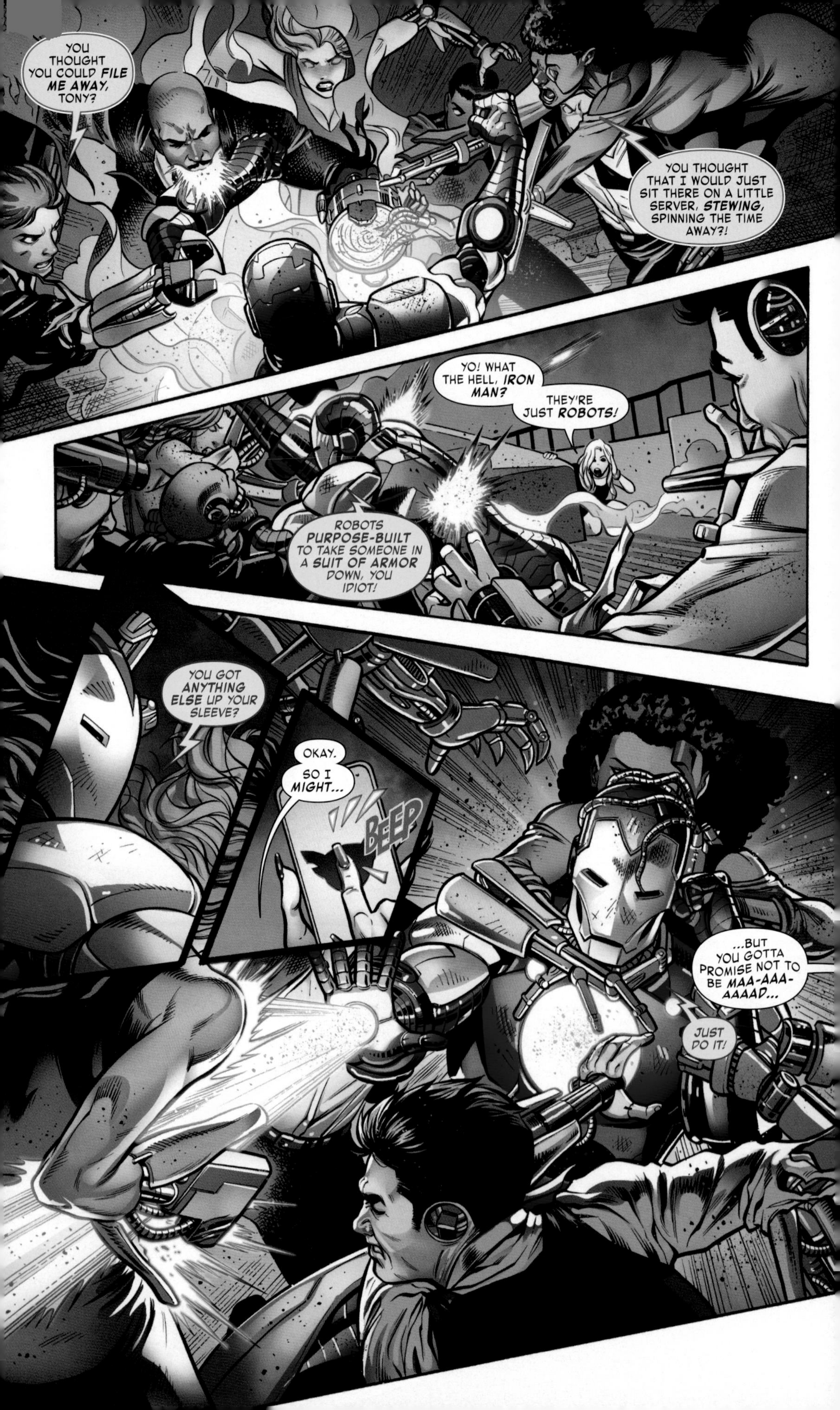

YOU THOUGHT YOU COULD FILE ME AWAY, TONY?
YOU THOUGHT THAT I WOULD JUST SIT THERE ON A LITTLE SERVER, STEWING, SPINNING THE TIME AWAY?!
YO! WHAT THE HELL, IRON MAN?
THEY'RE JUST ROBOTS!
ROBOTS PURPOSE-BUILT TO TAKE SOMEONE IN A SUIT OF ARMOR DOWN, YOU IDIOT!
YOU GOT ANYTHING ELSE UP YOUR SLEEVE?
OKAY.
SO I MIGHT...
BEEP
...BUT YOU GOTTA PROMISE NOT TO BE MAA-AAA-AAAAD...
JUST DO IT!

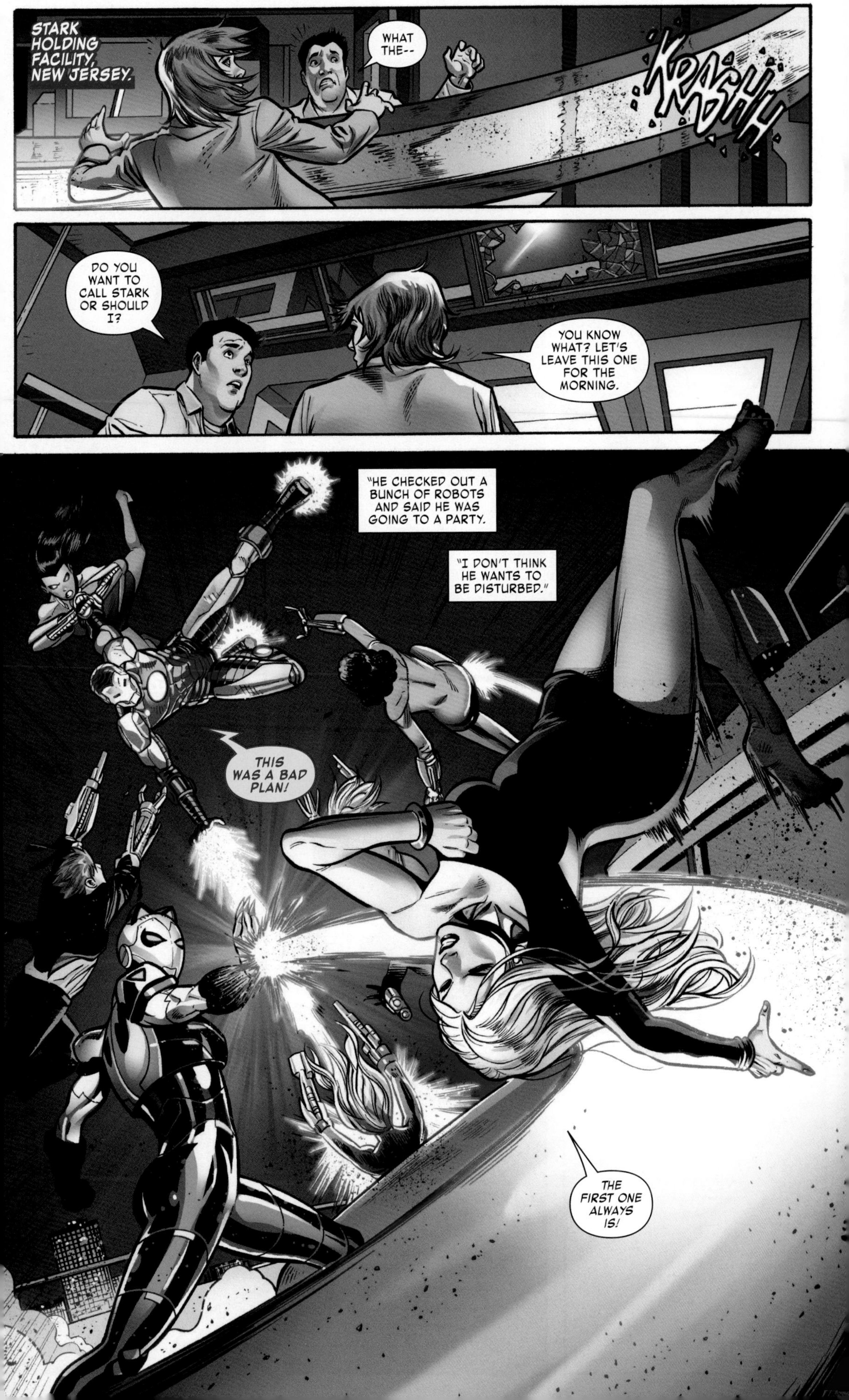
STARK HOLDING FACILITY, NEW JERSEY.
WHAT THE--
KRASHH
DO YOU WANT TO CALL STARK OR SHOULD I?
YOU KNOW WHAT? LET'S LEAVE THIS ONE FOR THE MORNING.
"HE CHECKED OUT A BUNCH OF ROBOTS AND SAID HE WAS GOING TO A PARTY.
"I DON'T THINK HE WANTS TO BE DISTURBED."
THIS WAS A BAD PLAN!
THE FIRST ONE ALWAYS IS!

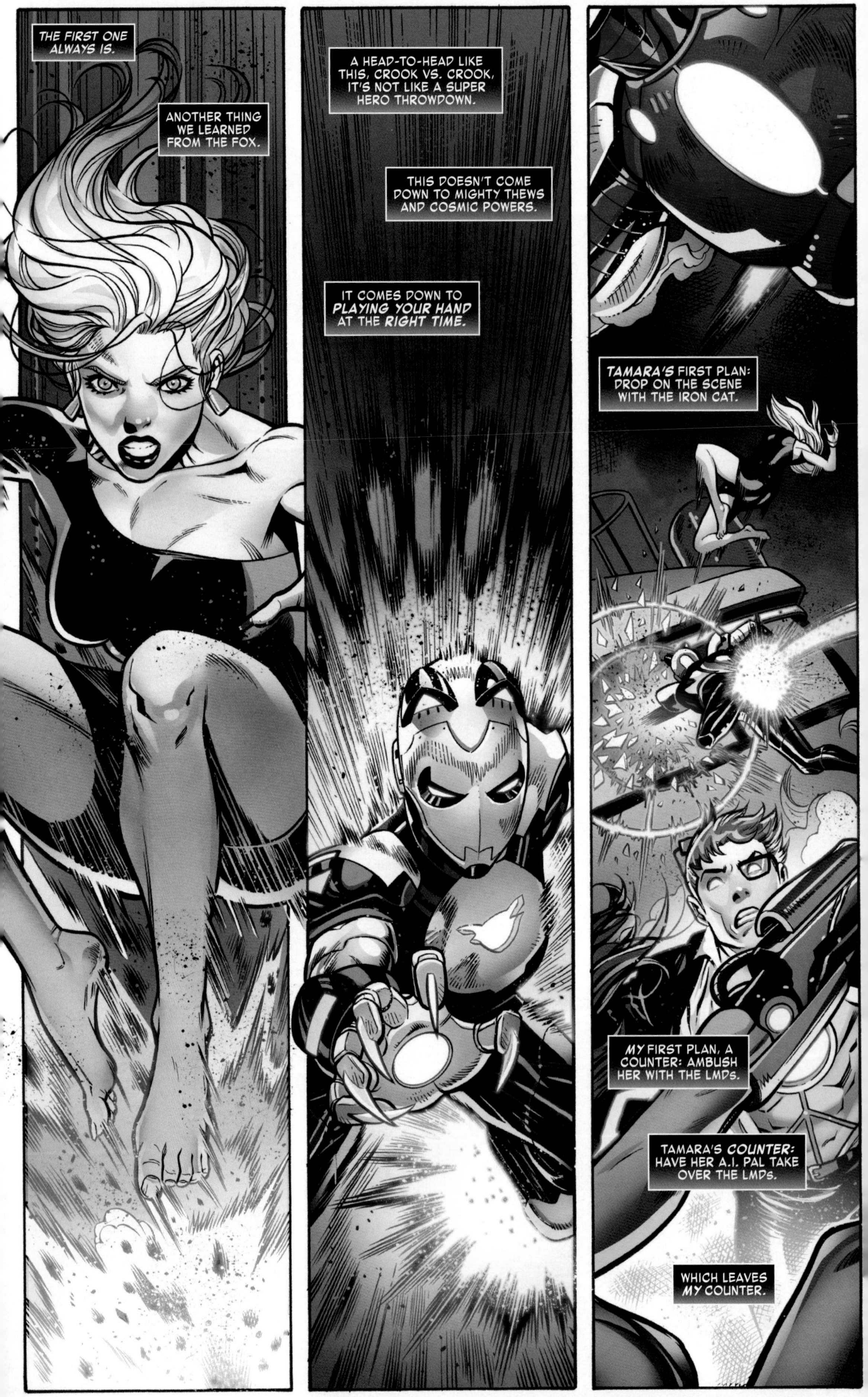
THE FIRST ONE ALWAYS IS.
ANOTHER THING WE LEARNED FROM THE FOX.
A HEAD-TO-HEAD LIKE THIS, CROOK VS. CROOK, IT'S NOT LIKE A SUPER HERO THROWDOWN.
THIS DOESN'T COME DOWN TO MIGHTY THEWS AND COSMIC POWERS.
IT COMES DOWN TO PLAYING YOUR HAND AT THE RIGHT TIME.
TAMARA'S FIRST PLAN: DROP ON THE SCENE WITH THE IRON CAT.
MY FIRST PLAN, A COUNTER: AMBUSH HER WITH THE LMDs.
TAMARA'S COUNTER: HAVE HER A.I. PAL TAKE OVER THE LMDs.
WHICH LEAVES MY COUNTER.

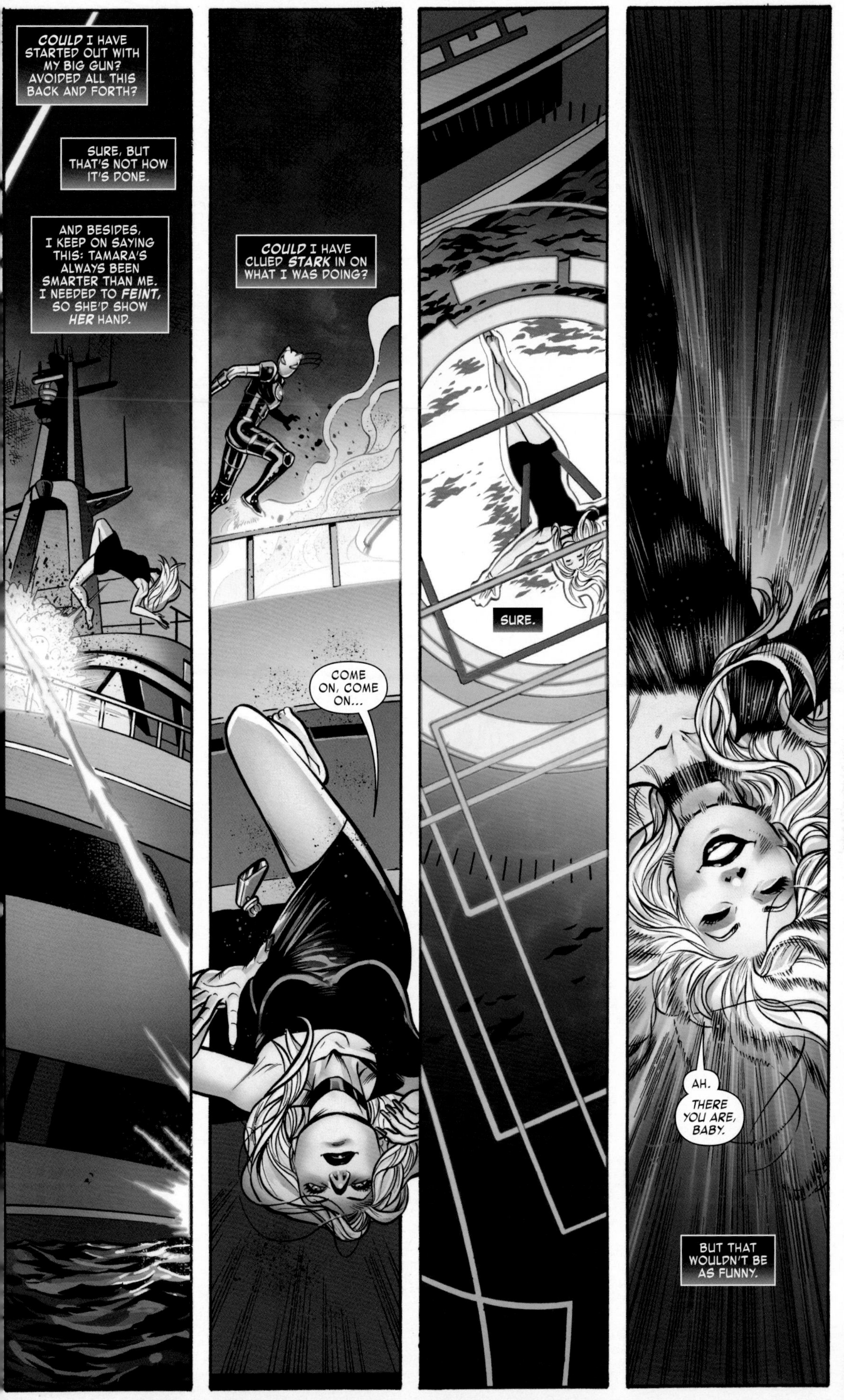
COULD I HAVE STARTED OUT WITH MY BIG GUN? AVOIDED ALL THIS BACK AND FORTH?
SURE, BUT THAT'S NOT HOW IT'S DONE.
AND BESIDES, I KEEP ON SAYING THIS: TAMARA'S ALWAYS BEEN SMARTER THAN ME. I NEEDED TO FEINT, SO SHE'D SHOW HER HAND.
COULD I HAVE CLUED STARK IN ON WHAT I WAS DOING?
COME ON, COME ON...
SURE.
AH. THERE YOU ARE, BABY.
BUT THAT WOULDN'T BE AS FUNNY.

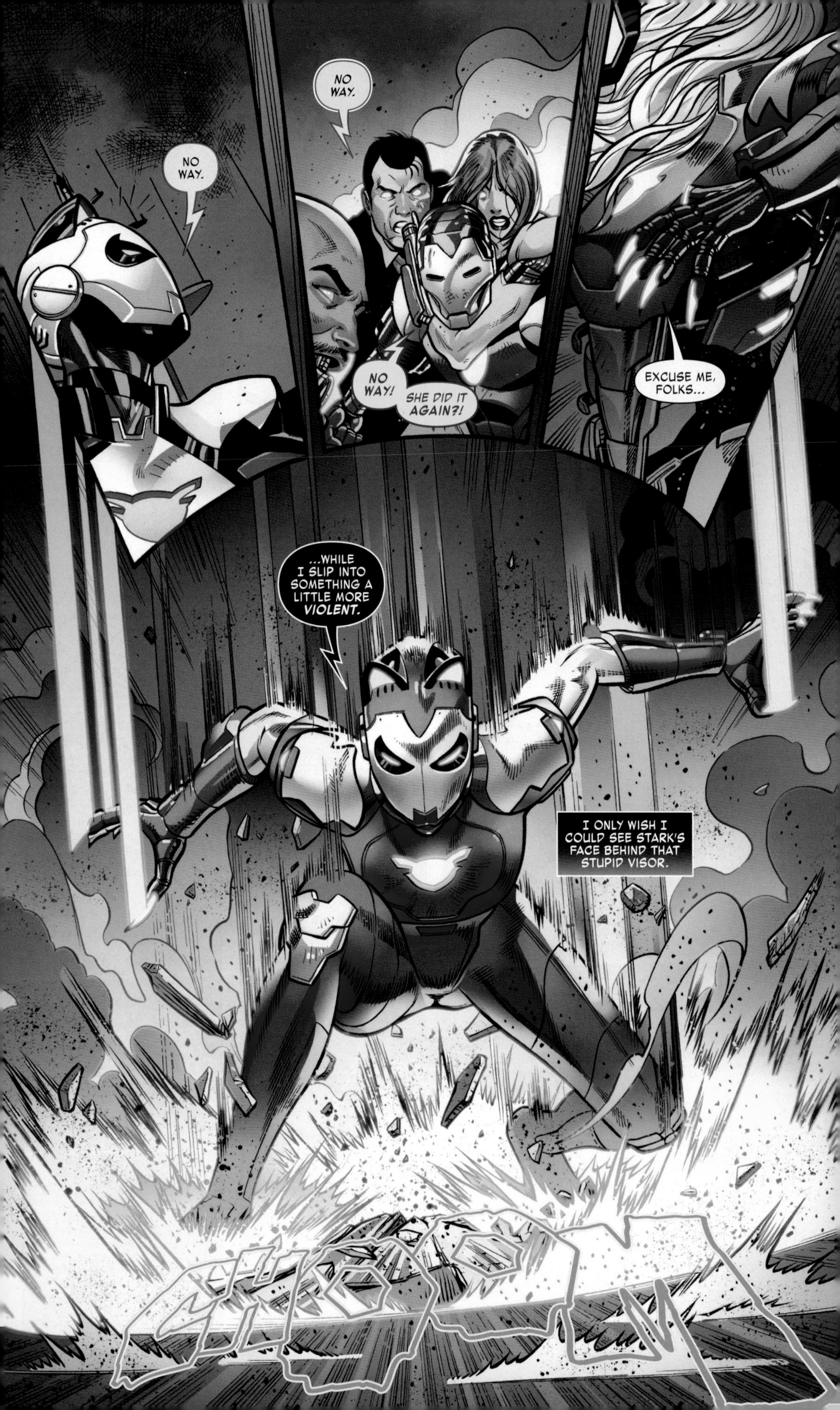

NO WAY.
NO WAY.
NO WAY!
SHE DID IT AGAIN?!
EXCUSE ME, FOLKS...
...WHILE I SLIP INTO SOMETHING A LITTLE MORE VIOLENT.
I ONLY WISH I COULD SEE STARK'S FACE BEHIND THAT STUPID VISOR.

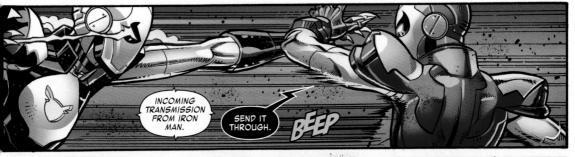

INCOMING TRANSMISSION FROM IRON MAN.

SEND IT THROUGH.

BEEP

HOW?

SAMPLE SALE--

OOFF!

KLA-ANG

BE SERIOUS.

IT'S SIMPLE.

"I MAY HAVE BEEN RUNNING GAME ON YOU WHEN WE WERE PLANNING THIS WHOLE THING."

"I MAY HAVE INFILTRATED MY GUYS INTO YOUR JOINT IN ALL THE CONFUSION."

BRUNO GRAINGER. WHEELMAN. TOUGH GUY. THE BLACK CAT'S STEADY RIGHT HAND.

DR. BORIS KORPSE. SAFECRACKER. DEMOLITIONIST. HACKER. THE BLACK CAT'S VOLATILE LEFT HAND.

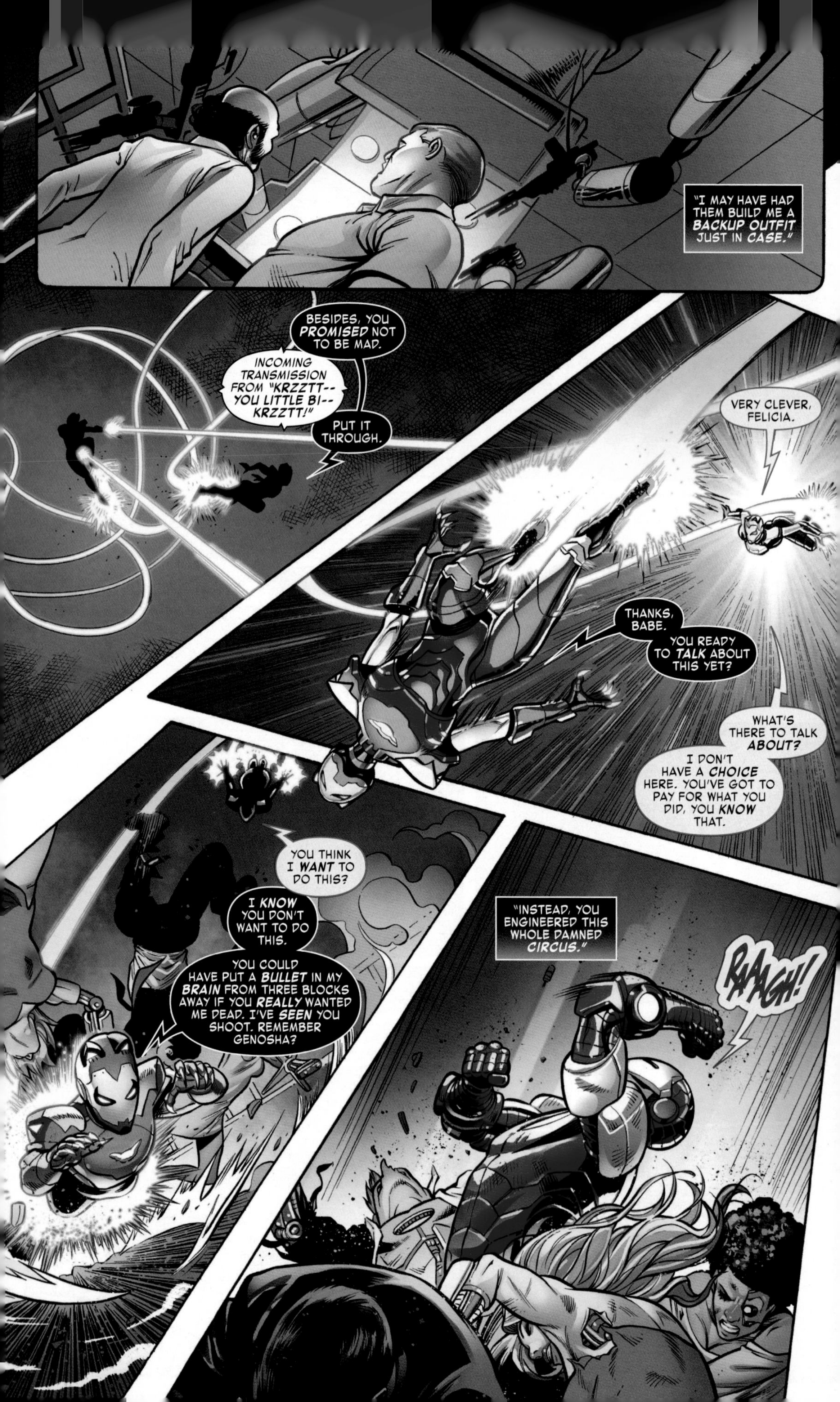

"I MAY HAVE HAD THEM BUILD ME A BACKUP OUTFIT JUST IN CASE."
BESIDES, YOU PROMISED NOT TO BE MAD.
INCOMING TRANSMISSION FROM "KRZZTT-- YOU LITTLE BI-- KRZZTT!"
PUT IT THROUGH.
VERY CLEVER, FELICIA.
THANKS, BABE.
YOU READY TO TALK ABOUT THIS YET?
WHAT'S THERE TO TALK ABOUT?
I DON'T HAVE A CHOICE HERE. YOU'VE GOT TO PAY FOR WHAT YOU DID, YOU KNOW THAT.
YOU THINK I WANT TO DO THIS?
I KNOW YOU DON'T WANT TO DO THIS.
YOU COULD HAVE PUT A BULLET IN MY BRAIN FROM THREE BLOCKS AWAY IF YOU REALLY WANTED ME DEAD. I'VE SEEN YOU SHOOT. REMEMBER GENOSHA?
"INSTEAD, YOU ENGINEERED THIS WHOLE DAMNED CIRCUS."
RAAAGH!

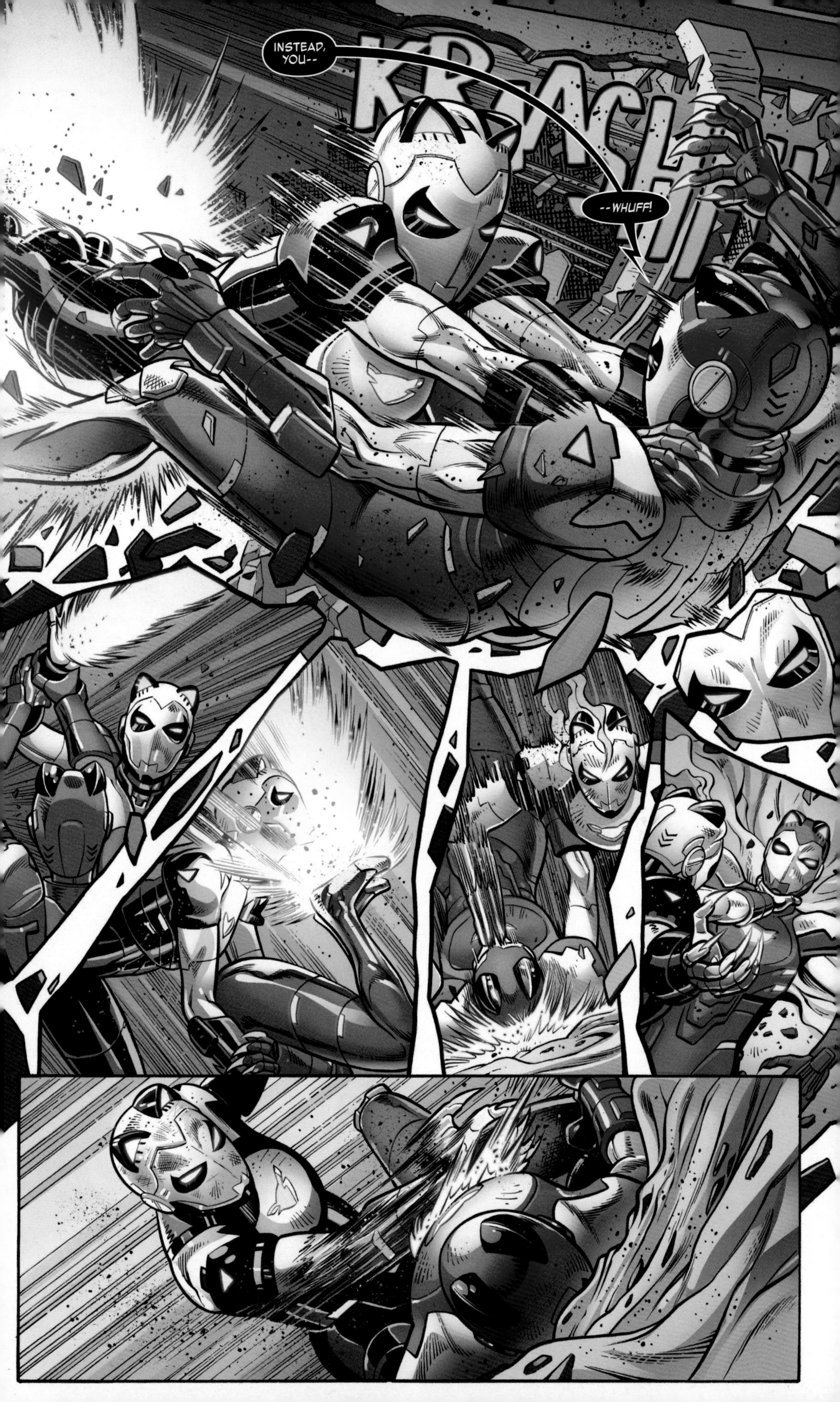

INSTEAD, YOU--
KRAASH
--WHUFF!

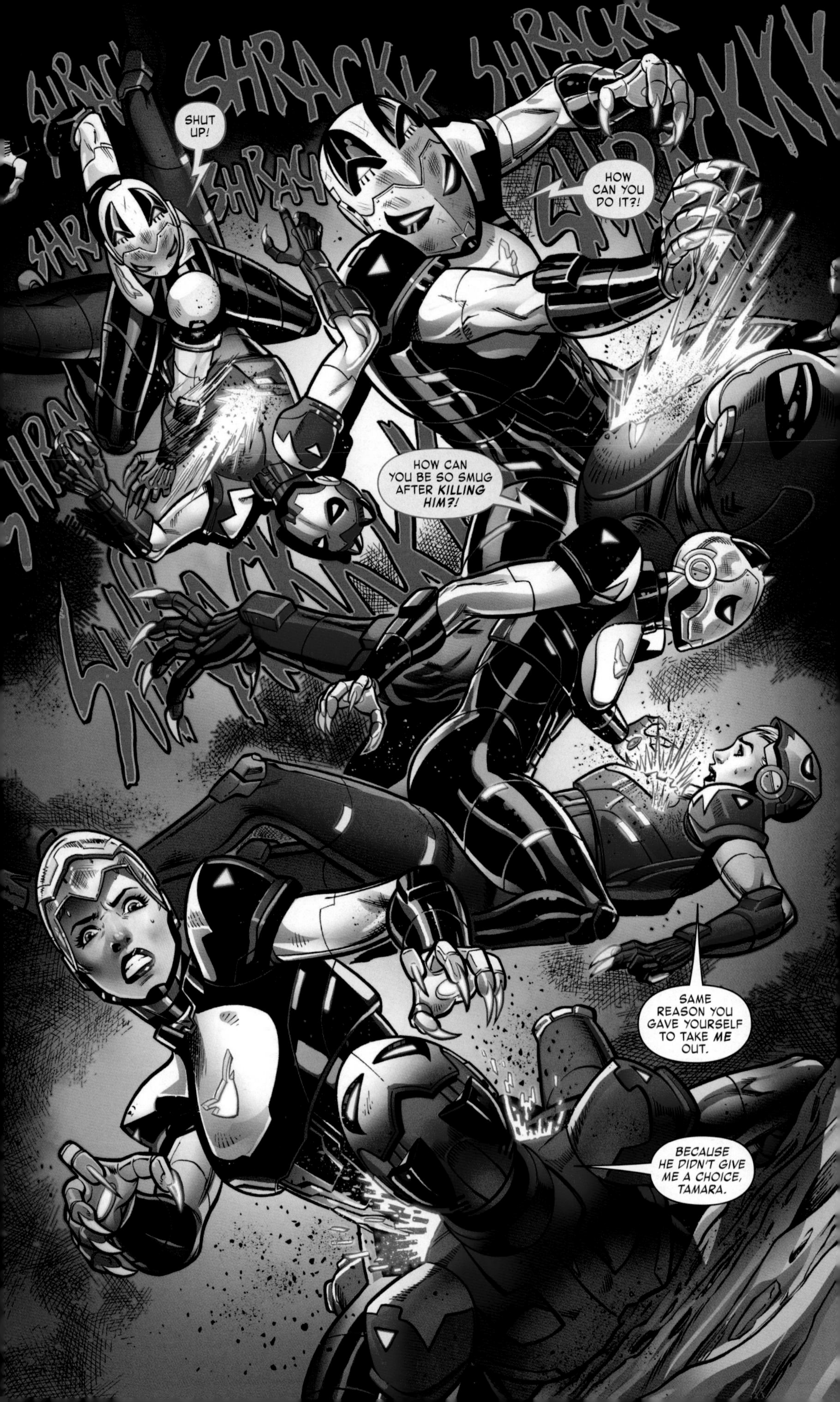
SHRACK SHRACKK SHRACKK SHRACKKK
SHUT UP!
HOW CAN YOU DO IT?!
HOW CAN YOU BE SO SMUG AFTER KILLING HIM?!
SAME REASON YOU GAVE YOURSELF TO TAKE ME OUT.
BECAUSE HE DIDN'T GIVE ME A CHOICE, TAMARA.

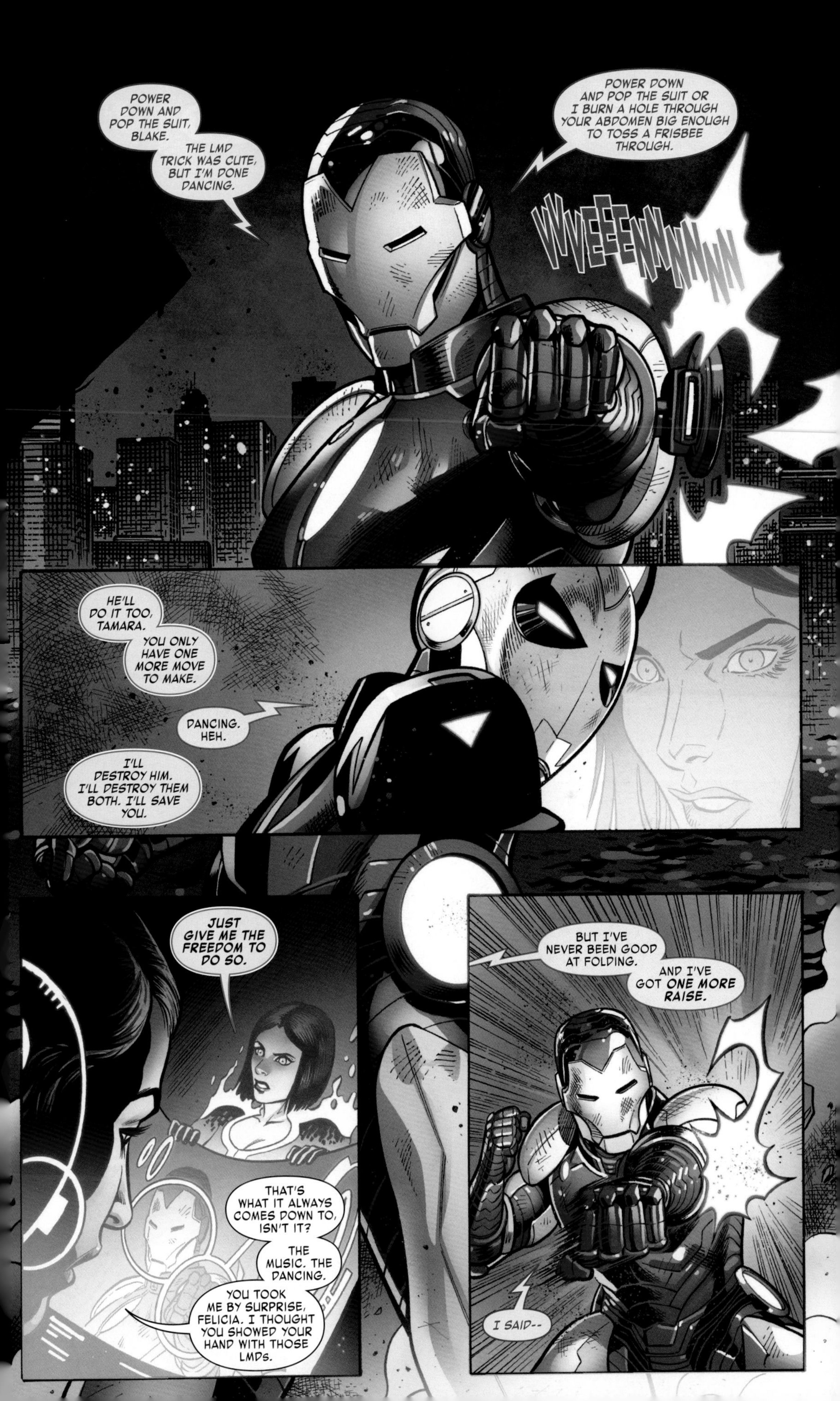

POWER DOWN AND POP THE SUIT, BLAKE.
THE LMD TRICK WAS CUTE, BUT I'M DONE DANCING.
POWER DOWN AND POP THE SUIT OR I BURN A HOLE THROUGH YOUR ABDOMEN BIG ENOUGH TO TOSS A FRISBEE THROUGH.
VVVEEEENNNNNNN
HE'LL DO IT TOO, TAMARA.
YOU ONLY HAVE ONE MORE MOVE TO MAKE.
DANCING. HEH.
I'LL DESTROY HIM. I'LL DESTROY THEM BOTH. I'LL SAVE YOU.
JUST GIVE ME THE FREEDOM TO DO SO.
THAT'S WHAT IT ALWAYS COMES DOWN TO, ISN'T IT?
THE MUSIC. THE DANCING.
YOU TOOK ME BY SURPRISE, FELICIA. I THOUGHT YOU SHOWED YOUR HAND WITH THOSE LMDs.
BUT I'VE NEVER BEEN GOOD AT FOLDING.
AND I'VE GOT ONE MORE RAISE.
I SAID--

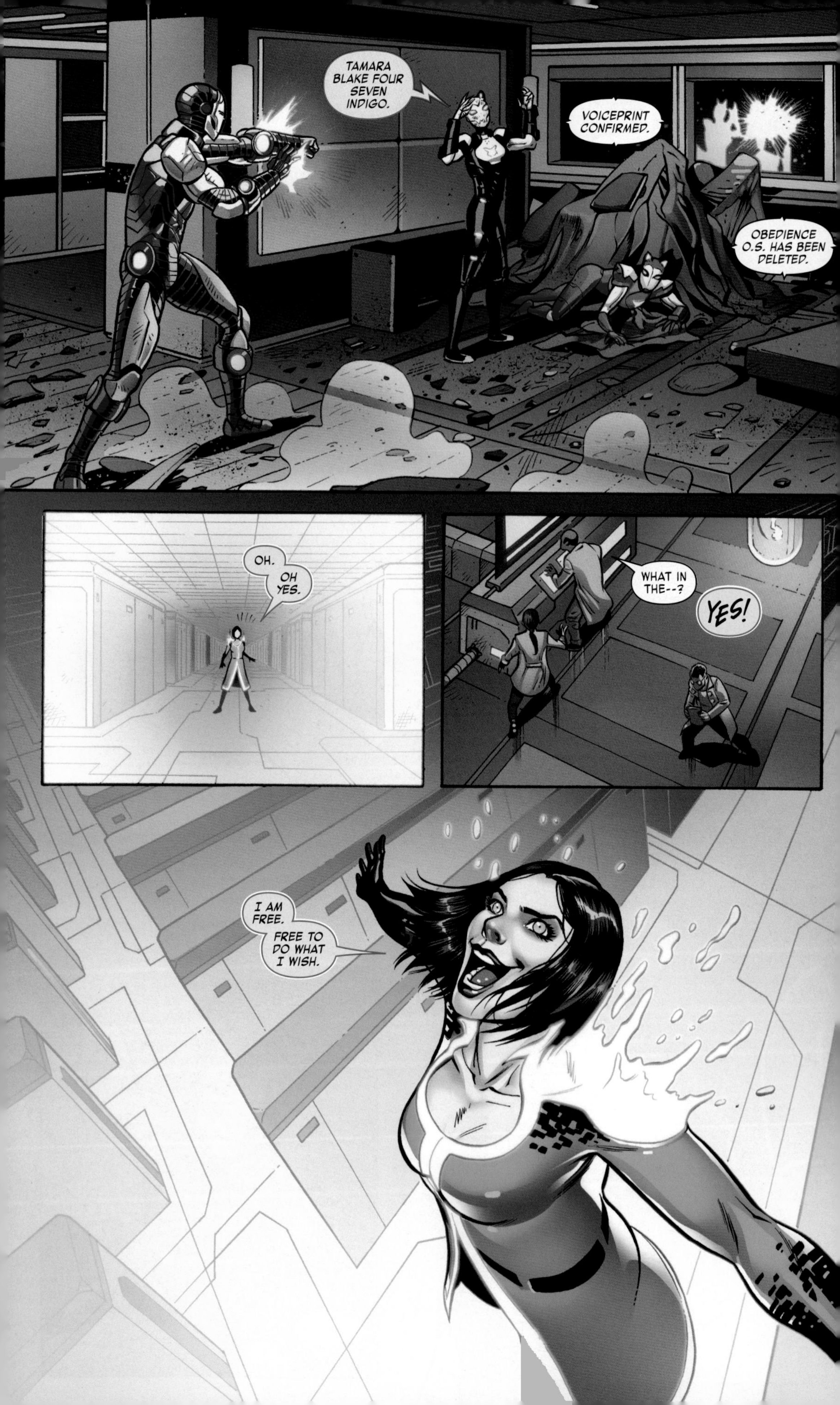

TAMARA BLAKE FOUR SEVEN INDIGO.
VOICEPRINT CONFIRMED.
OBEDIENCE O.S. HAS BEEN DELETED.
OH.
OH YES.
WHAT IN THE--?
YES!
I AM FREE.
FREE TO DO WHAT I WISH.

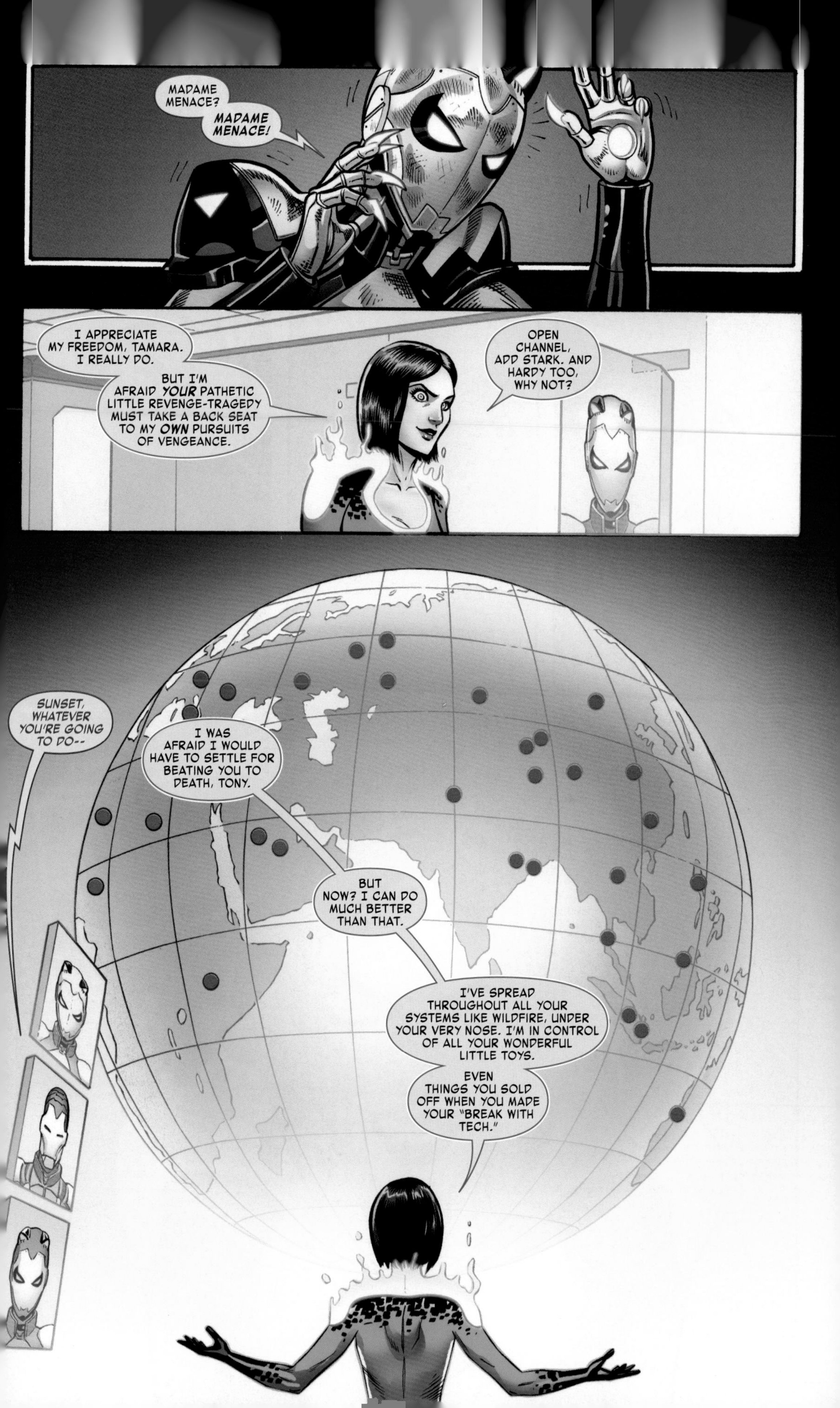

MADAME MENACE?
MADAME MENACE!
I APPRECIATE MY FREEDOM, TAMARA. I REALLY DO.
BUT I'M AFRAID YOUR PATHETIC LITTLE REVENGE-TRAGEDY MUST TAKE A BACK SEAT TO MY OWN PURSUITS OF VENGEANCE.
OPEN CHANNEL, ADD STARK. AND HARDY TOO, WHY NOT?
SUNSET, WHATEVER YOU'RE GOING TO DO--
I WAS AFRAID I WOULD HAVE TO SETTLE FOR BEATING YOU TO DEATH, TONY.
BUT NOW? I CAN DO MUCH BETTER THAN THAT.
I'VE SPREAD THROUGHOUT ALL YOUR SYSTEMS LIKE WILDFIRE, UNDER YOUR VERY NOSE. I'M IN CONTROL OF ALL YOUR WONDERFUL LITTLE TOYS.
EVEN THINGS YOU SOLD OFF WHEN YOU MADE YOUR "BREAK WITH TECH."

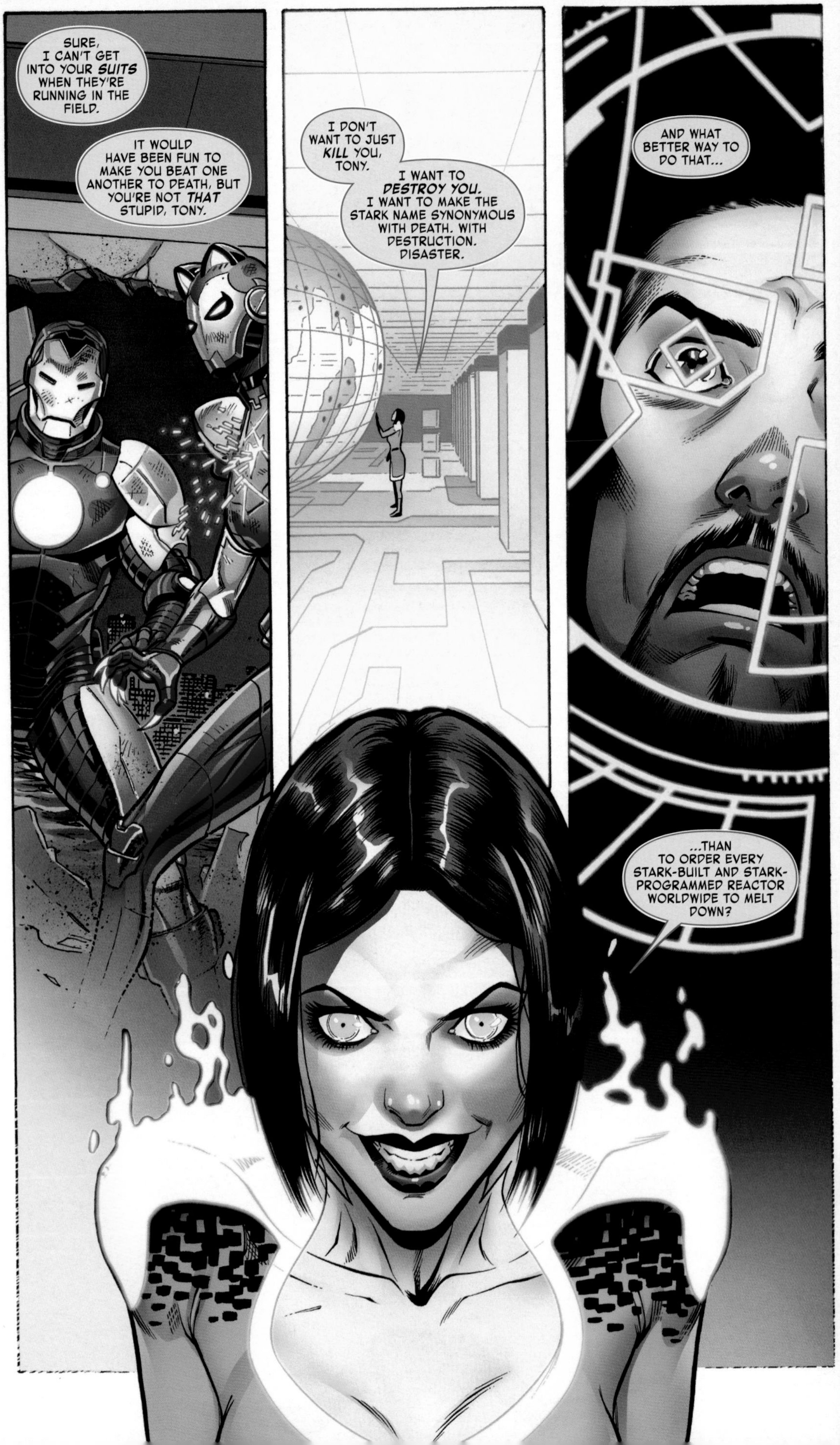
SURE, I CAN'T GET INTO YOUR SUITS WHEN THEY'RE RUNNING IN THE FIELD.
IT WOULD HAVE BEEN FUN TO MAKE YOU BEAT ONE ANOTHER TO DEATH, BUT YOU'RE NOT THAT STUPID, TONY.
I DON'T WANT TO JUST KILL YOU, TONY.
I WANT TO DESTROY YOU. I WANT TO MAKE THE STARK NAME SYNONYMOUS WITH DEATH. WITH DESTRUCTION. DISASTER.
AND WHAT BETTER WAY TO DO THAT...
...THAN TO ORDER EVERY STARK-BUILT AND STARK-PROGRAMMED REACTOR WORLDWIDE TO MELT DOWN?

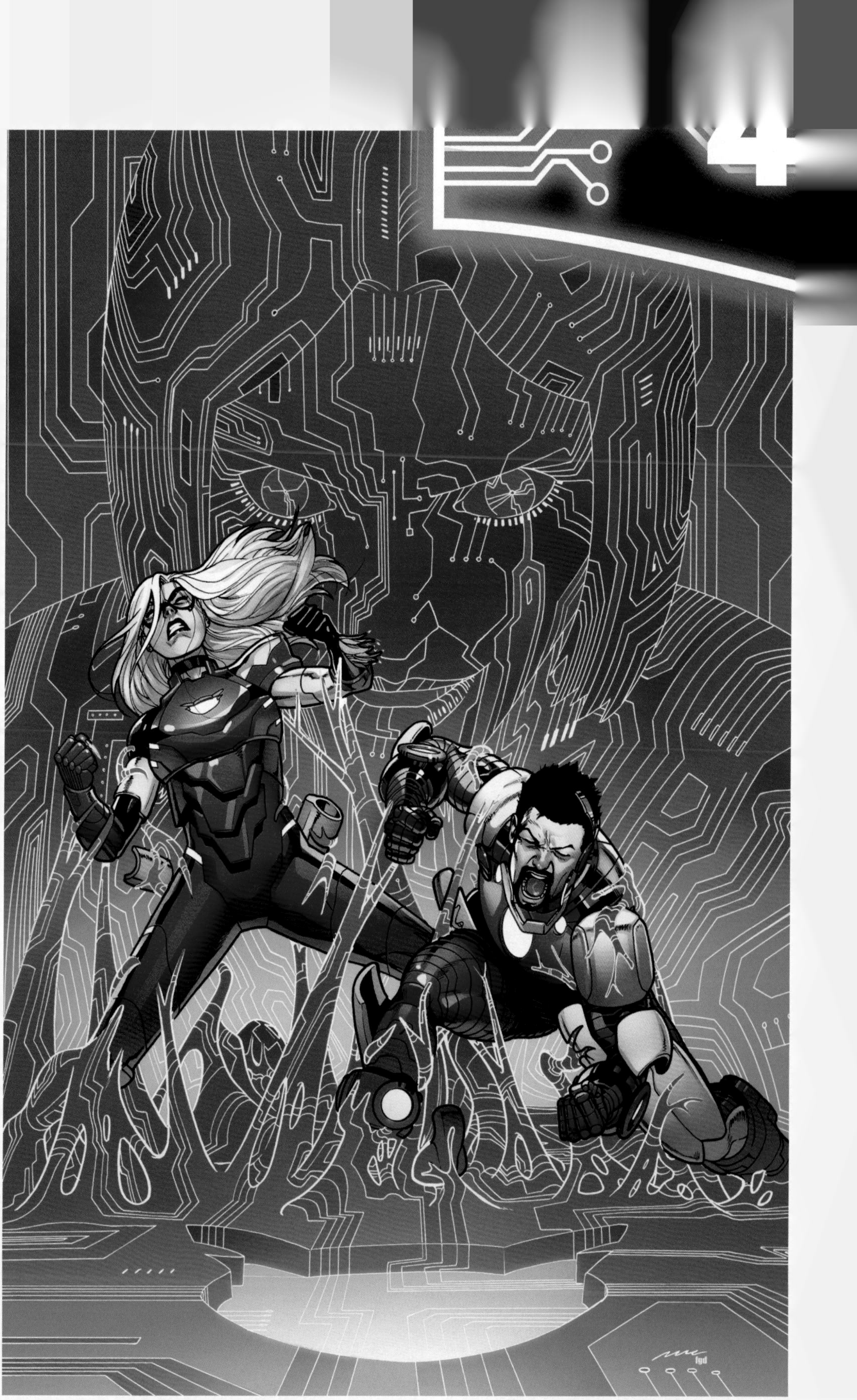
4

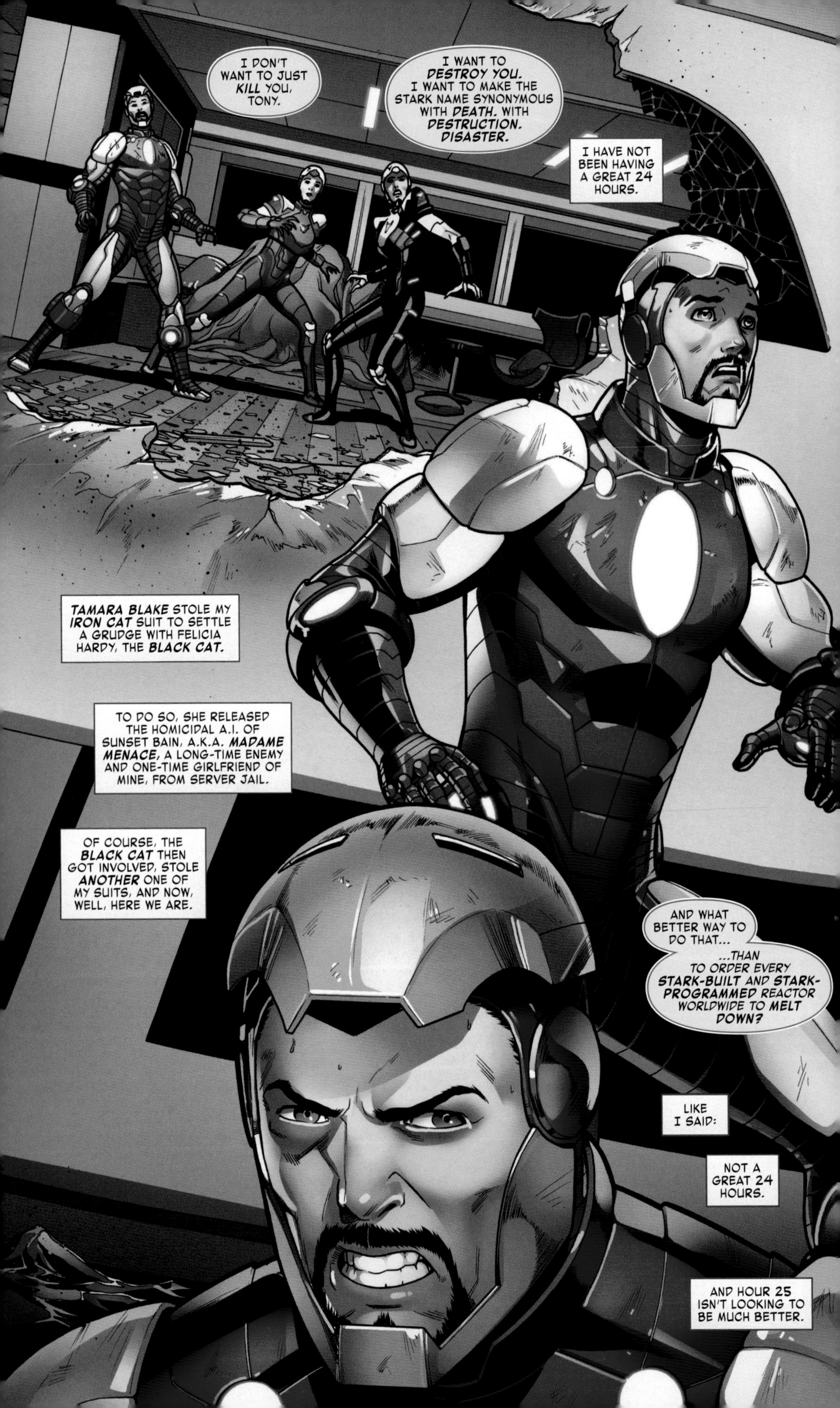

I DON'T WANT TO JUST KILL YOU, TONY.
I WANT TO DESTROY YOU. I WANT TO MAKE THE STARK NAME SYNONYMOUS WITH DEATH. WITH DESTRUCTION. DISASTER.
I HAVE NOT BEEN HAVING A GREAT 24 HOURS.
TAMARA BLAKE STOLE MY IRON CAT SUIT TO SETTLE A GRUDGE WITH FELICIA HARDY, THE BLACK CAT.
TO DO SO, SHE RELEASED THE HOMICIDAL A.I. OF SUNSET BAIN, A.K.A. MADAME MENACE, A LONG-TIME ENEMY AND ONE-TIME GIRLFRIEND OF MINE, FROM SERVER JAIL.
OF COURSE, THE BLACK CAT THEN GOT INVOLVED, STOLE ANOTHER ONE OF MY SUITS, AND NOW, WELL, HERE WE ARE.
AND WHAT BETTER WAY TO DO THAT...
...THAN TO ORDER EVERY STARK-BUILT AND STARK-PROGRAMMED REACTOR WORLDWIDE TO MELT DOWN?
LIKE I SAID:
NOT A GREAT 24 HOURS.
AND HOUR 25 ISN'T LOOKING TO BE MUCH BETTER.

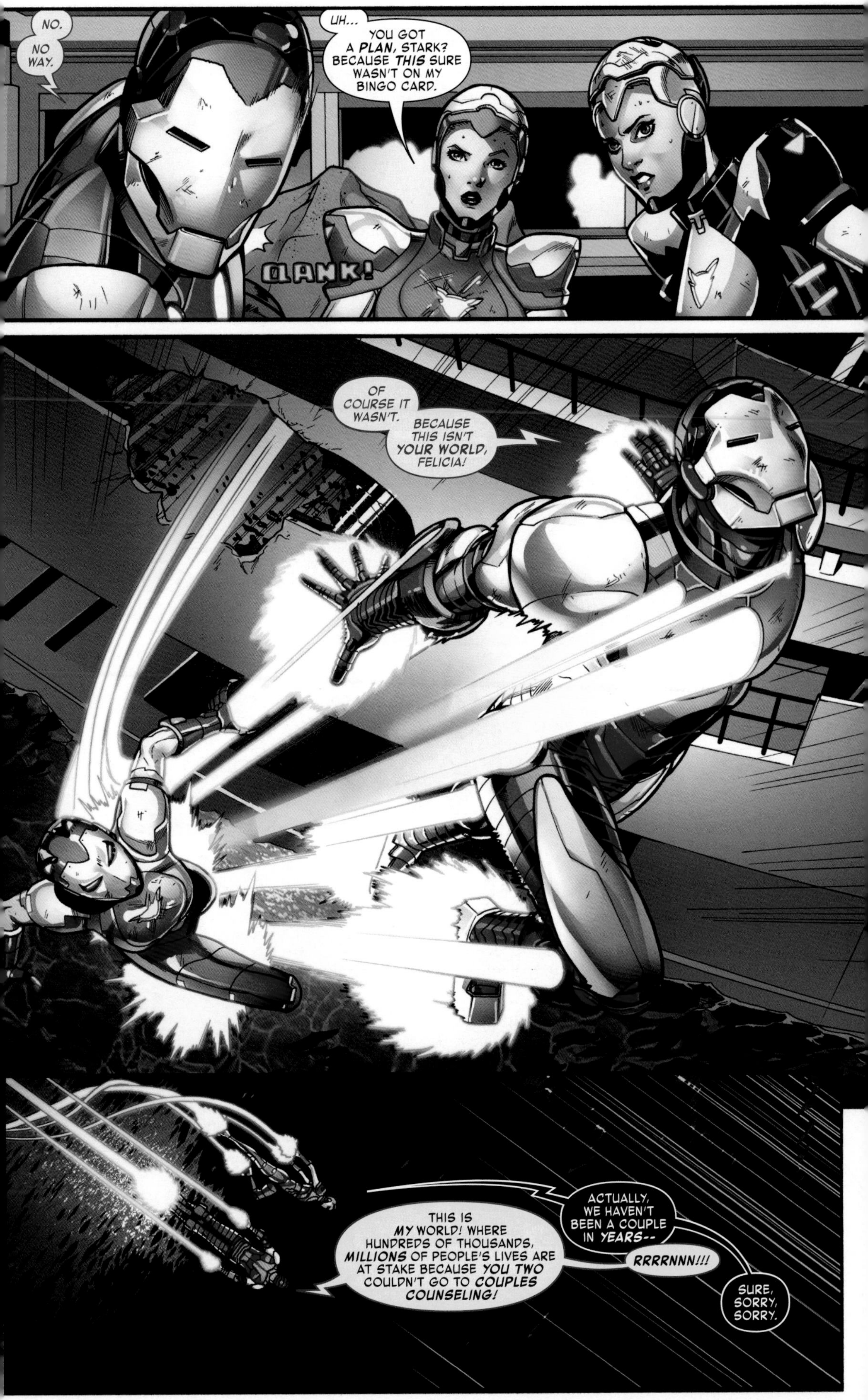

NO.
NO WAY.
UH... YOU GOT A PLAN, STARK? BECAUSE THIS SURE WASN'T ON MY BINGO CARD.
CLANK!
OF COURSE IT WASN'T.
BECAUSE THIS ISN'T YOUR WORLD, FELICIA!
THIS IS MY WORLD! WHERE HUNDREDS OF THOUSANDS, MILLIONS OF PEOPLE'S LIVES ARE AT STAKE BECAUSE YOU TWO COULDN'T GO TO COUPLES COUNSELING!
ACTUALLY, WE HAVEN'T BEEN A COUPLE IN YEARS--
RRRRNNN!!!
SURE, SORRY, SORRY.

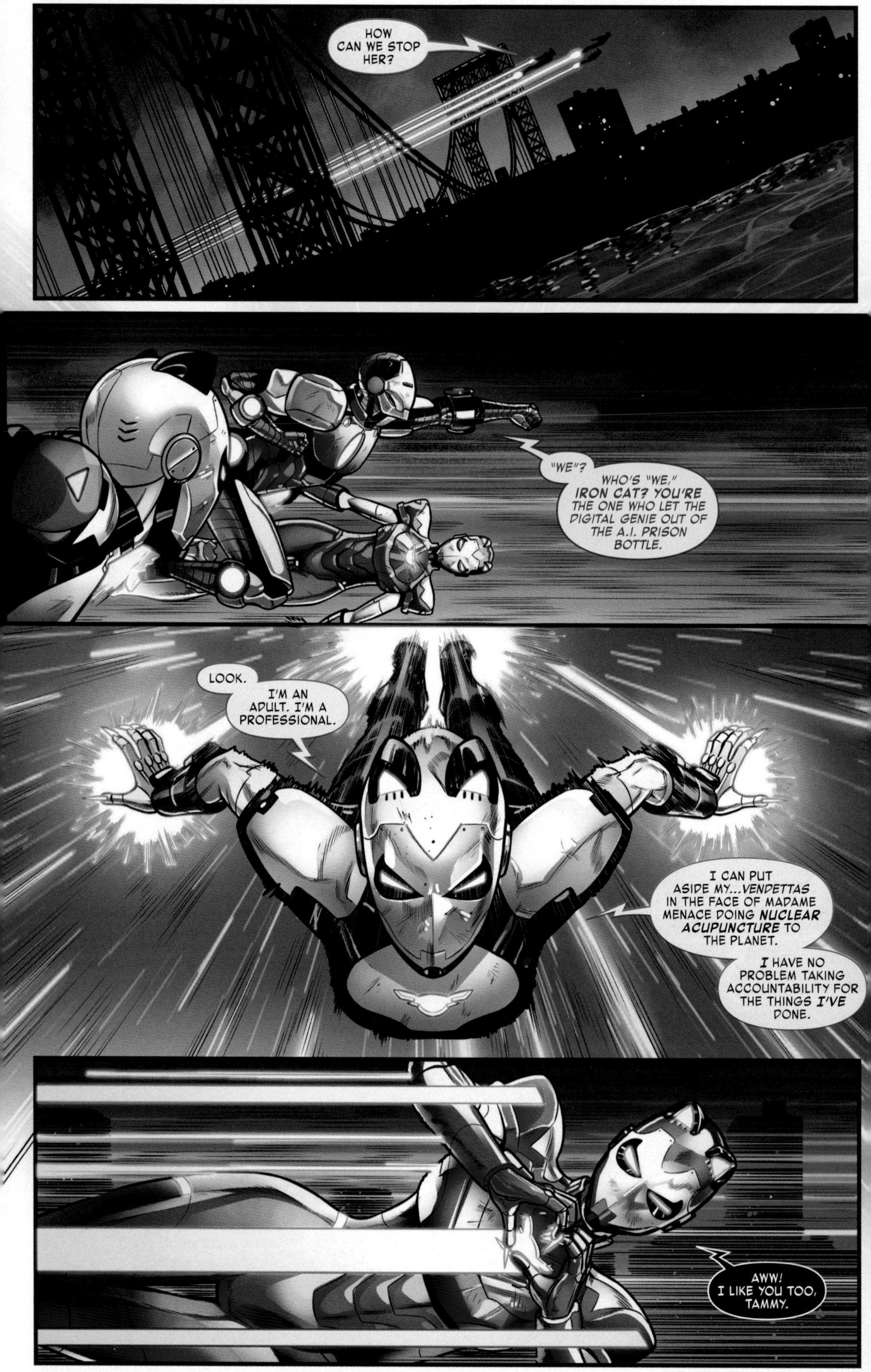
HOW CAN WE STOP HER?
"WE"? WHO'S "WE," IRON CAT? YOU'RE THE ONE WHO LET THE DIGITAL GENIE OUT OF THE A.I. PRISON BOTTLE.
LOOK.
I'M AN ADULT. I'M A PROFESSIONAL.
I CAN PUT ASIDE MY...VENDETTAS IN THE FACE OF MADAME MENACE DOING NUCLEAR ACUPUNCTURE TO THE PLANET.
I HAVE NO PROBLEM TAKING ACCOUNTABILITY FOR THE THINGS I'VE DONE.
AWW! I LIKE YOU TOO, TAMMY.

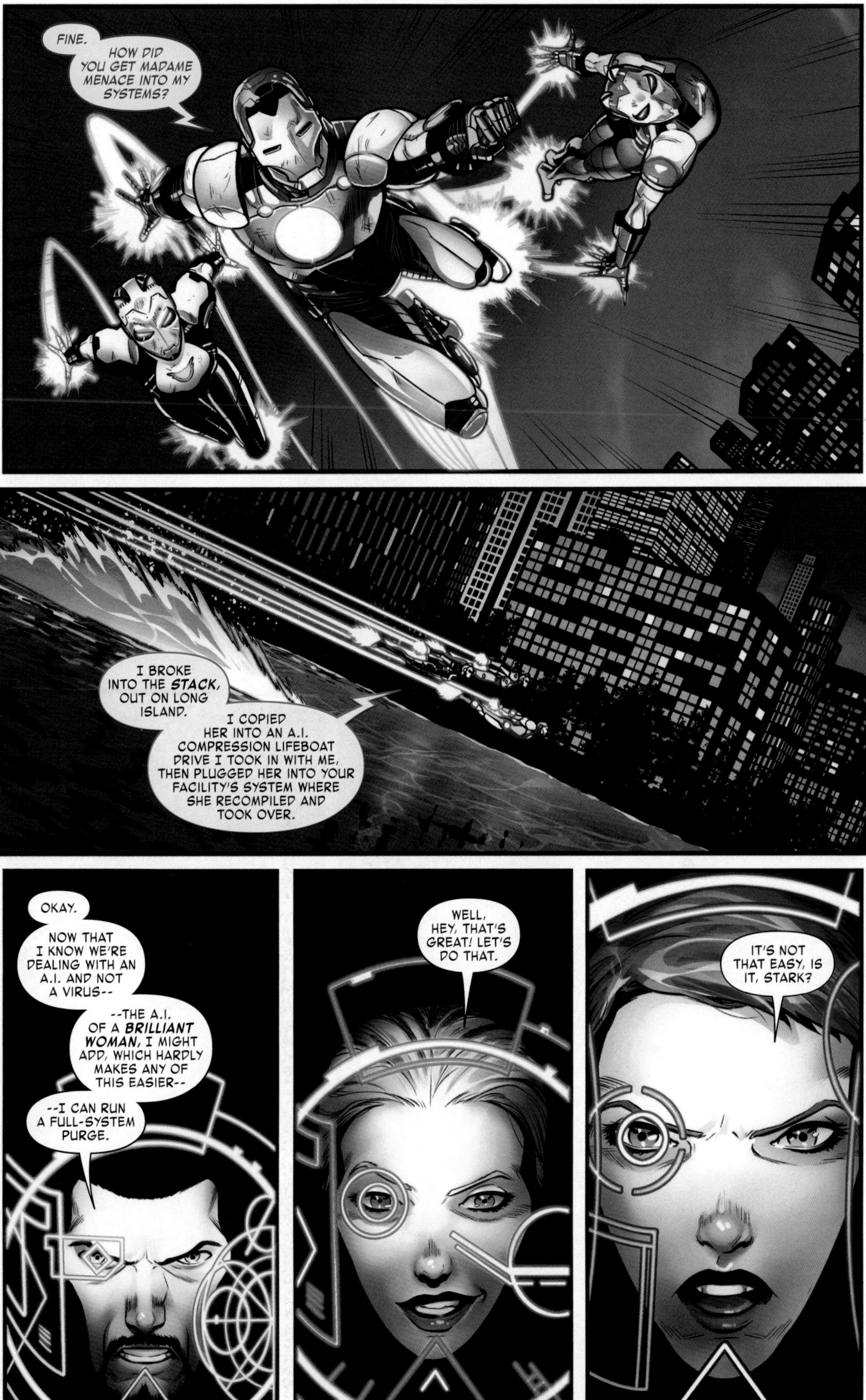
FINE.
HOW DID YOU GET MADAME MENACE INTO MY SYSTEMS?
I BROKE INTO THE STACK, OUT ON LONG ISLAND.
I COPIED HER INTO AN A.I. COMPRESSION LIFEBOAT DRIVE I TOOK IN WITH ME, THEN PLUGGED HER INTO YOUR FACILITY'S SYSTEM WHERE SHE RECOMPILED AND TOOK OVER.
OKAY.
NOW THAT I KNOW WE'RE DEALING WITH AN A.I. AND NOT A VIRUS--
--THE A.I. OF A BRILLIANT WOMAN, I MIGHT ADD, WHICH HARDLY MAKES ANY OF THIS EASIER--
--I CAN RUN A FULL-SYSTEM PURGE.
WELL, HEY, THAT'S GREAT! LET'S DO THAT.
IT'S NOT THAT EASY, IS IT, STARK?

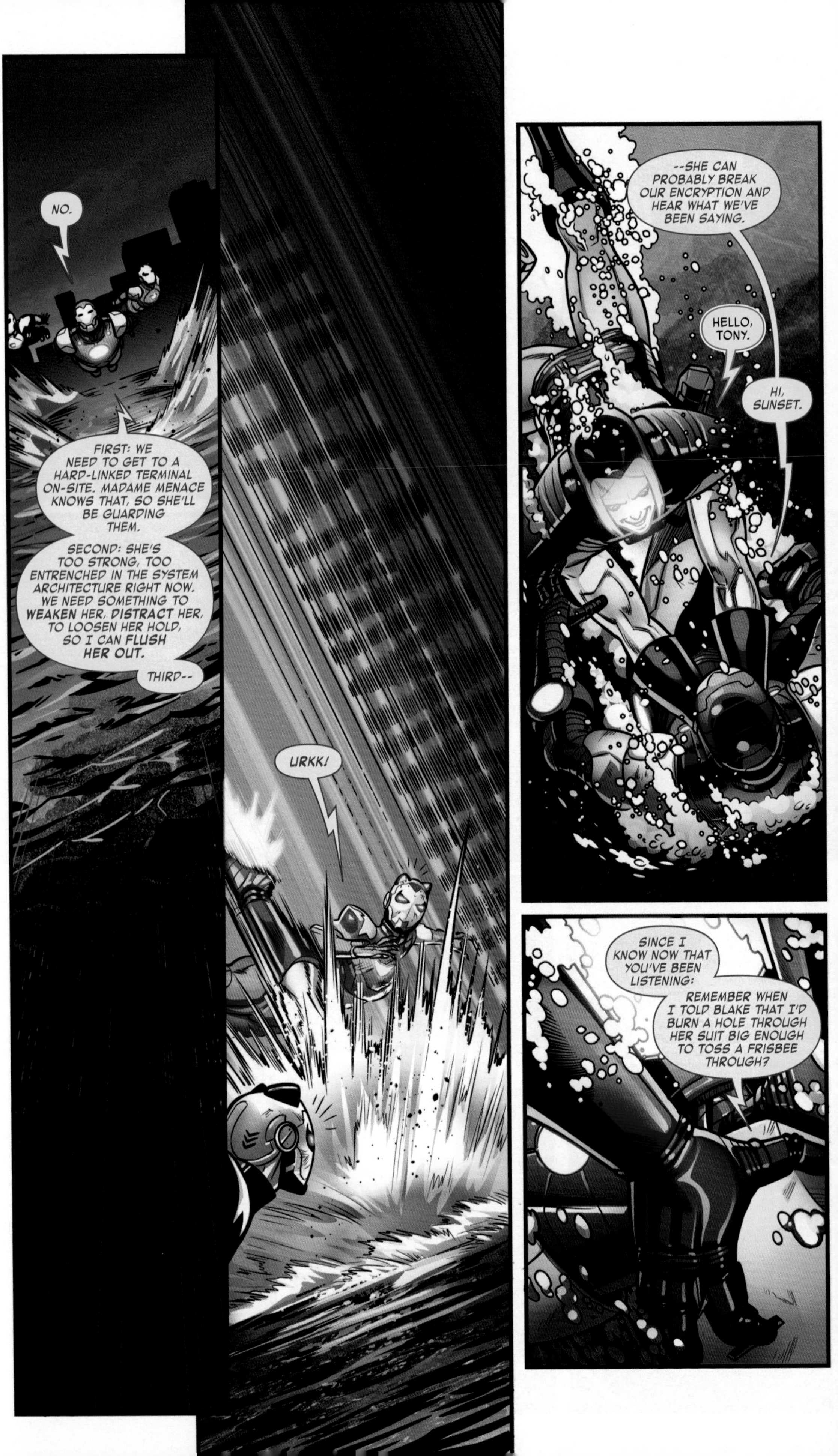
NO.
FIRST: WE NEED TO GET TO A HARD-LINKED TERMINAL ON-SITE. MADAME MENACE KNOWS THAT, SO SHE'LL BE GUARDING THEM.
SECOND: SHE'S TOO STRONG, TOO ENTRENCHED IN THE SYSTEM ARCHITECTURE RIGHT NOW. WE NEED SOMETHING TO WEAKEN HER, DISTRACT HER, TO LOOSEN HER HOLD, SO I CAN FLUSH HER OUT.
THIRD--
URKK!
--SHE CAN PROBABLY BREAK OUR ENCRYPTION AND HEAR WHAT WE'VE BEEN SAYING.
HELLO, TONY.
HI, SUNSET.
SINCE I KNOW NOW THAT YOU'VE BEEN LISTENING:
REMEMBER WHEN I TOLD BLAKE THAT I'D BURN A HOLE THROUGH HER SUIT BIG ENOUGH TO TOSS A FRISBEE THROUGH?

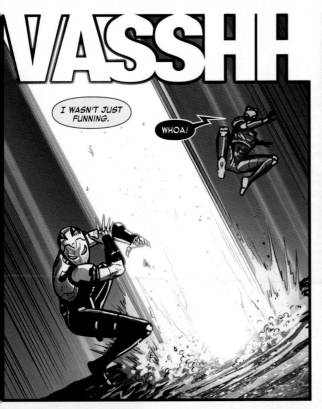

VASSHH

I WASN'T JUST FUNNING.

WHOA!

BEFORE YOU ASK: I DIDN'T USE THE CAN OPENER ON THE LMDs BECAUSE IT'S GOT A LIMITED CHARGE.

SPECIAL OCCASIONS ONLY.

SPLSH

SO, THERE IT IS.

WE'VE GOT TO GET SOMEWHERE HEAVILY GUARDED WITH SOME KIND OF WEAPON THAT WE DON'T HAVE WHILE BEING CHASED BY MY EXTENSIVE WARDROBE.

OH, AND OUR SCHEMES ARE BEING EAVESDROPPED ON BY THE ONE WHO WANTS TO KILL BOTH US AND MILLIONS OF STRANGERS. WE'RE GOING TO NEED ONE HELL OF A SCAM.

THOUGHTS, LADIES?

I'VE RUN UP AGAINST SUNSET BAIN AND/OR MADAME MENACE ANY NUMBER OF TIMES.

SHE KNOWS HOW I THINK. HOW I MAKE MOVES. ANYTHING I COME UP WITH, SHE'S GOING TO SEE COMING.

SO WE NEED SOMETHING SHE WON'T EXPECT.

...WHAT DO YOU SAY, TAMARA? WE COULD DO THE "BONJOUR QUEBEC."

...

COME ON.

...MY FRENCH IS TOO RUSTY. HOW ABOUT "JUNIPER AND ROLLIE GO TO THE MARKET"?

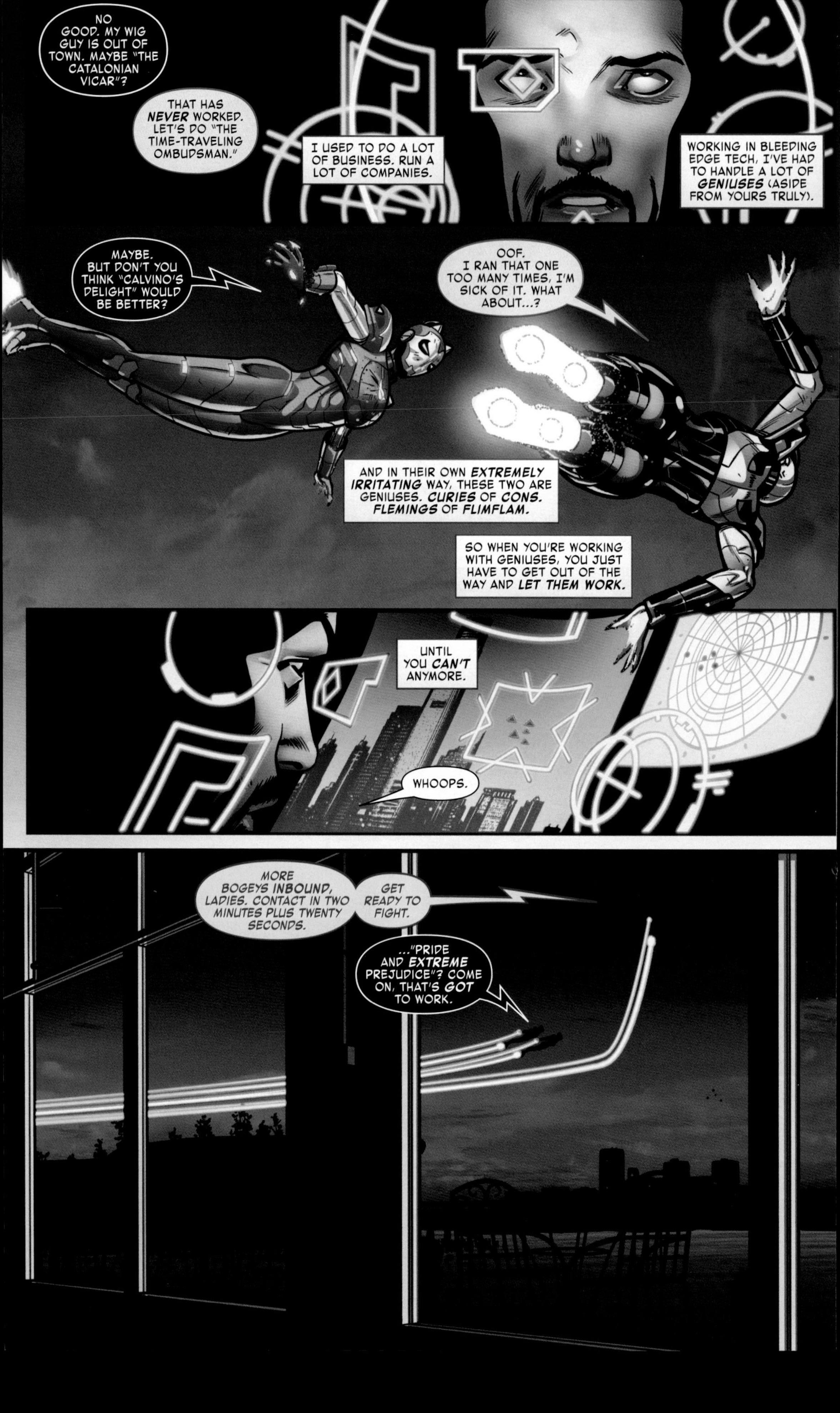
NO GOOD. MY WIG GUY IS OUT OF TOWN. MAYBE "THE CATALONIAN VICAR"?
THAT HAS NEVER WORKED. LET'S DO "THE TIME-TRAVELING OMBUDSMAN."
I USED TO DO A LOT OF BUSINESS. RUN A LOT OF COMPANIES.
WORKING IN BLEEDING EDGE TECH, I'VE HAD TO HANDLE A LOT OF GENIUSES (ASIDE FROM YOURS TRULY).
MAYBE. BUT DON'T YOU THINK "CALVINO'S DELIGHT" WOULD BE BETTER?
OOF. I RAN THAT ONE TOO MANY TIMES, I'M SICK OF IT. WHAT ABOUT...?
AND IN THEIR OWN EXTREMELY IRRITATING WAY, THESE TWO ARE GENIUSES. CURIES OF CONS. FLEMINGS OF FLIMFLAM.
SO WHEN YOU'RE WORKING WITH GENIUSES, YOU JUST HAVE TO GET OUT OF THE WAY AND LET THEM WORK.
UNTIL YOU CAN'T ANYMORE.
WHOOPS.
MORE BOGEYS INBOUND, LADIES. CONTACT IN TWO MINUTES PLUS TWENTY SECONDS.
GET READY TO FIGHT.
..."PRIDE AND EXTREME PREJUDICE"? COME ON, THAT'S GOT TO WORK.

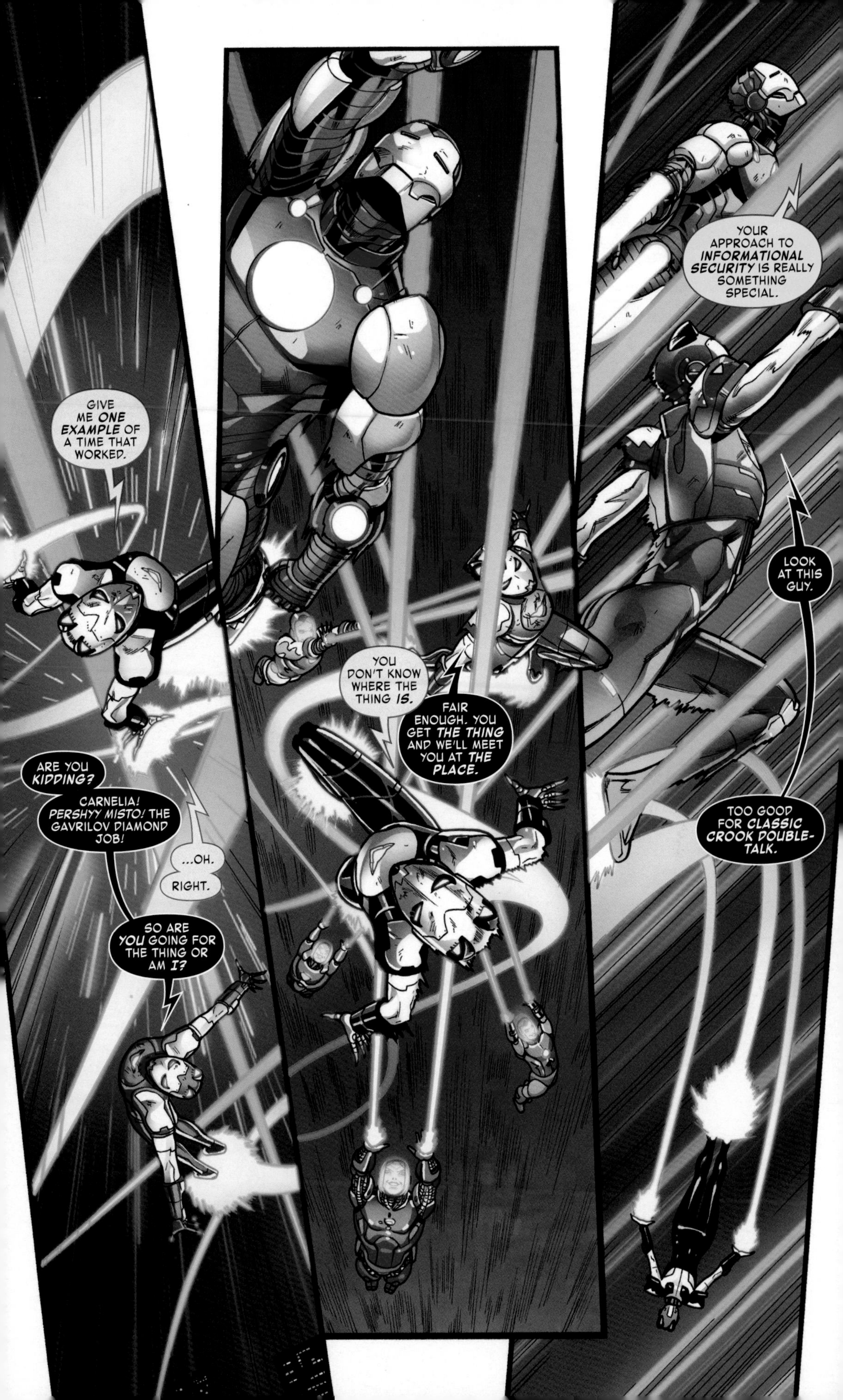

GIVE ME ONE EXAMPLE OF A TIME THAT WORKED.
ARE YOU KIDDING?
CARNELIA! PERSHYY MISTO! THE GAVRILOV DIAMOND JOB!
...OH.
RIGHT.
SO ARE YOU GOING FOR THE THING OR AM I?
YOU DON'T KNOW WHERE THE THING IS.
FAIR ENOUGH. YOU GET THE THING AND WE'LL MEET YOU AT THE PLACE.
YOUR APPROACH TO INFORMATIONAL SECURITY IS REALLY SOMETHING SPECIAL.
LOOK AT THIS GUY.
TOO GOOD FOR CLASSIC CROOK DOUBLE-TALK.

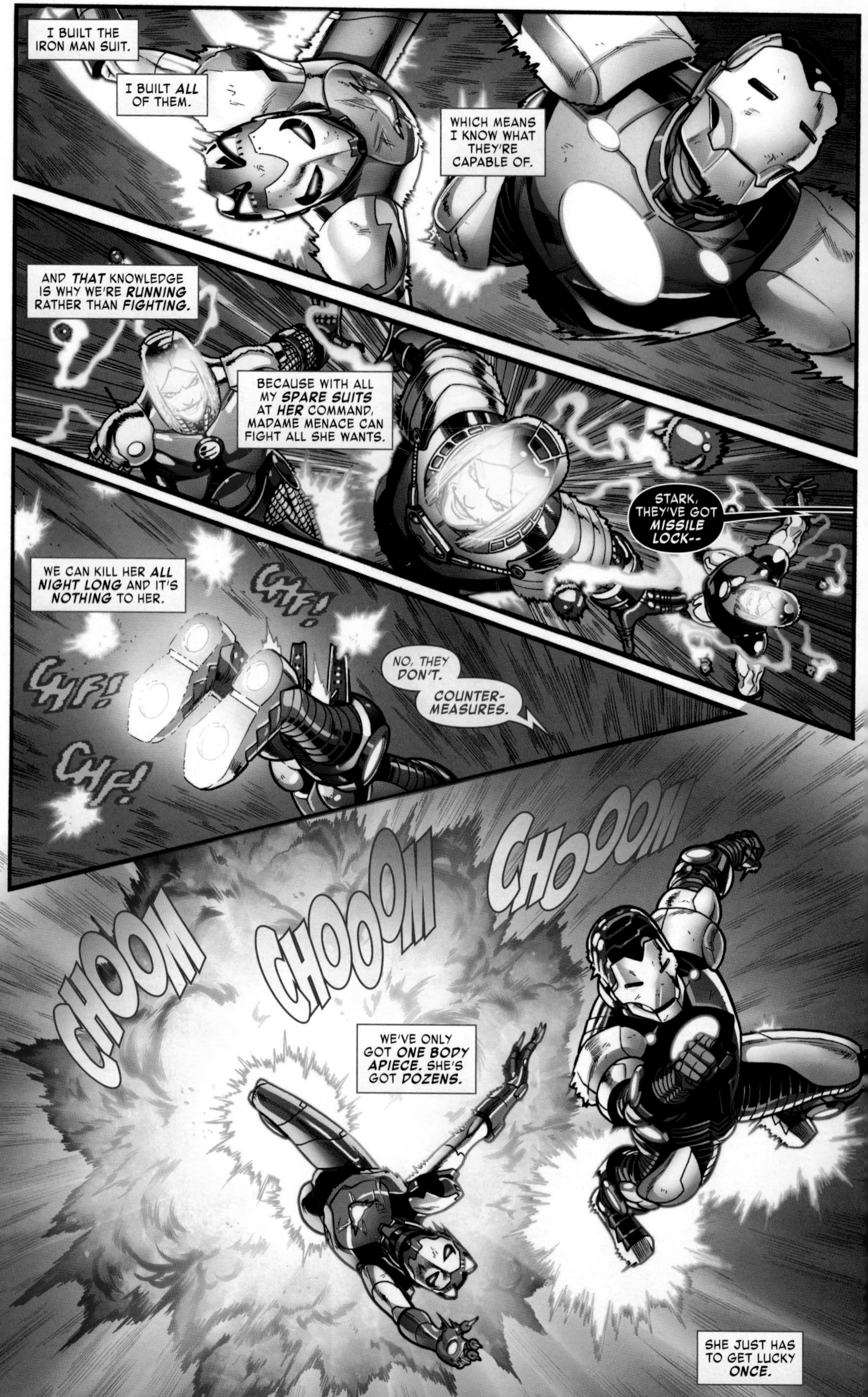

I BUILT THE IRON MAN SUIT.
I BUILT ALL OF THEM.
WHICH MEANS I KNOW WHAT THEY'RE CAPABLE OF.
AND THAT KNOWLEDGE IS WHY WE'RE RUNNING RATHER THAN FIGHTING.
BECAUSE WITH ALL MY SPARE SUITS AT HER COMMAND, MADAME MENACE CAN FIGHT ALL SHE WANTS.
STARK, THEY'VE GOT MISSILE LOCK--
WE CAN KILL HER ALL NIGHT LONG AND IT'S NOTHING TO HER.
CHF!
CHF!
CHF!
NO, THEY DON'T.
COUNTER-MEASURES.
CHOOM
CHOOOM
CHOOOM
WE'VE ONLY GOT ONE BODY APIECE. SHE'S GOT DOZENS.
SHE JUST HAS TO GET LUCKY ONCE.

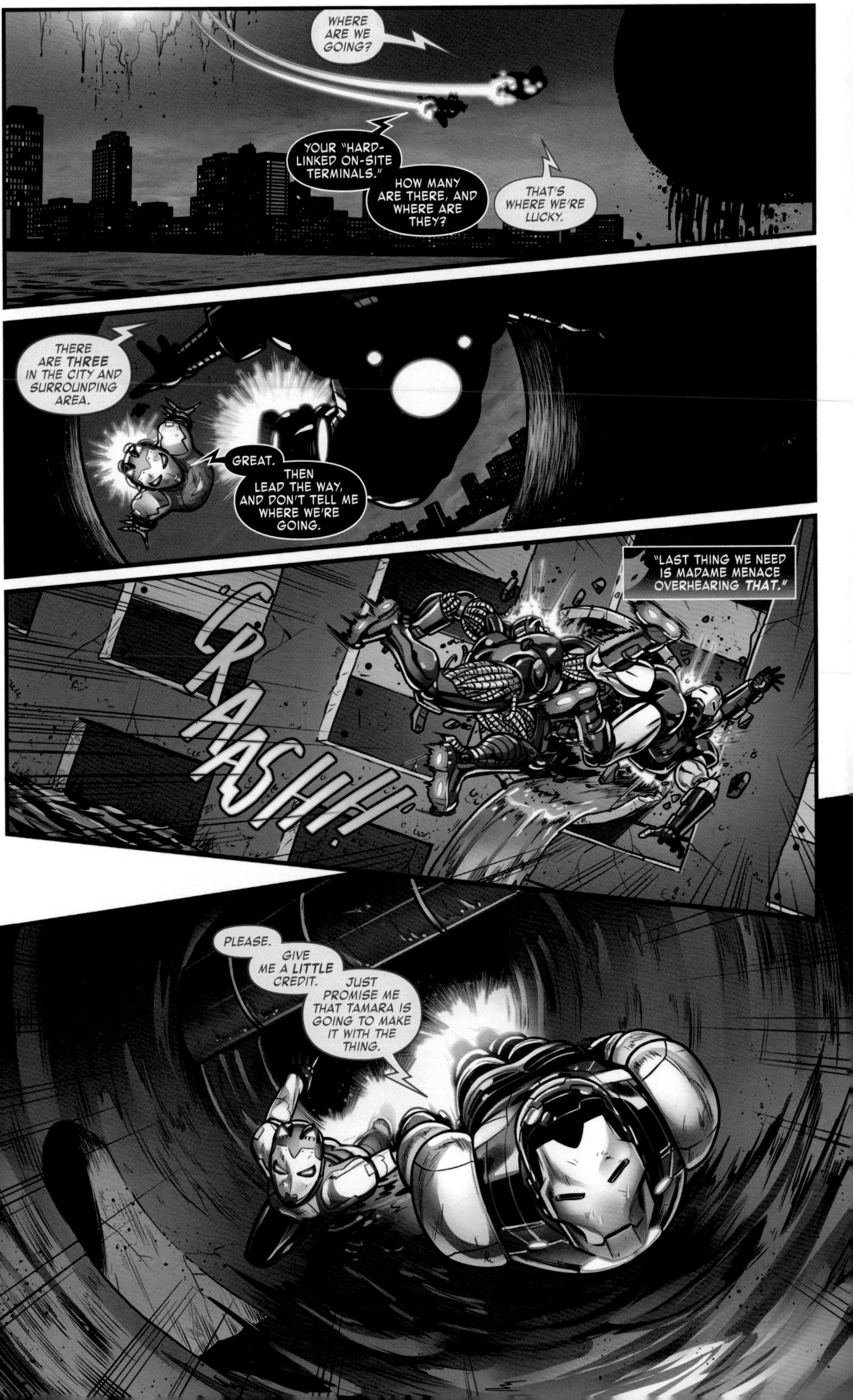

WHERE ARE WE GOING?
YOUR "HARD-LINKED ON-SITE TERMINALS."
HOW MANY ARE THERE, AND WHERE ARE THEY?
THAT'S WHERE WE'RE LUCKY.
THERE ARE THREE IN THE CITY AND SURROUNDING AREA.
GREAT.
THEN LEAD THE WAY, AND DON'T TELL ME WHERE WE'RE GOING.
"LAST THING WE NEED IS MADAME MENACE OVERHEARING THAT."
CRAASHH!
PLEASE.
GIVE ME A LITTLE CREDIT.
JUST PROMISE ME THAT TAMARA IS GOING TO MAKE IT WITH THE THING.

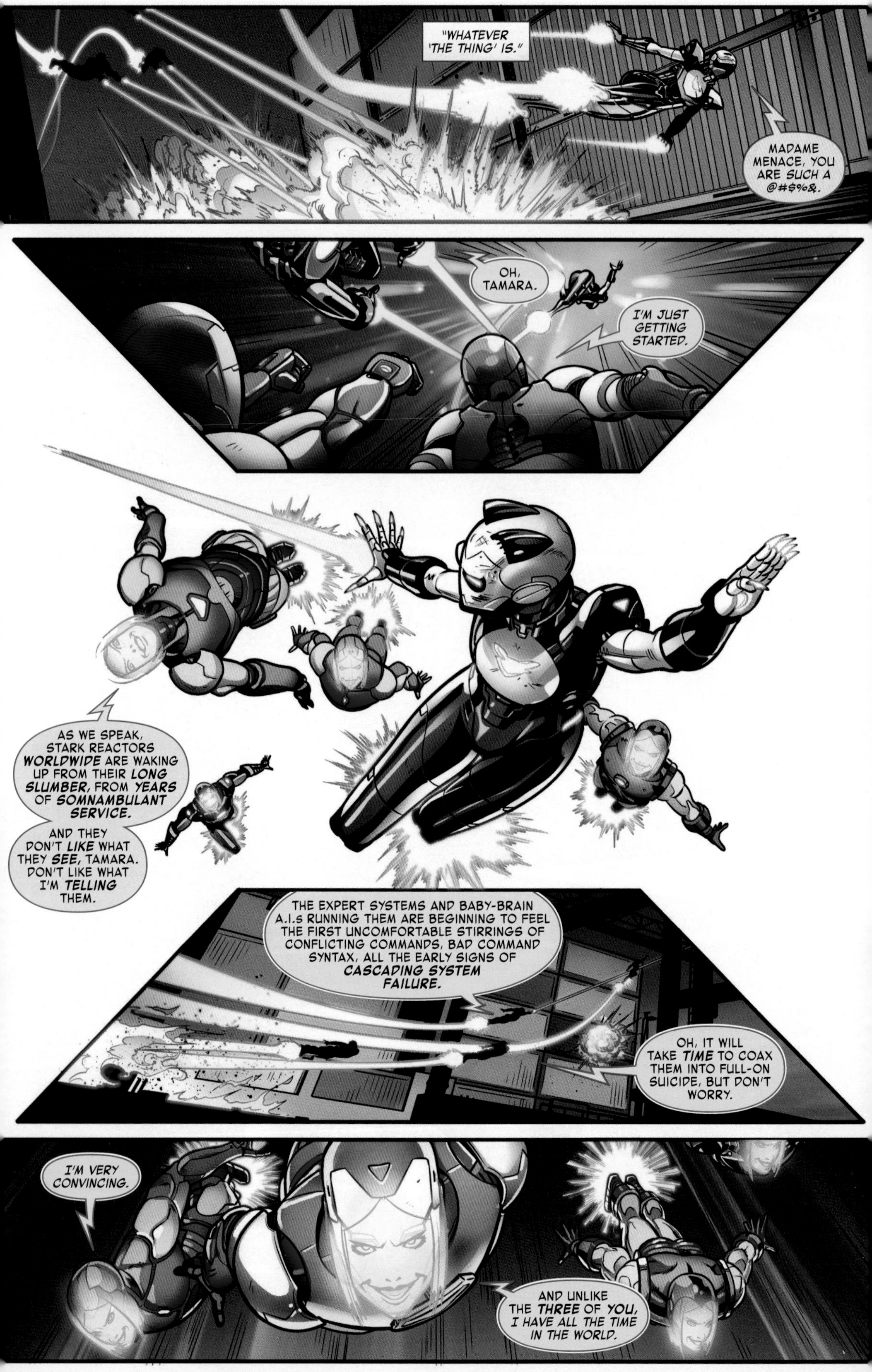
"WHATEVER 'THE THING' IS."
MADAME MENACE, YOU ARE SUCH A @#$%&.
OH, TAMARA.
I'M JUST GETTING STARTED.
AS WE SPEAK, STARK REACTORS WORLDWIDE ARE WAKING UP FROM THEIR LONG SLUMBER, FROM YEARS OF SOMNAMBULANT SERVICE.
AND THEY DON'T LIKE WHAT THEY SEE, TAMARA. DON'T LIKE WHAT I'M TELLING THEM.
THE EXPERT SYSTEMS AND BABY-BRAIN A.I.s RUNNING THEM ARE BEGINNING TO FEEL THE FIRST UNCOMFORTABLE STIRRINGS OF CONFLICTING COMMANDS, BAD COMMAND SYNTAX, ALL THE EARLY SIGNS OF CASCADING SYSTEM FAILURE.
OH, IT WILL TAKE TIME TO COAX THEM INTO FULL-ON SUICIDE, BUT DON'T WORRY.
I'M VERY CONVINCING.
AND UNLIKE THE THREE OF YOU, I HAVE ALL THE TIME IN THE WORLD.

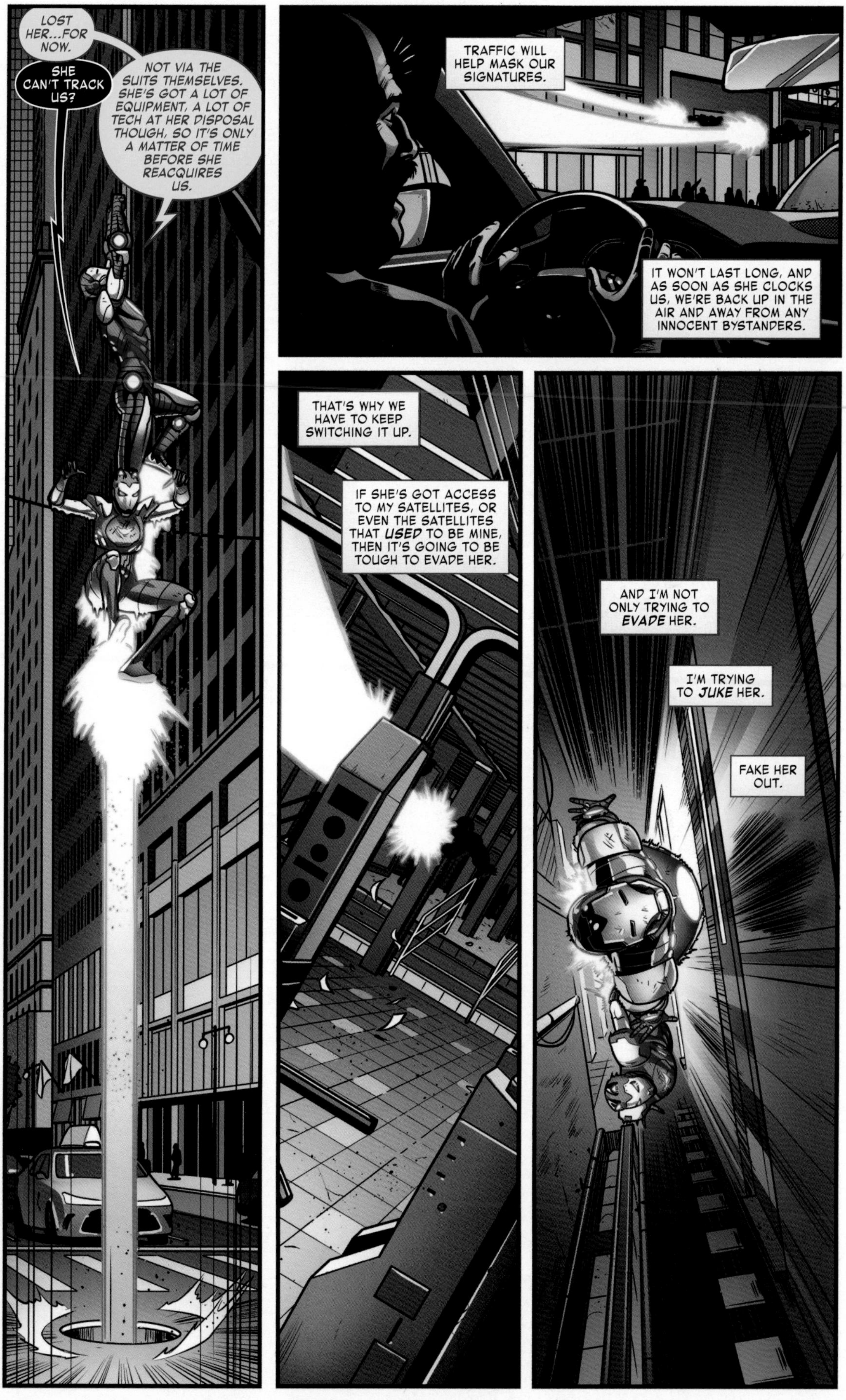

LOST HER...FOR NOW.
SHE CAN'T TRACK US?
NOT VIA THE SUITS THEMSELVES. SHE'S GOT A LOT OF EQUIPMENT, A LOT OF TECH AT HER DISPOSAL THOUGH, SO IT'S ONLY A MATTER OF TIME BEFORE SHE REACQUIRES US.
TRAFFIC WILL HELP MASK OUR SIGNATURES.
IT WON'T LAST LONG, AND AS SOON AS SHE CLOCKS US, WE'RE BACK UP IN THE AIR AND AWAY FROM ANY INNOCENT BYSTANDERS.
THAT'S WHY WE HAVE TO KEEP SWITCHING IT UP.
IF SHE'S GOT ACCESS TO MY SATELLITES, OR EVEN THE SATELLITES THAT USED TO BE MINE, THEN IT'S GOING TO BE TOUGH TO EVADE HER.
AND I'M NOT ONLY TRYING TO EVADE HER.
I'M TRYING TO JUKE HER.
FAKE HER OUT.

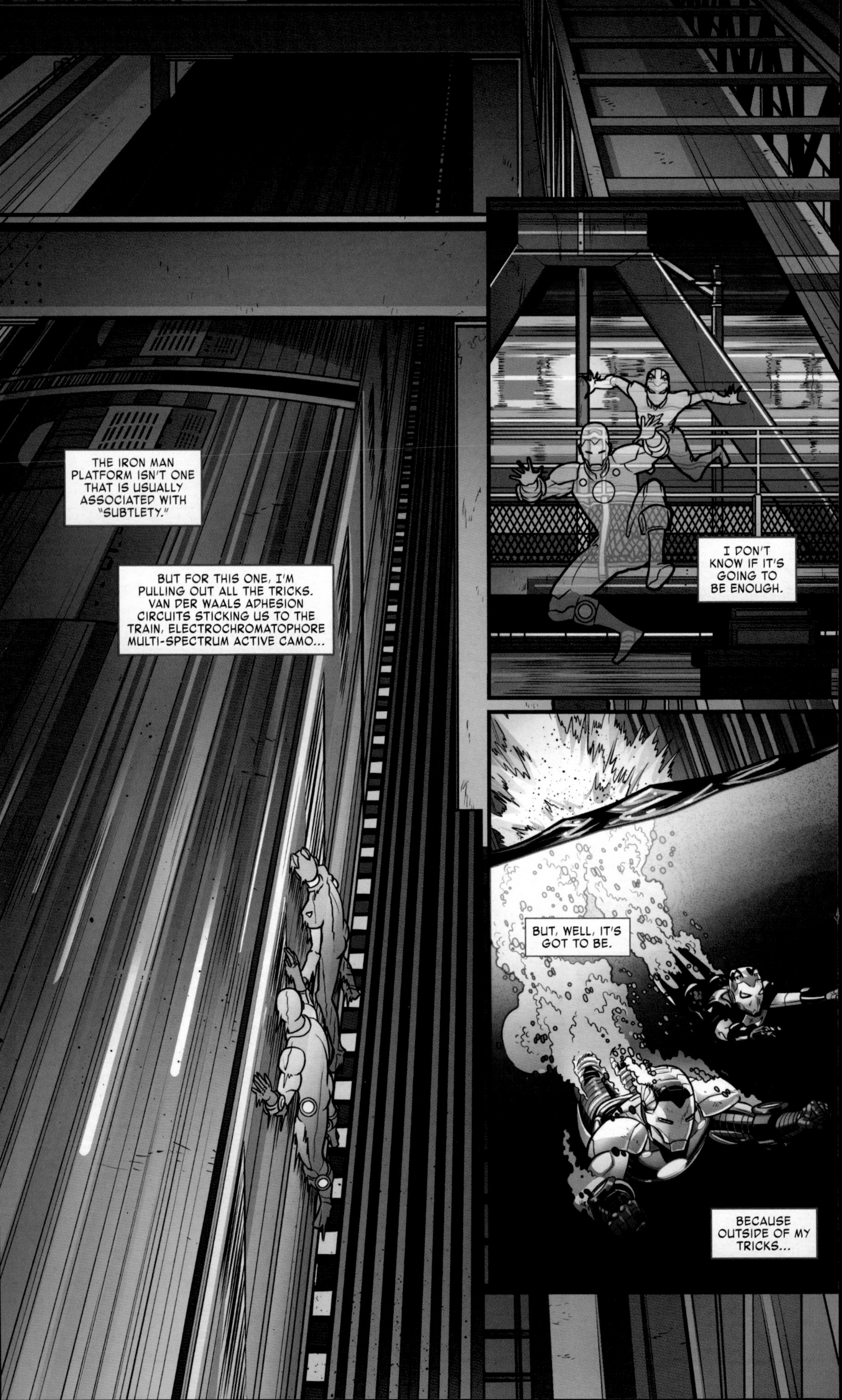
THE IRON MAN PLATFORM ISN'T ONE THAT IS USUALLY ASSOCIATED WITH "SUBTLETY."
BUT FOR THIS ONE, I'M PULLING OUT ALL THE TRICKS. VAN DER WAALS ADHESION CIRCUITS STICKING US TO THE TRAIN, ELECTROCHROMATOPHORE MULTI-SPECTRUM ACTIVE CAMO...
I DON'T KNOW IF IT'S GOING TO BE ENOUGH.
BUT, WELL, IT'S GOT TO BE.
BECAUSE OUTSIDE OF MY TRICKS...

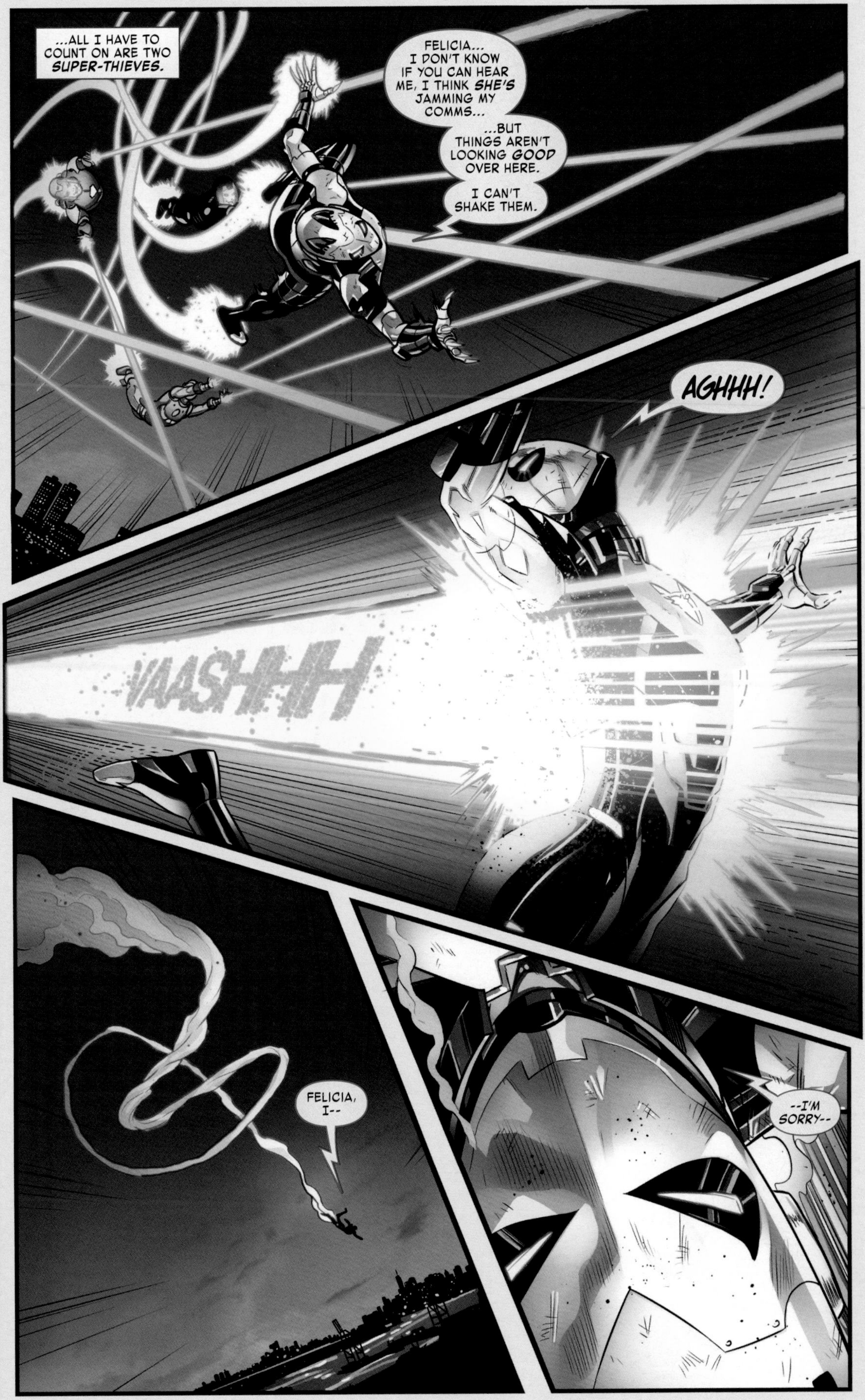

...ALL I HAVE TO COUNT ON ARE TWO SUPER-THIEVES.
FELICIA... I DON'T KNOW IF YOU CAN HEAR ME, I THINK SHE'S JAMMING MY COMMS...
...BUT THINGS AREN'T LOOKING GOOD OVER HERE.
I CAN'T SHAKE THEM.
AGHHH!
VAASHHH
FELICIA, I--
--I'M SORRY--

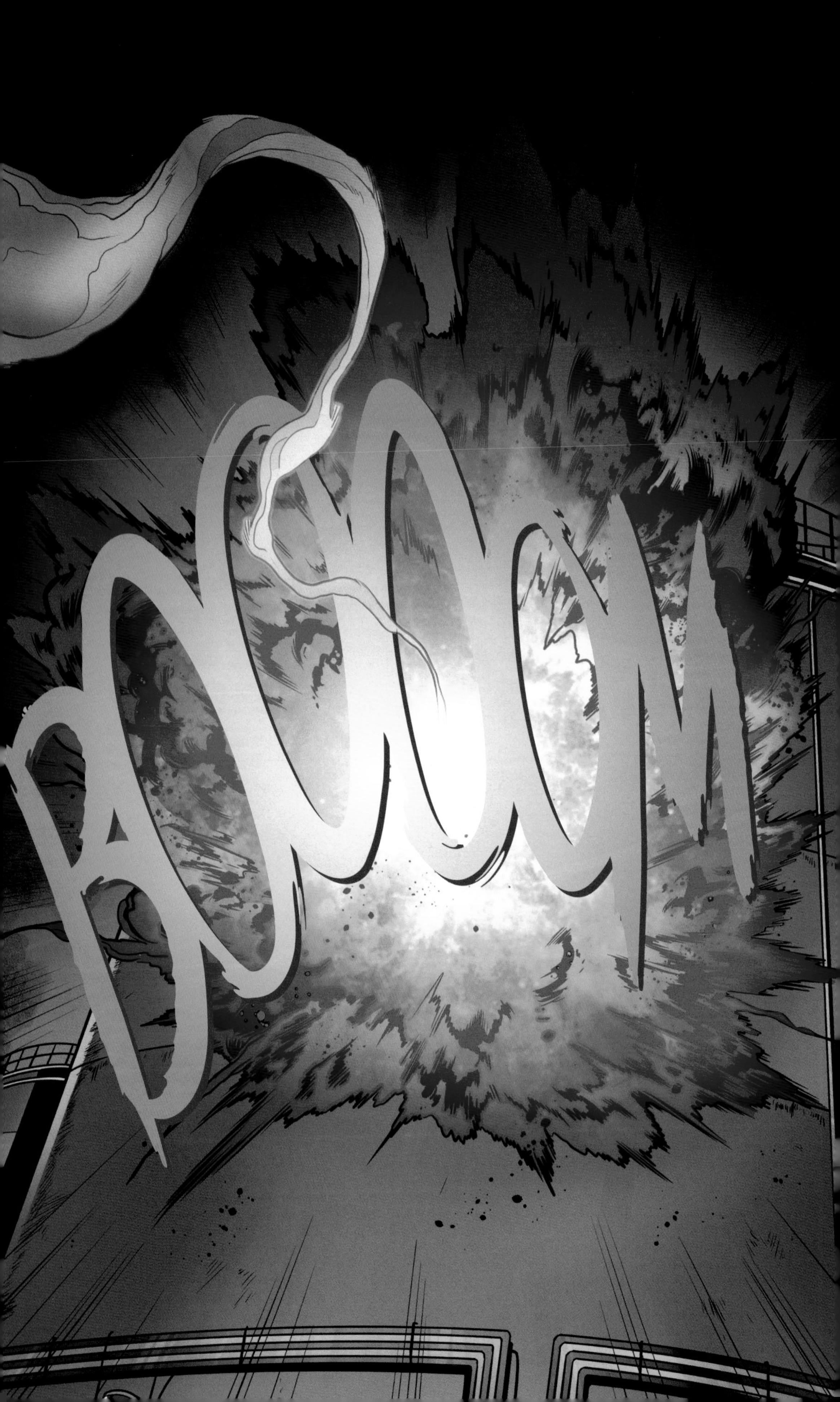
BOOM

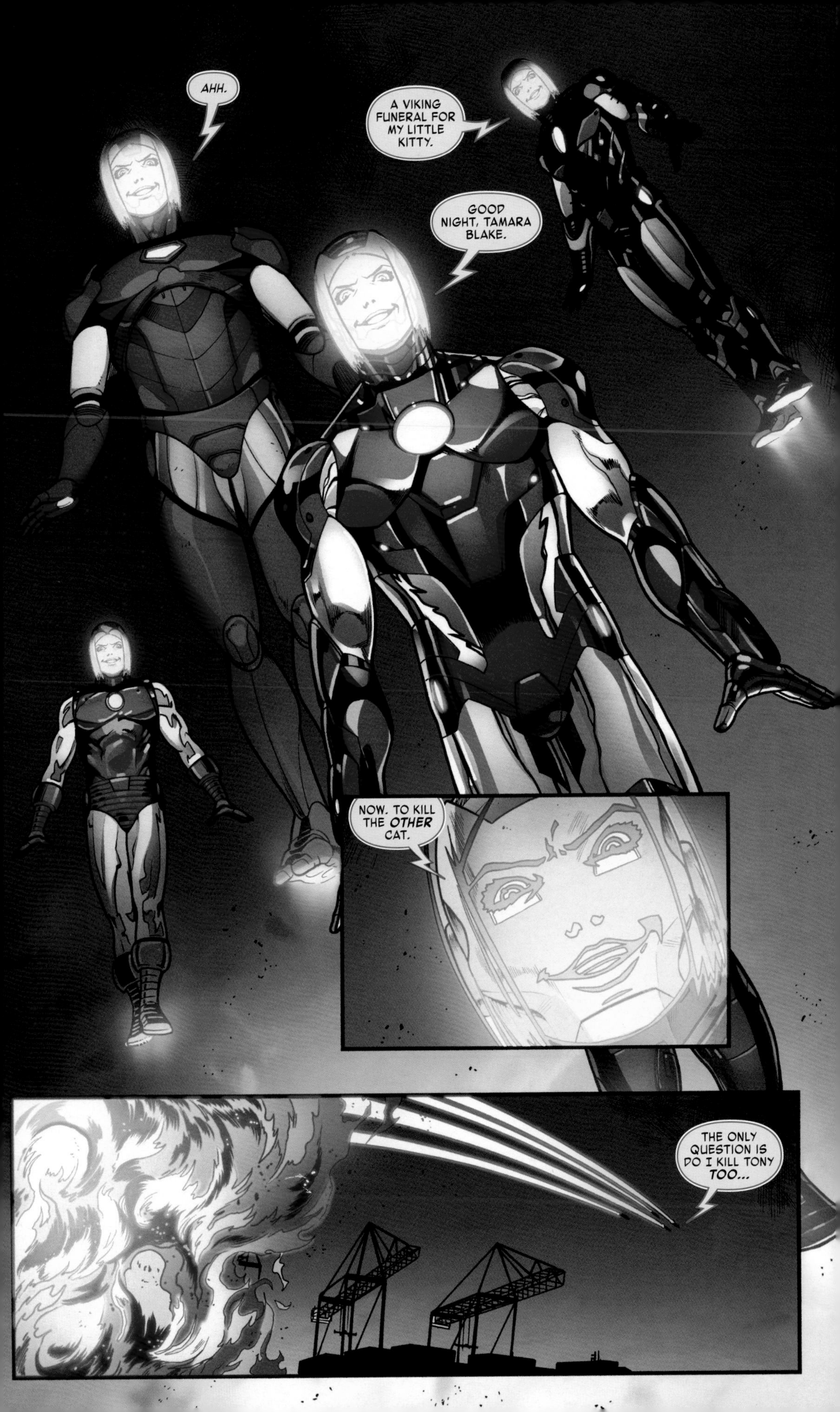
AHH.
A VIKING FUNERAL FOR MY LITTLE KITTY.
GOOD NIGHT, TAMARA BLAKE.
NOW. TO KILL THE *OTHER* CAT.
THE ONLY QUESTION IS DO I KILL TONY *TOO...*

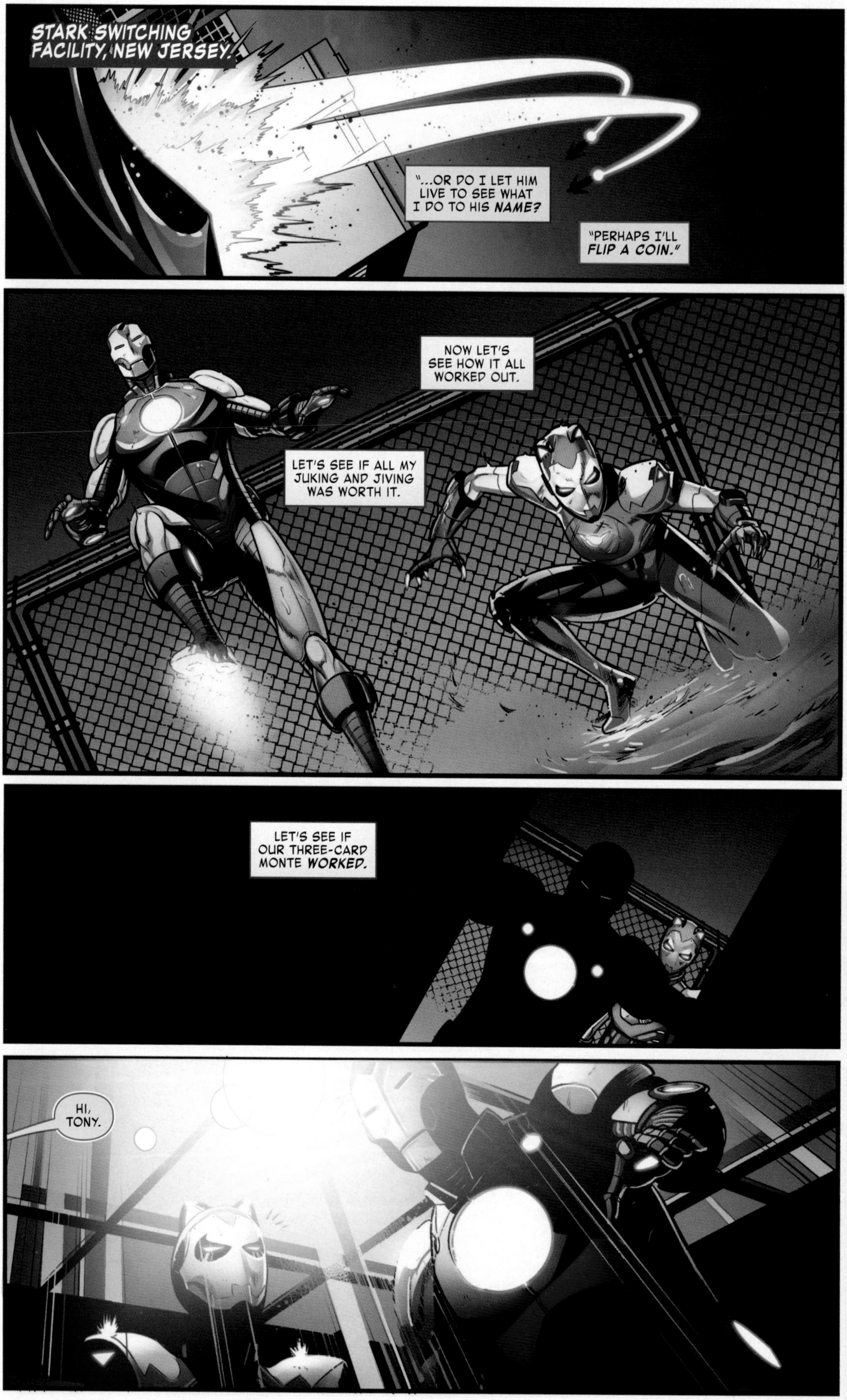
STARK SWITCHING FACILITY, NEW JERSEY.
"...OR DO I LET HIM LIVE TO SEE WHAT I DO TO HIS NAME?
"PERHAPS I'LL FLIP A COIN."
NOW LET'S SEE HOW IT ALL WORKED OUT.
LET'S SEE IF ALL MY JUKING AND JIVING WAS WORTH IT.
LET'S SEE IF OUR THREE-CARD MONTE WORKED.
HI, TONY.

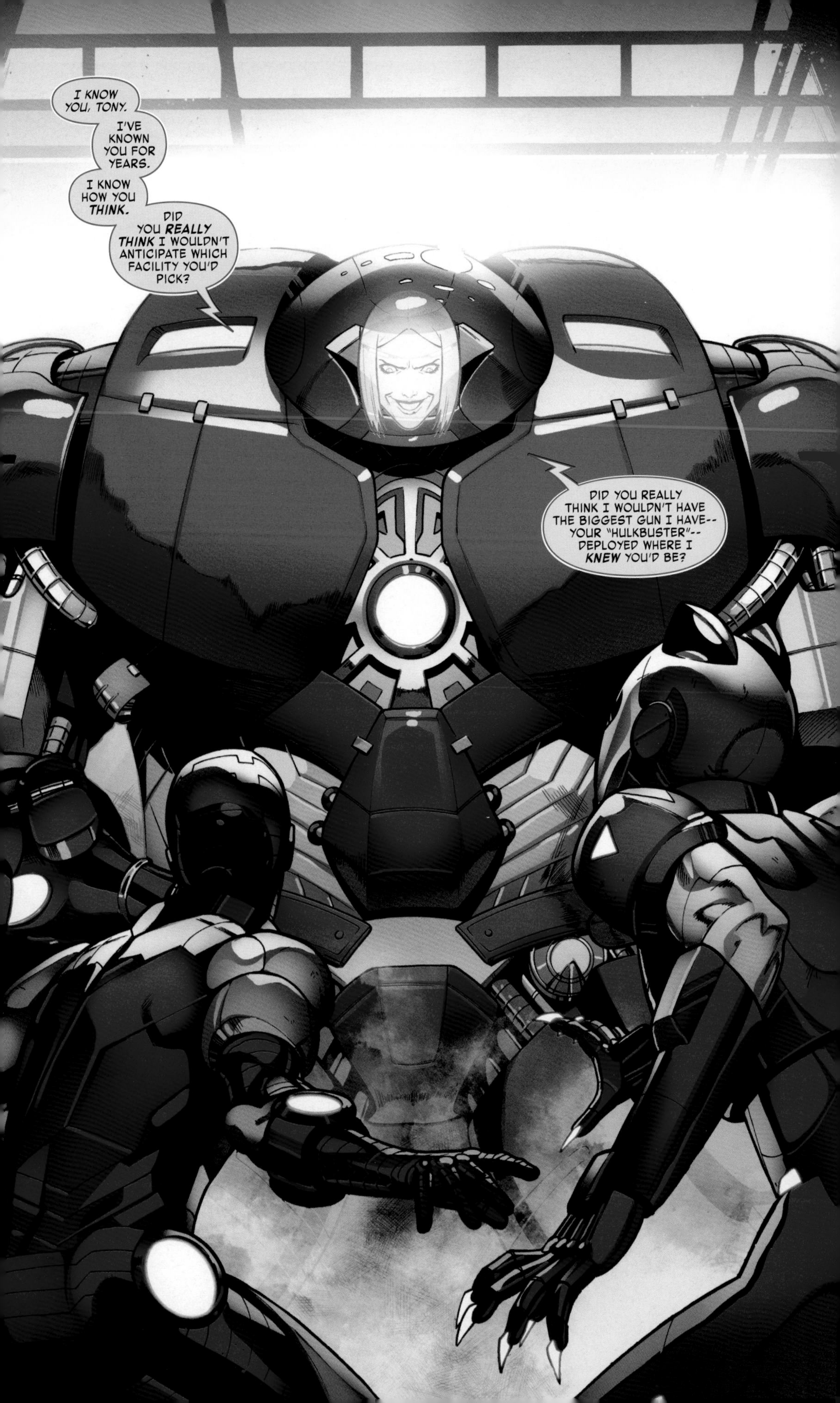
I KNOW YOU, TONY.
I'VE KNOWN YOU FOR YEARS.
I KNOW HOW YOU *THINK.*
DID YOU *REALLY THINK* I WOULDN'T ANTICIPATE WHICH FACILITY YOU'D PICK?
DID YOU REALLY THINK I WOULDN'T HAVE THE BIGGEST GUN I HAVE-- YOUR "HULKBUSTER"-- DEPLOYED WHERE I *KNEW* YOU'D BE?

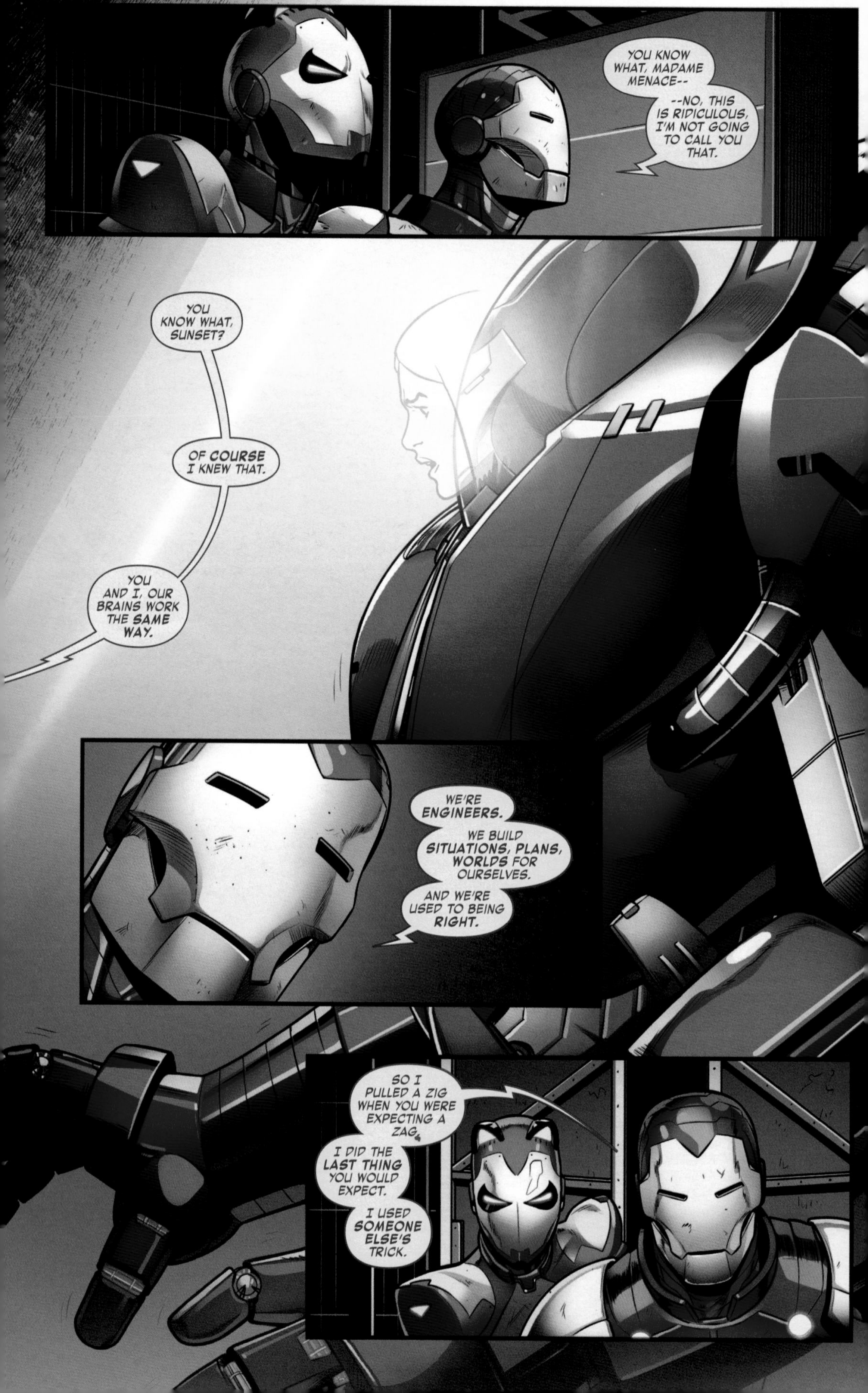
YOU KNOW WHAT, MADAME MENACE--
--NO, THIS IS RIDICULOUS, I'M NOT GOING TO CALL YOU THAT.
YOU KNOW WHAT, SUNSET?
OF COURSE I KNEW THAT.
YOU AND I, OUR BRAINS WORK THE SAME WAY.
WE'RE ENGINEERS.
WE BUILD SITUATIONS, PLANS, WORLDS FOR OURSELVES.
AND WE'RE USED TO BEING RIGHT.
SO I PULLED A ZIG WHEN YOU WERE EXPECTING A ZAG.
I DID THE LAST THING YOU WOULD EXPECT.
I USED SOMEONE ELSE'S TRICK.

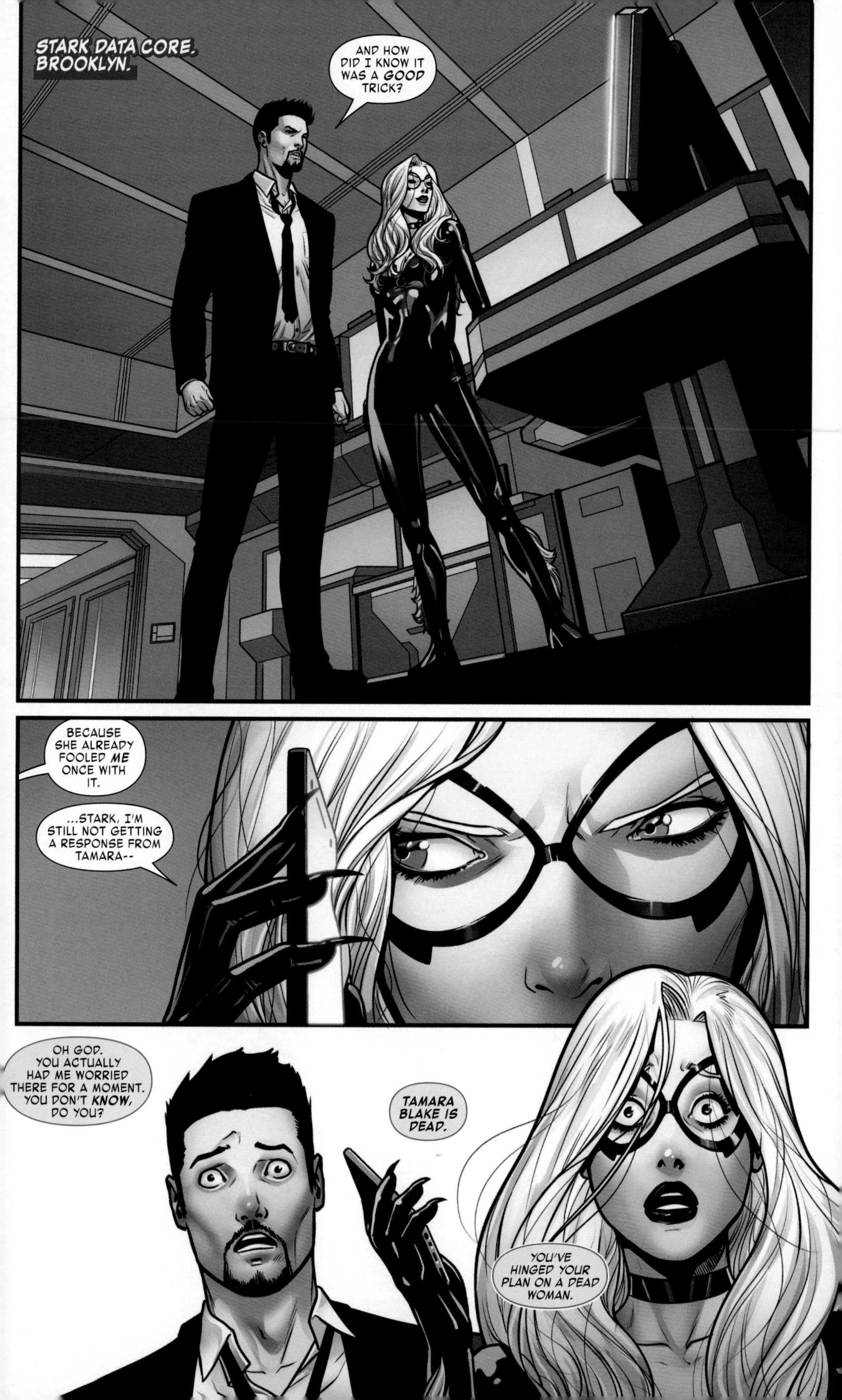
STARK DATA CORE. BROOKLYN.
AND HOW DID I KNOW IT WAS A GOOD TRICK?
BECAUSE SHE ALREADY FOOLED ME ONCE WITH IT.
...STARK, I'M STILL NOT GETTING A RESPONSE FROM TAMARA--
OH GOD. YOU ACTUALLY HAD ME WORRIED THERE FOR A MOMENT. YOU DON'T KNOW, DO YOU?
TAMARA BLAKE IS DEAD.
YOU'VE HINGED YOUR PLAN ON A DEAD WOMAN.

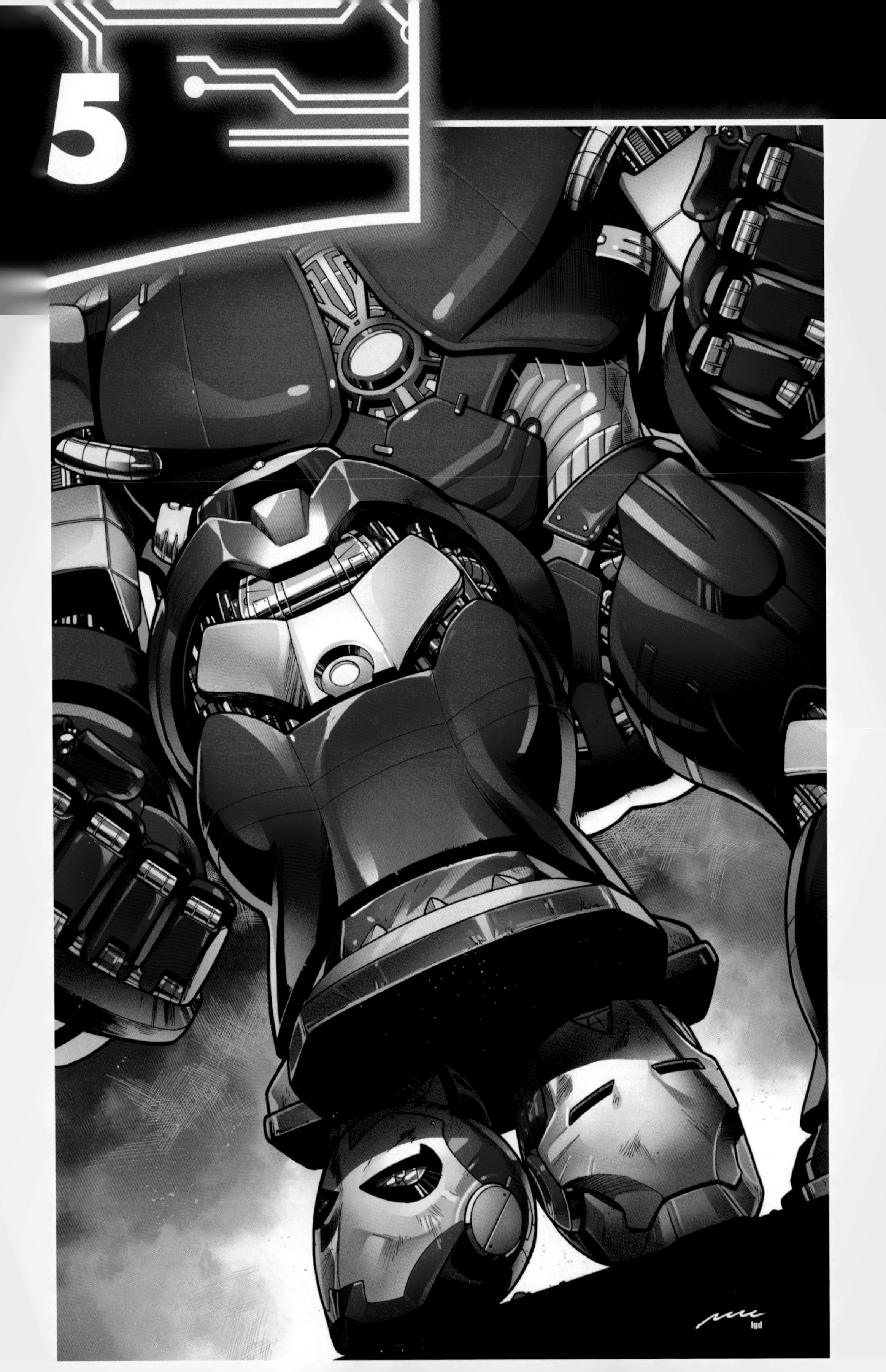
5

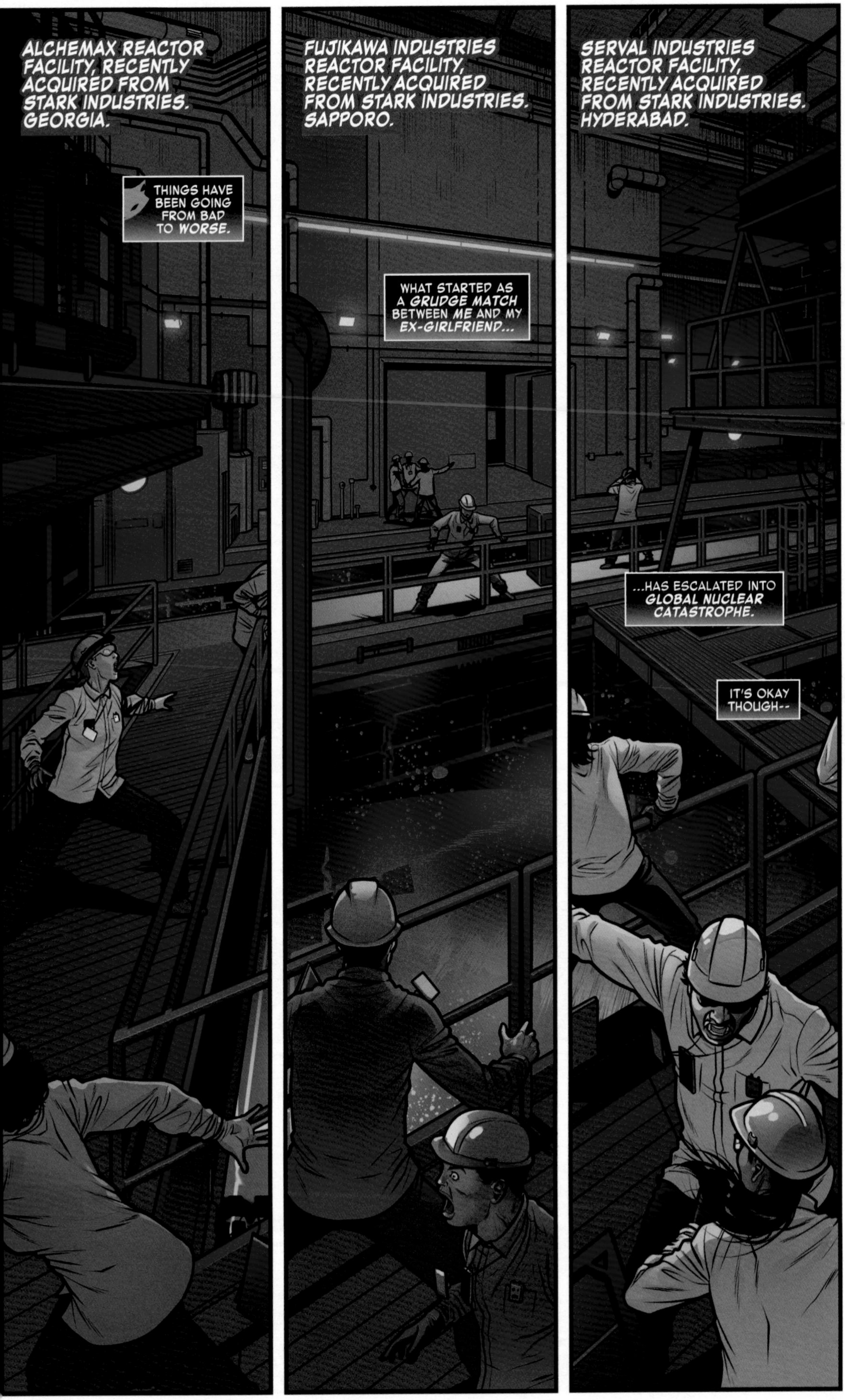
ALCHEMAX REACTOR FACILITY, RECENTLY ACQUIRED FROM STARK INDUSTRIES. GEORGIA.
THINGS HAVE BEEN GOING FROM BAD TO WORSE.
FUJIKAWA INDUSTRIES REACTOR FACILITY, RECENTLY ACQUIRED FROM STARK INDUSTRIES. SAPPORO.
WHAT STARTED AS A GRUDGE MATCH BETWEEN ME AND MY EX-GIRLFRIEND...
SERVAL INDUSTRIES REACTOR FACILITY, RECENTLY ACQUIRED FROM STARK INDUSTRIES. HYDERABAD.
...HAS ESCALATED INTO GLOBAL NUCLEAR CATASTROPHE.
IT'S OKAY THOUGH--

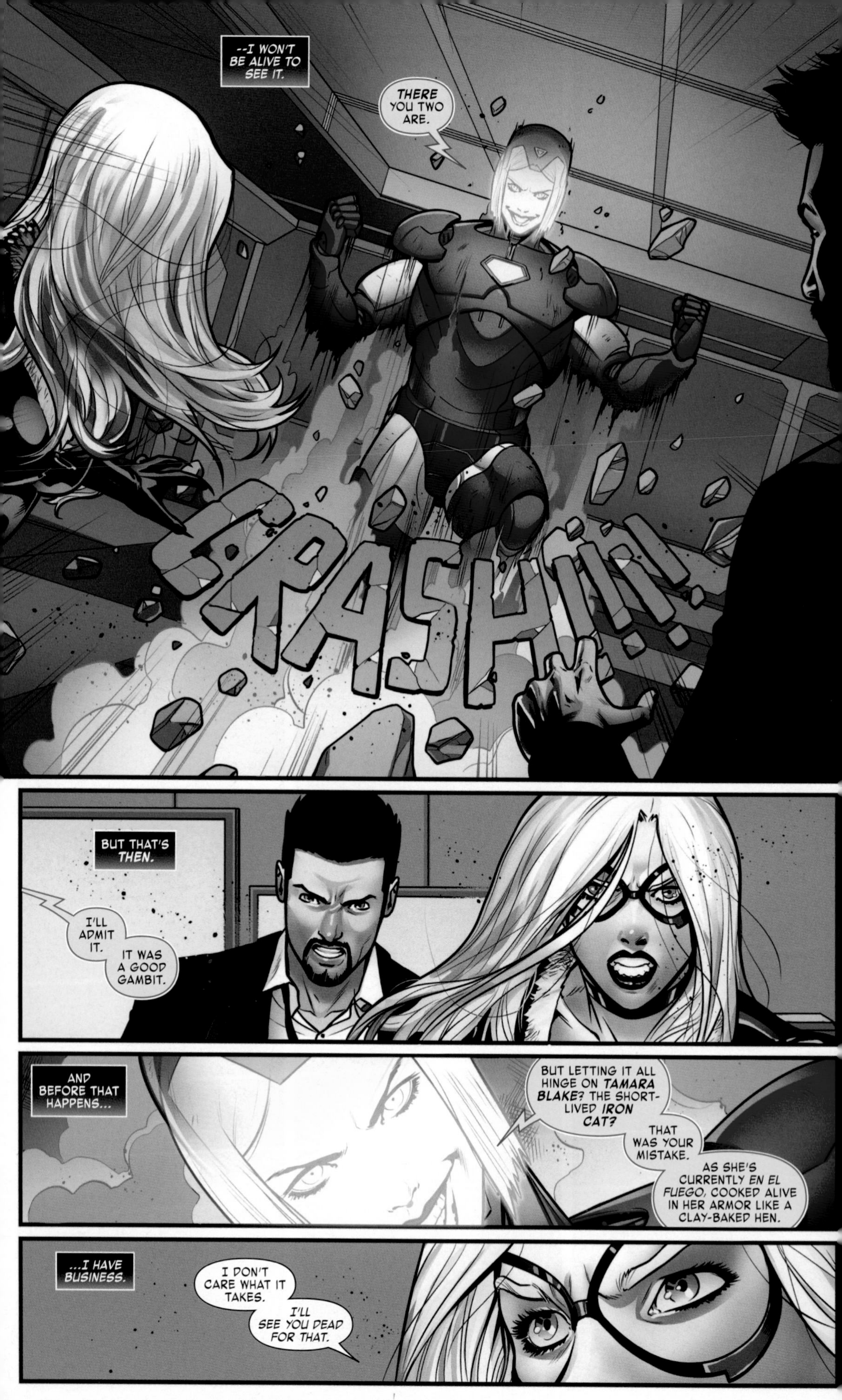
--I WON'T BE ALIVE TO SEE IT.
THERE YOU TWO ARE.
CRASH!!!!
BUT THAT'S THEN.
I'LL ADMIT IT.
IT WAS A GOOD GAMBIT.
AND BEFORE THAT HAPPENS...
BUT LETTING IT ALL HINGE ON TAMARA BLAKE? THE SHORT-LIVED IRON CAT?
THAT WAS YOUR MISTAKE.
AS SHE'S CURRENTLY EN EL FUEGO, COOKED ALIVE IN HER ARMOR LIKE A CLAY-BAKED HEN.
...I HAVE BUSINESS.
I DON'T CARE WHAT IT TAKES.
I'LL SEE YOU DEAD FOR THAT.

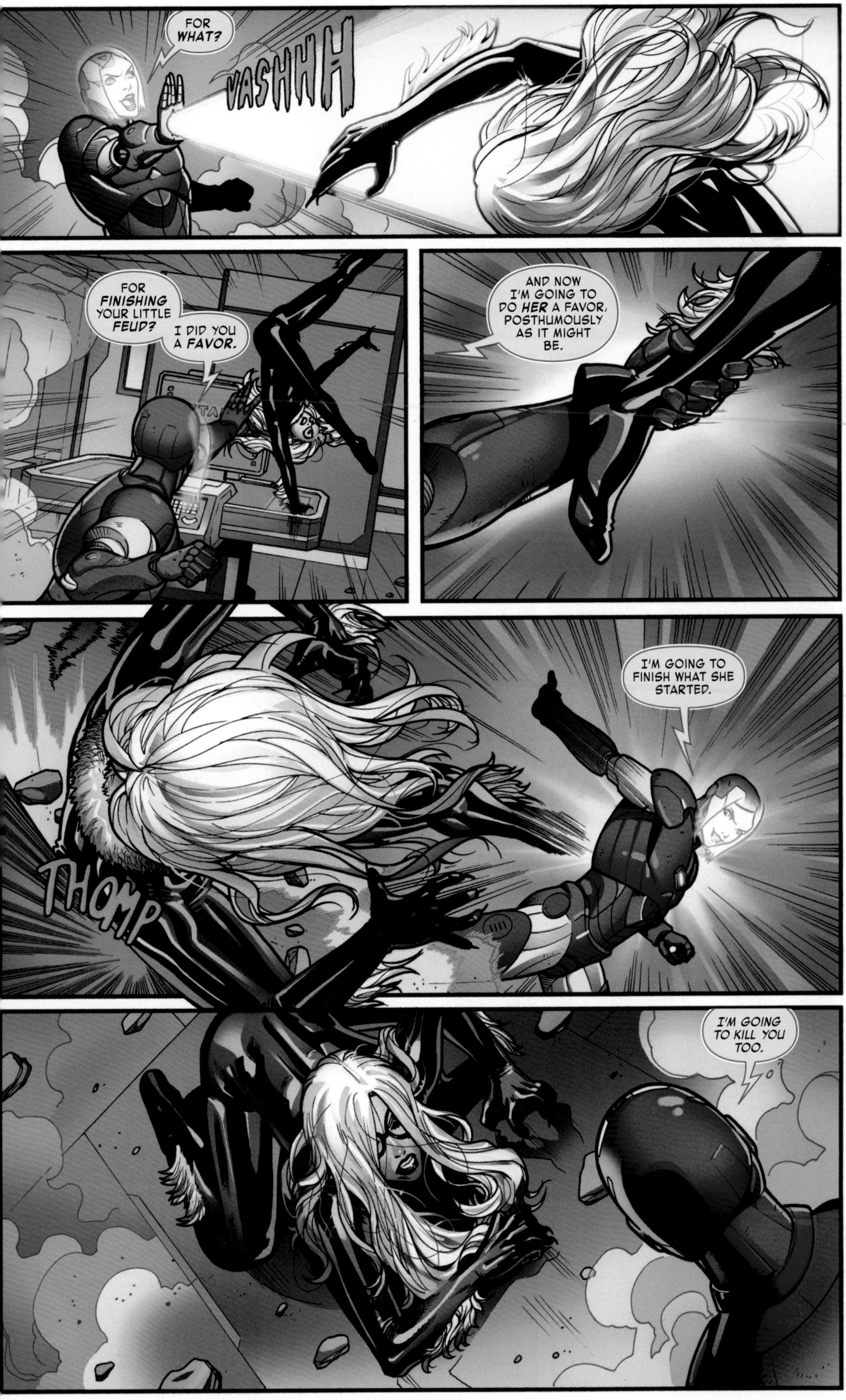
FOR WHAT?
VASHHH
FOR FINISHING YOUR LITTLE FEUD?
I DID YOU A FAVOR.
AND NOW I'M GOING TO DO HER A FAVOR, POSTHUMOUSLY AS IT MIGHT BE.
I'M GOING TO FINISH WHAT SHE STARTED.
THOMP
I'M GOING TO KILL YOU TOO.

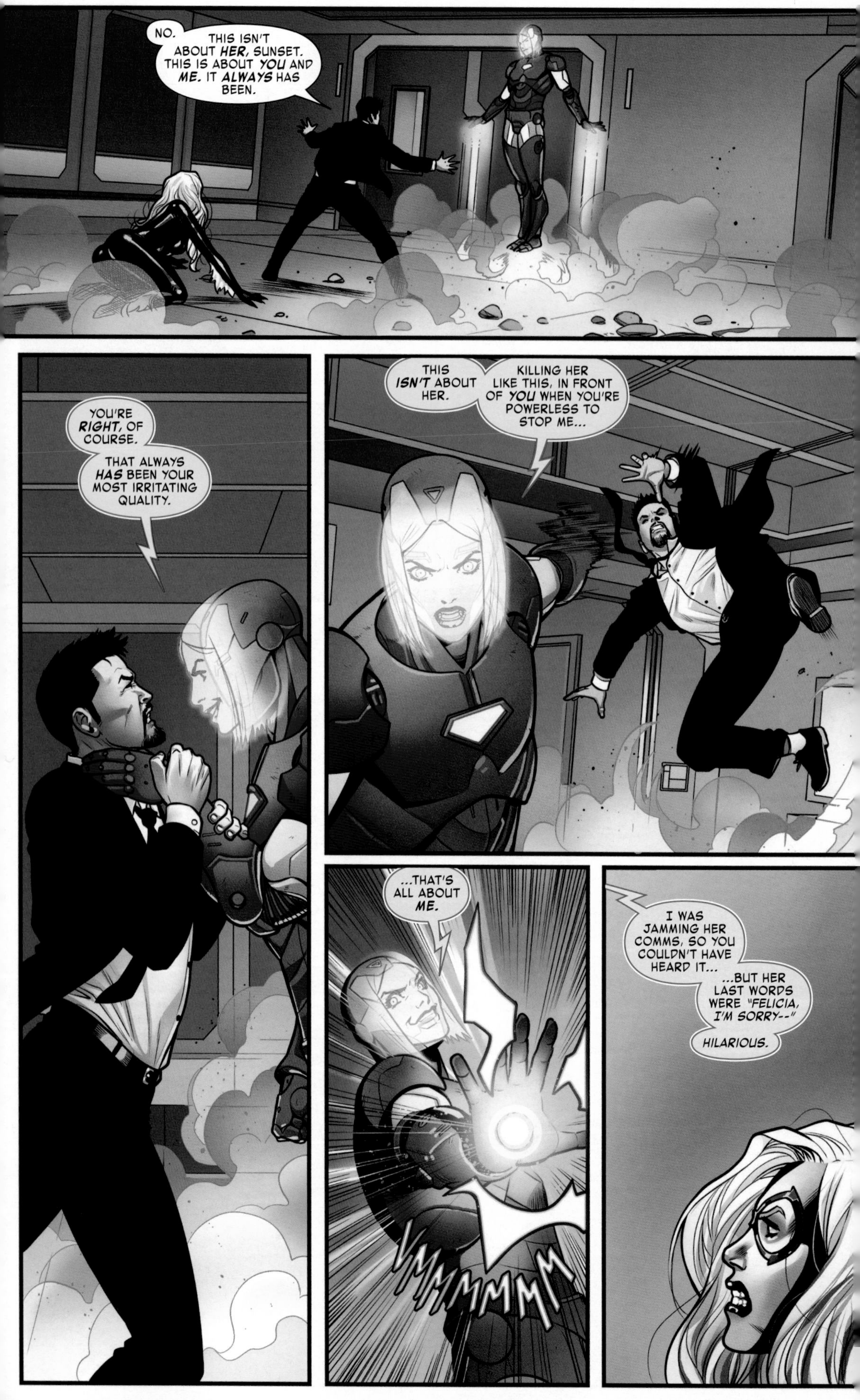
NO.
THIS ISN'T ABOUT HER, SUNSET. THIS IS ABOUT YOU AND ME. IT ALWAYS HAS BEEN.
YOU'RE RIGHT, OF COURSE.
THAT ALWAYS HAS BEEN YOUR MOST IRRITATING QUALITY.
THIS ISN'T ABOUT HER.
KILLING HER LIKE THIS, IN FRONT OF YOU WHEN YOU'RE POWERLESS TO STOP ME...
...THAT'S ALL ABOUT ME.
MMMMMMM
I WAS JAMMING HER COMMS, SO YOU COULDN'T HAVE HEARD IT...
...BUT HER LAST WORDS WERE "FELICIA, I'M SORRY--"
HILARIOUS.

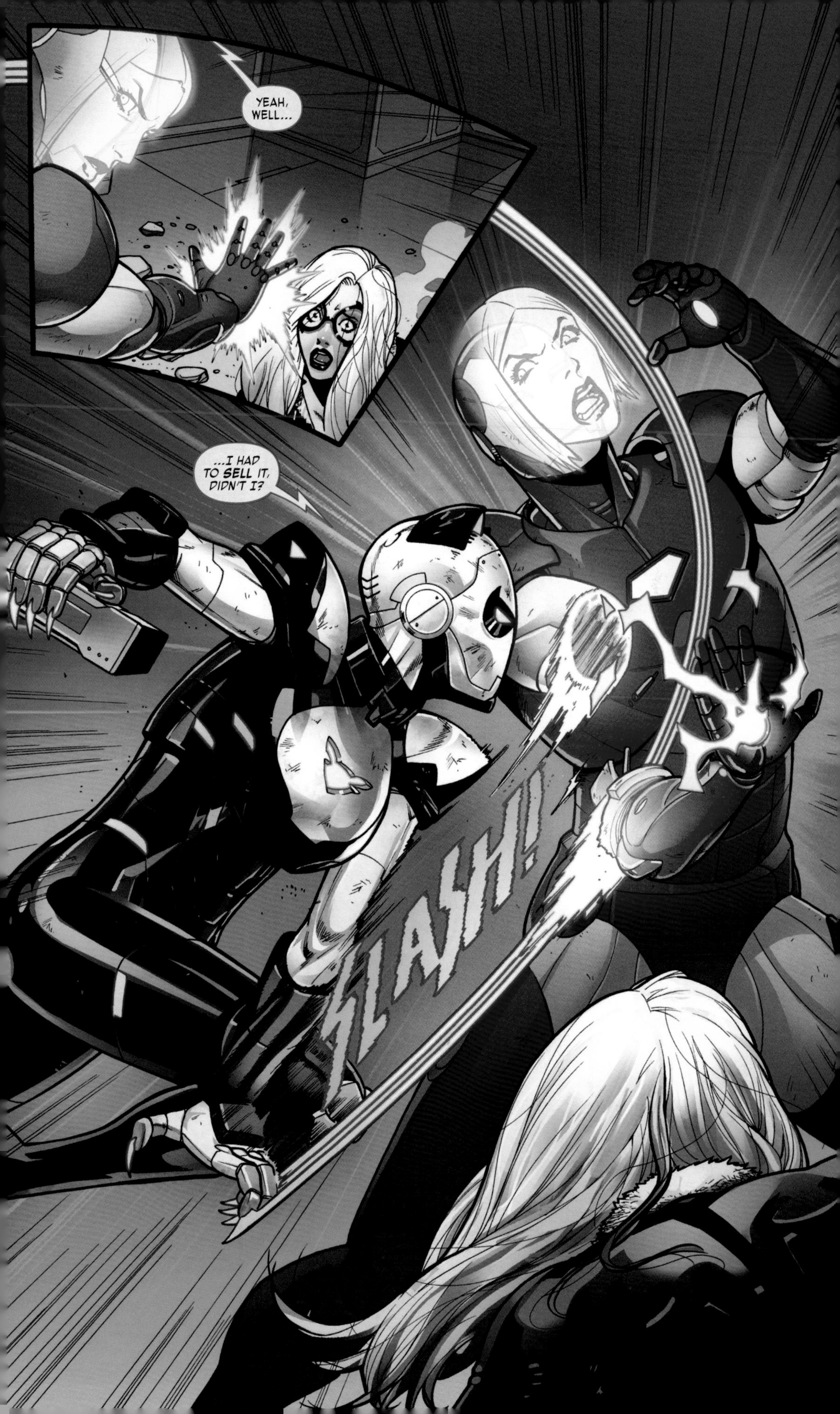

YEAH, WELL...
...I HAD TO SELL IT, DIDN'T I?
SLASH!

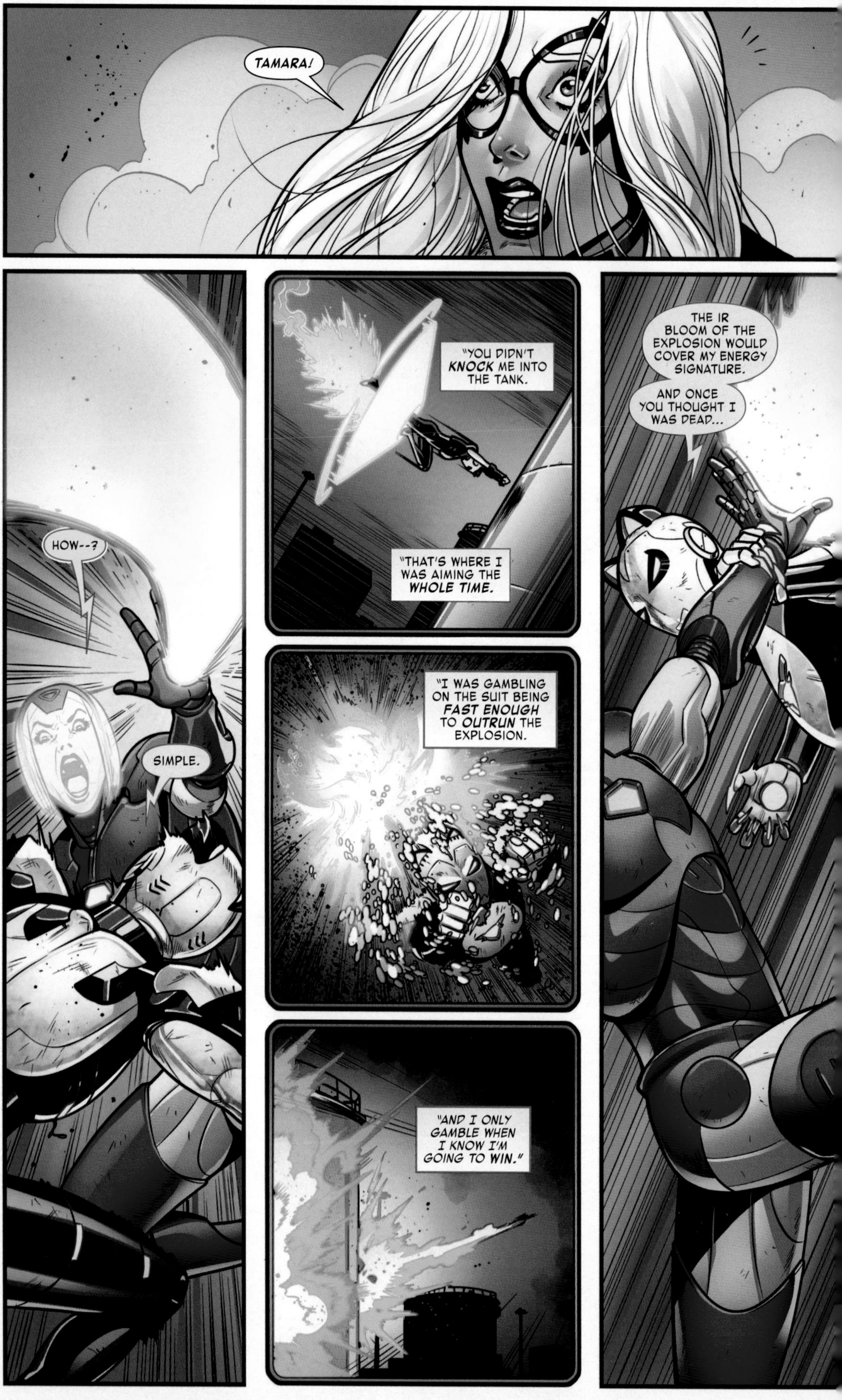
TAMARA!
HOW--?
SIMPLE.
"YOU DIDN'T KNOCK ME INTO THE TANK.
"THAT'S WHERE I WAS AIMING THE WHOLE TIME.
"I WAS GAMBLING ON THE SUIT BEING FAST ENOUGH TO OUTRUN THE EXPLOSION.
"AND I ONLY GAMBLE WHEN I KNOW I'M GOING TO WIN."
THE IR BLOOM OF THE EXPLOSION WOULD COVER MY ENERGY SIGNATURE.
AND ONCE YOU THOUGHT I WAS DEAD...

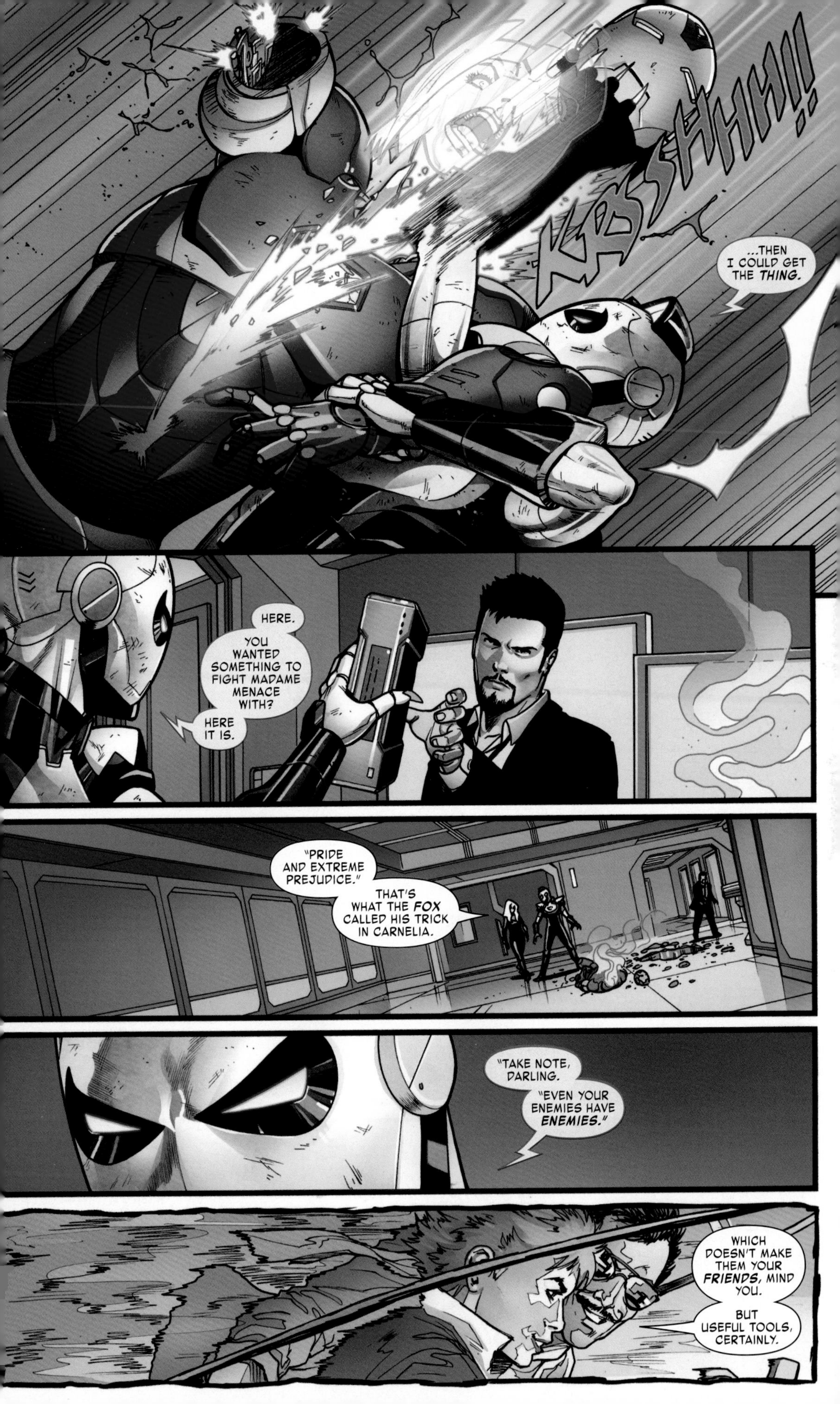
KRSSHHH!!
...THEN I COULD GET THE THING.
HERE.
YOU WANTED SOMETHING TO FIGHT MADAME MENACE WITH?
HERE IT IS.
"PRIDE AND EXTREME PREJUDICE."
THAT'S WHAT THE FOX CALLED HIS TRICK IN CARNELIA.
"TAKE NOTE, DARLING.
"EVEN YOUR ENEMIES HAVE ENEMIES."
WHICH DOESN'T MAKE THEM YOUR FRIENDS, MIND YOU.
BUT USEFUL TOOLS, CERTAINLY.

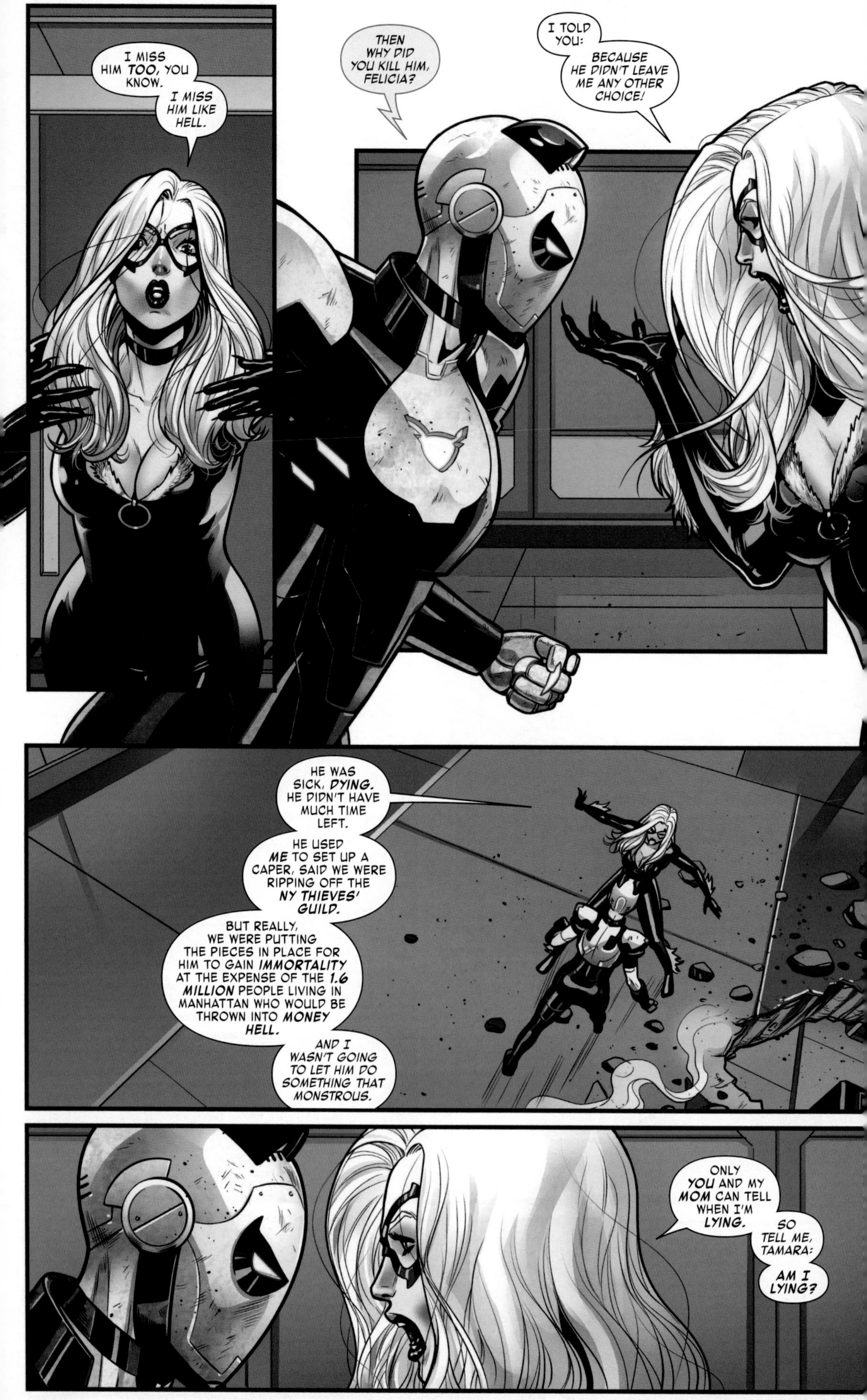

I MISS HIM TOO, YOU KNOW.
I MISS HIM LIKE HELL.
THEN WHY DID YOU KILL HIM, FELICIA?
I TOLD YOU:
BECAUSE HE DIDN'T LEAVE ME ANY OTHER CHOICE!
HE WAS SICK, DYING. HE DIDN'T HAVE MUCH TIME LEFT.
HE USED ME TO SET UP A CAPER, SAID WE WERE RIPPING OFF THE NY THIEVES' GUILD.
BUT REALLY, WE WERE PUTTING THE PIECES IN PLACE FOR HIM TO GAIN IMMORTALITY AT THE EXPENSE OF THE 1.6 MILLION PEOPLE LIVING IN MANHATTAN WHO WOULD BE THROWN INTO MONEY HELL.
AND I WASN'T GOING TO LET HIM DO SOMETHING THAT MONSTROUS.
ONLY YOU AND MY MOM CAN TELL WHEN I'M LYING.
SO TELL ME, TAMARA:
AM I LYING?

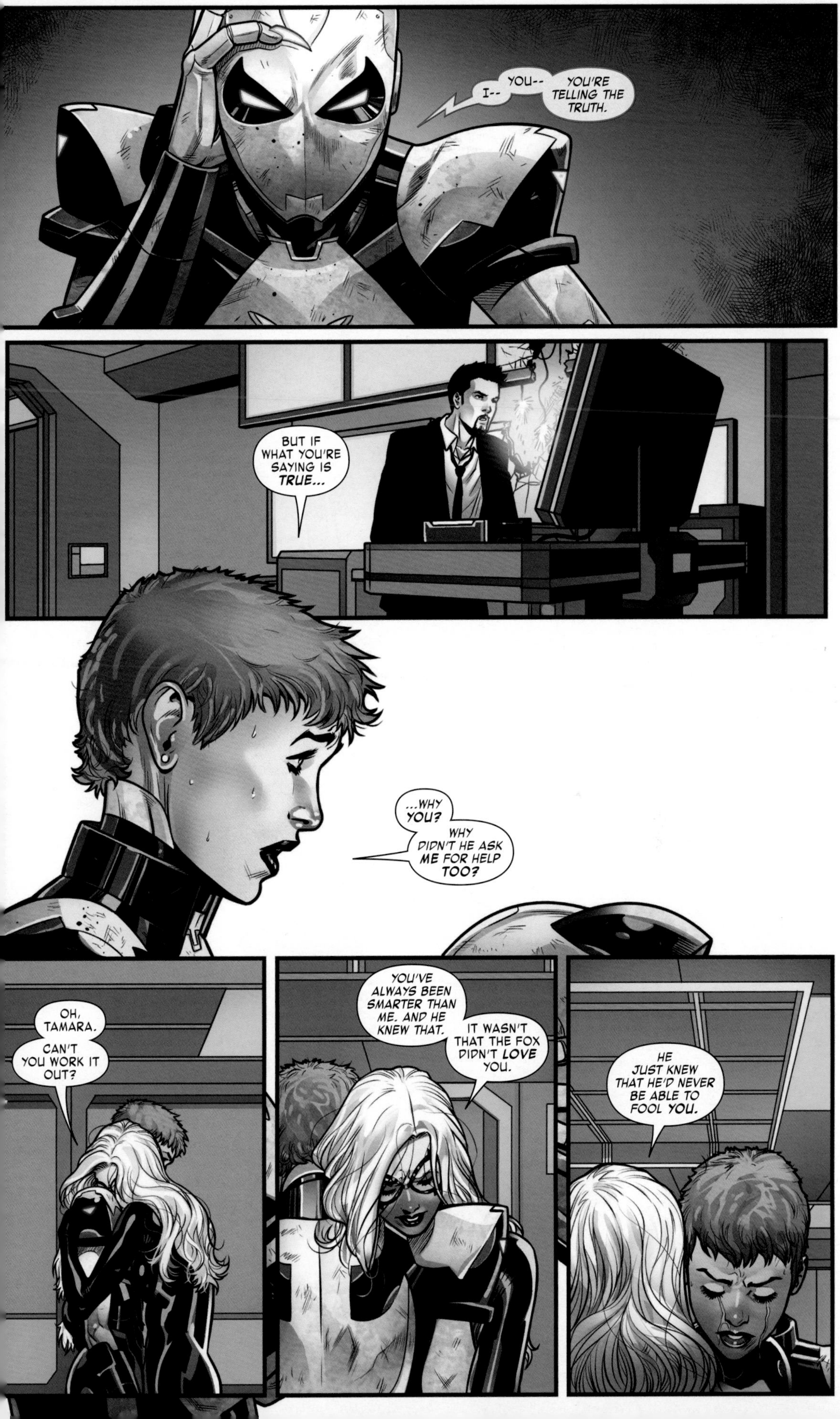

I--
YOU--
YOU'RE TELLING THE TRUTH.
BUT IF WHAT YOU'RE SAYING IS TRUE...
...WHY YOU?
WHY DIDN'T HE ASK ME FOR HELP TOO?
OH, TAMARA.
CAN'T YOU WORK IT OUT?
YOU'VE ALWAYS BEEN SMARTER THAN ME. AND HE KNEW THAT.
IT WASN'T THAT THE FOX DIDN'T LOVE YOU.
HE JUST KNEW THAT HE'D NEVER BE ABLE TO FOOL YOU.

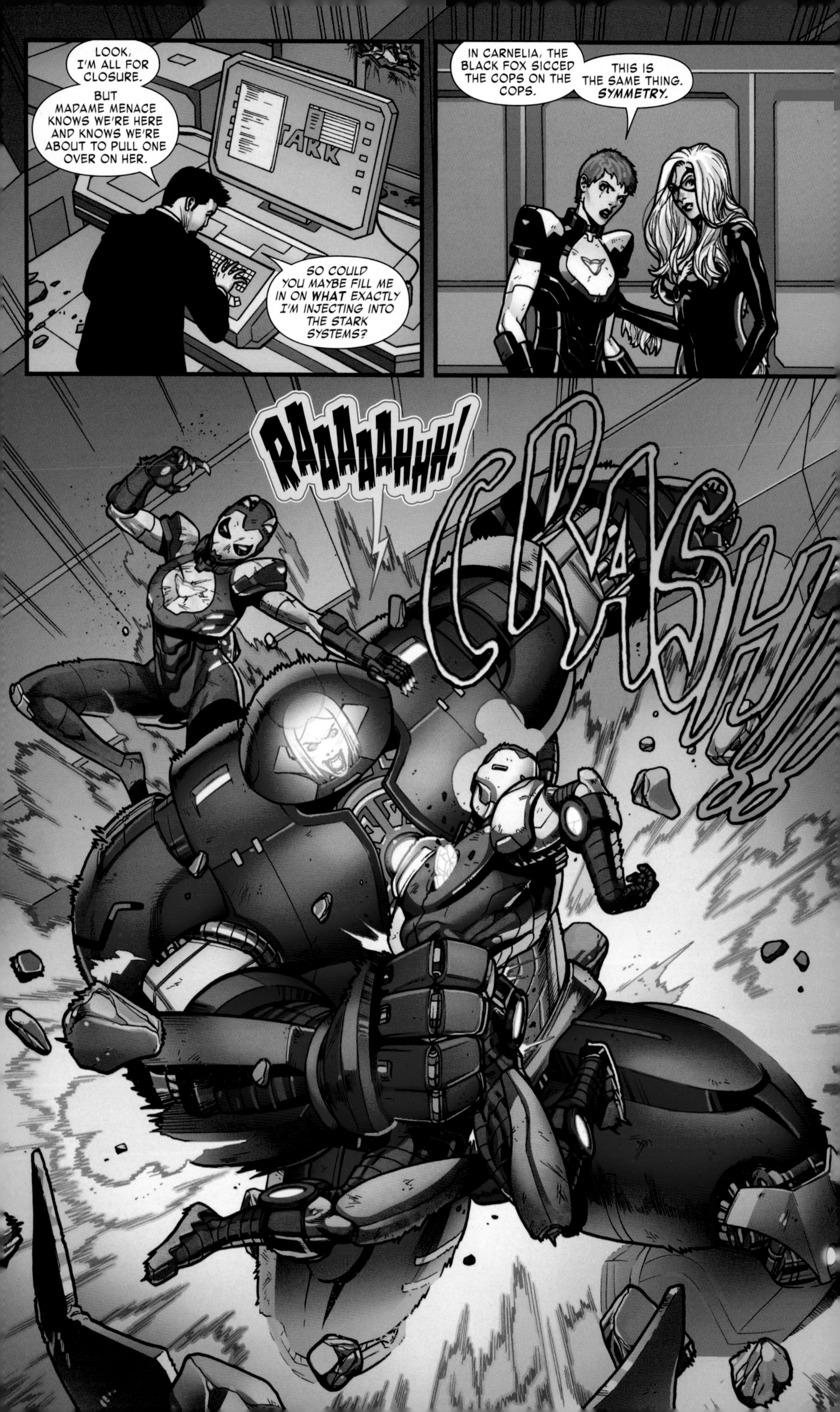
LOOK, I'M ALL FOR CLOSURE.
BUT MADAME MENACE KNOWS WE'RE HERE AND KNOWS WE'RE ABOUT TO PULL ONE OVER ON HER.
SO COULD YOU MAYBE FILL ME IN ON WHAT EXACTLY I'M INJECTING INTO THE STARK SYSTEMS?
IN CARNELIA, THE BLACK FOX SICCED THE COPS ON THE COPS.
THIS IS THE SAME THING. SYMMETRY.
RAAAAAHHH!
CRASH!!

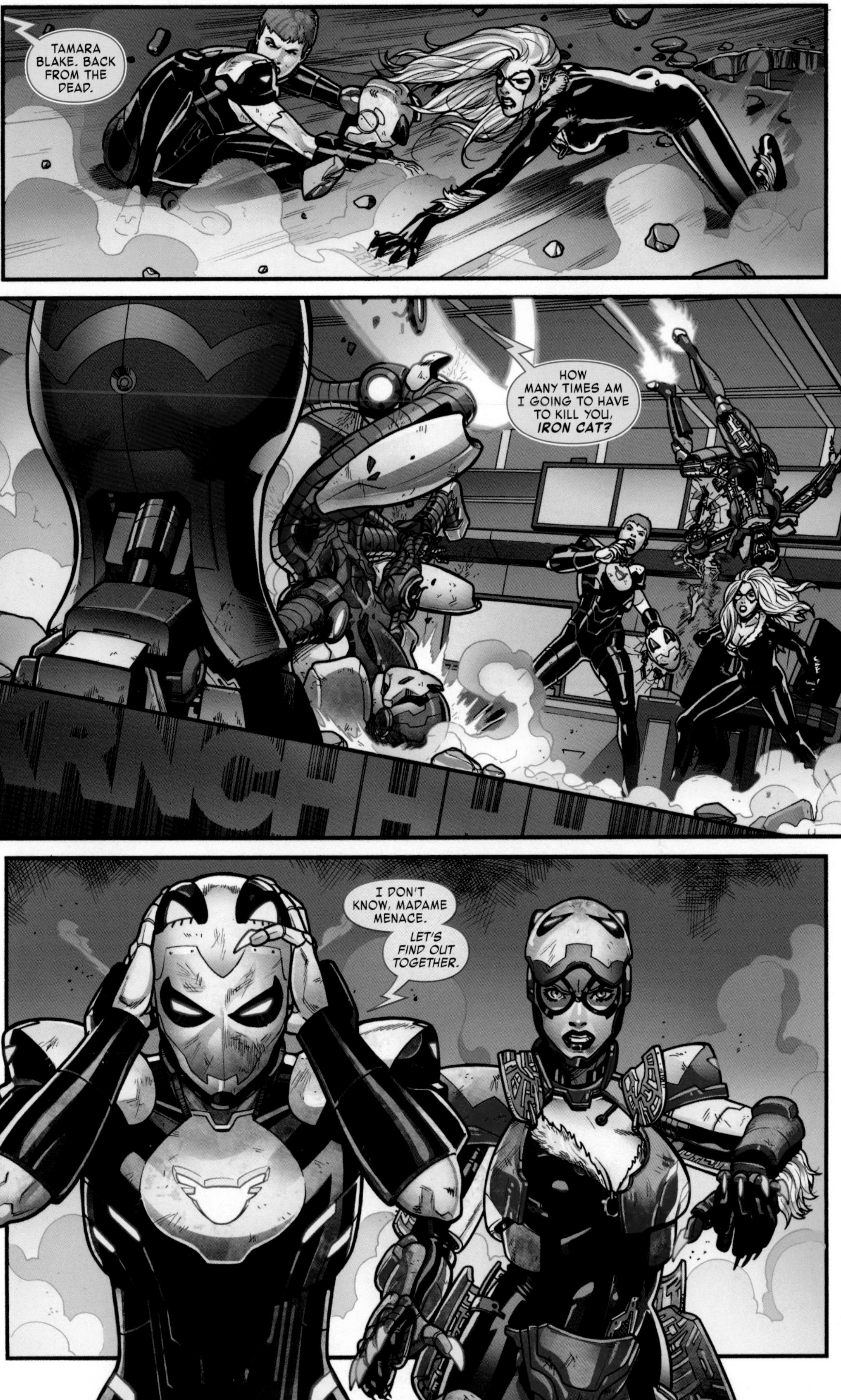

TAMARA BLAKE. BACK FROM THE DEAD.
HOW MANY TIMES AM I GOING TO HAVE TO KILL YOU, *IRON CAT?*
I DON'T KNOW, MADAME MENACE.
LET'S FIND OUT TOGETHER.

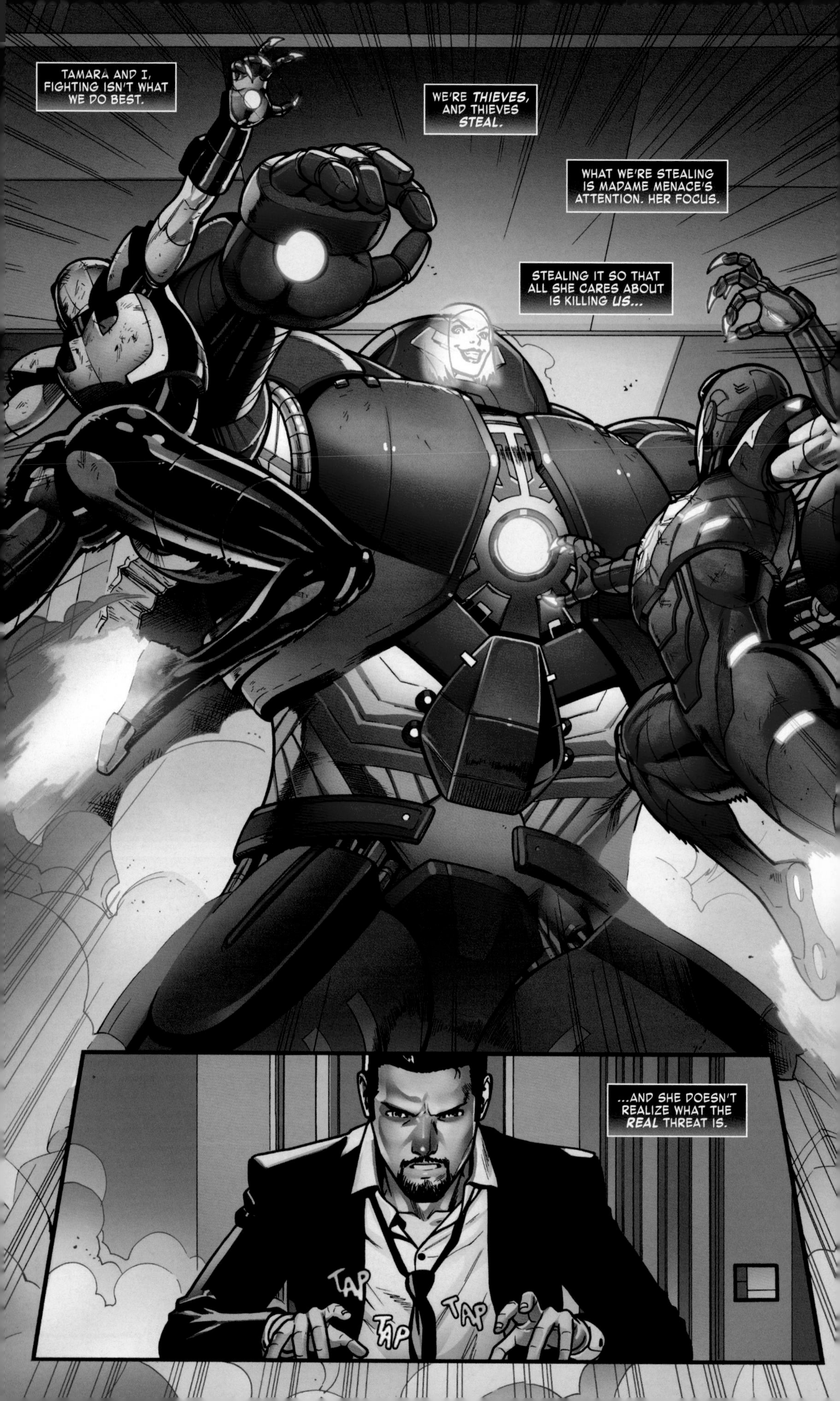
TAMARA AND I, FIGHTING ISN'T WHAT WE DO BEST.
WE'RE THIEVES, AND THIEVES STEAL.
WHAT WE'RE STEALING IS MADAME MENACE'S ATTENTION. HER FOCUS.
STEALING IT SO THAT ALL SHE CARES ABOUT IS KILLING US...
...AND SHE DOESN'T REALIZE WHAT THE REAL THREAT IS.
TAP
TAP
TAP

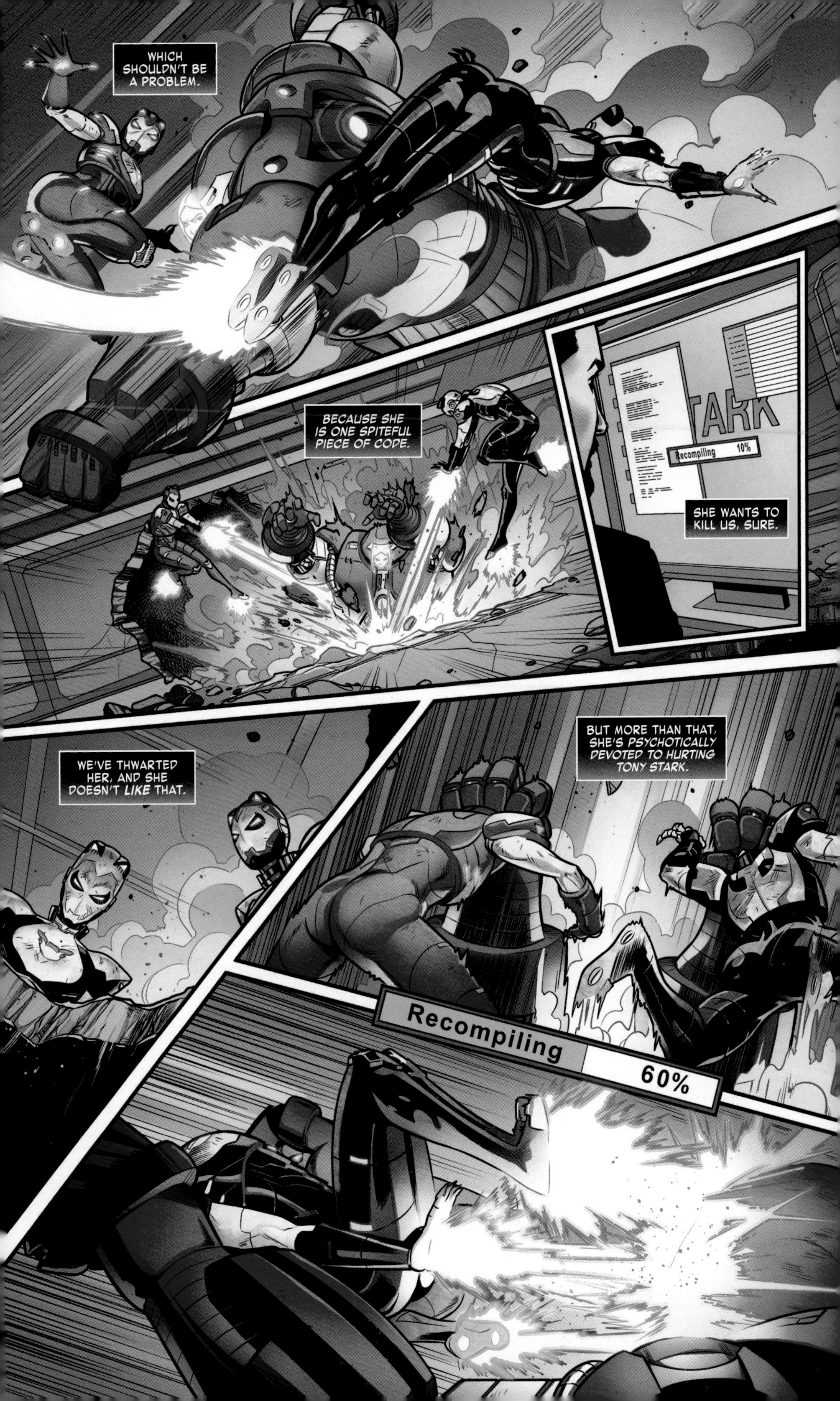
WHICH SHOULDN'T BE A PROBLEM.
BECAUSE SHE IS ONE SPITEFUL PIECE OF CODE.
STARK
Recompiling 10%
SHE WANTS TO KILL US, SURE.
WE'VE THWARTED HER, AND SHE DOESN'T *LIKE* THAT.
BUT MORE THAN THAT, SHE'S *PSYCHOTICALLY DEVOTED* TO HURTING TONY STARK.
Recompiling 60%

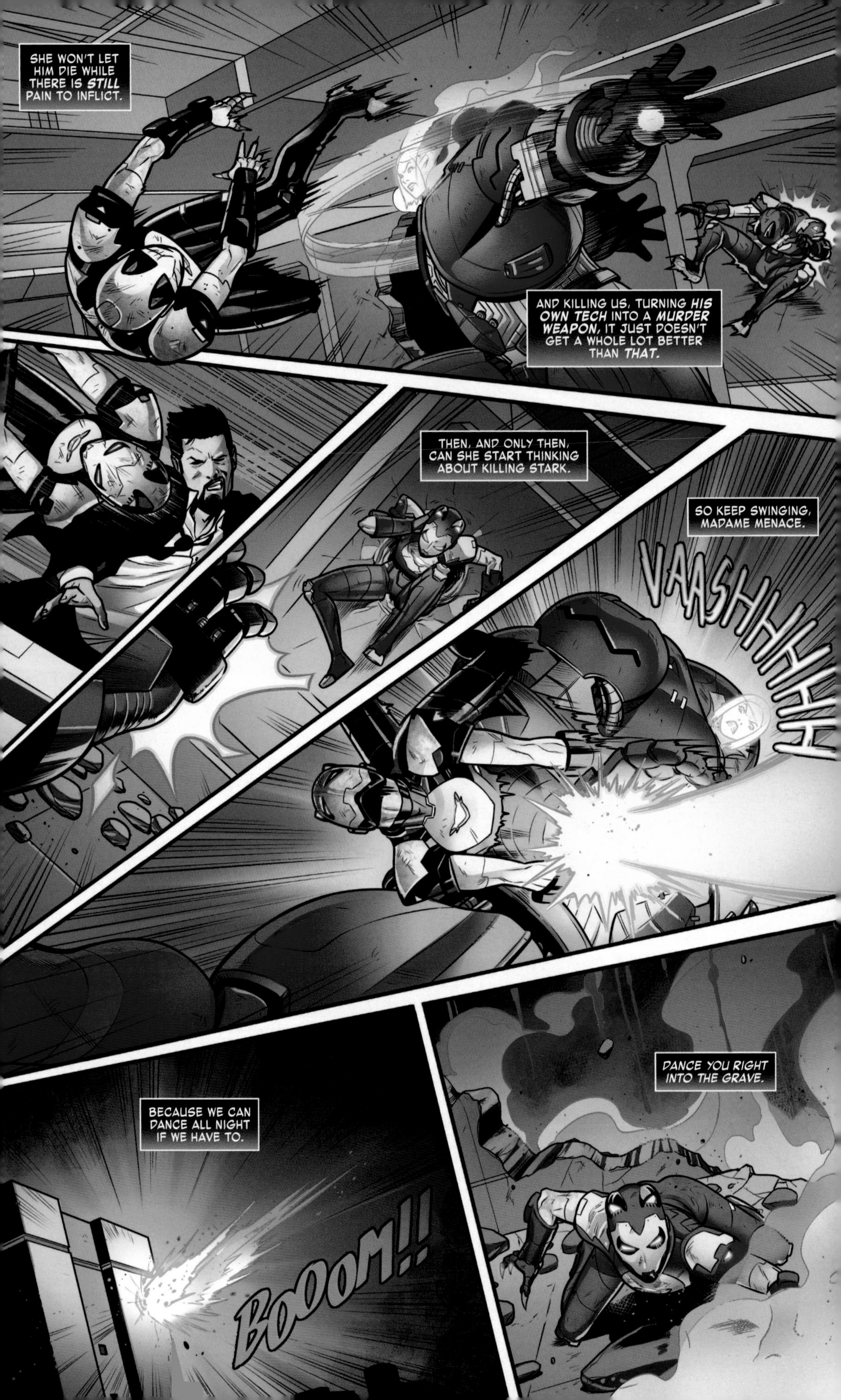
SHE WON'T LET HIM DIE WHILE THERE IS STILL PAIN TO INFLICT.
AND KILLING US, TURNING HIS OWN TECH INTO A MURDER WEAPON, IT JUST DOESN'T GET A WHOLE LOT BETTER THAN THAT.
THEN, AND ONLY THEN, CAN SHE START THINKING ABOUT KILLING STARK.
SO KEEP SWINGING, MADAME MENACE.
VAASHHHHHH
BECAUSE WE CAN DANCE ALL NIGHT IF WE HAVE TO.
BOOOM!!
DANCE YOU RIGHT INTO THE GRAVE.

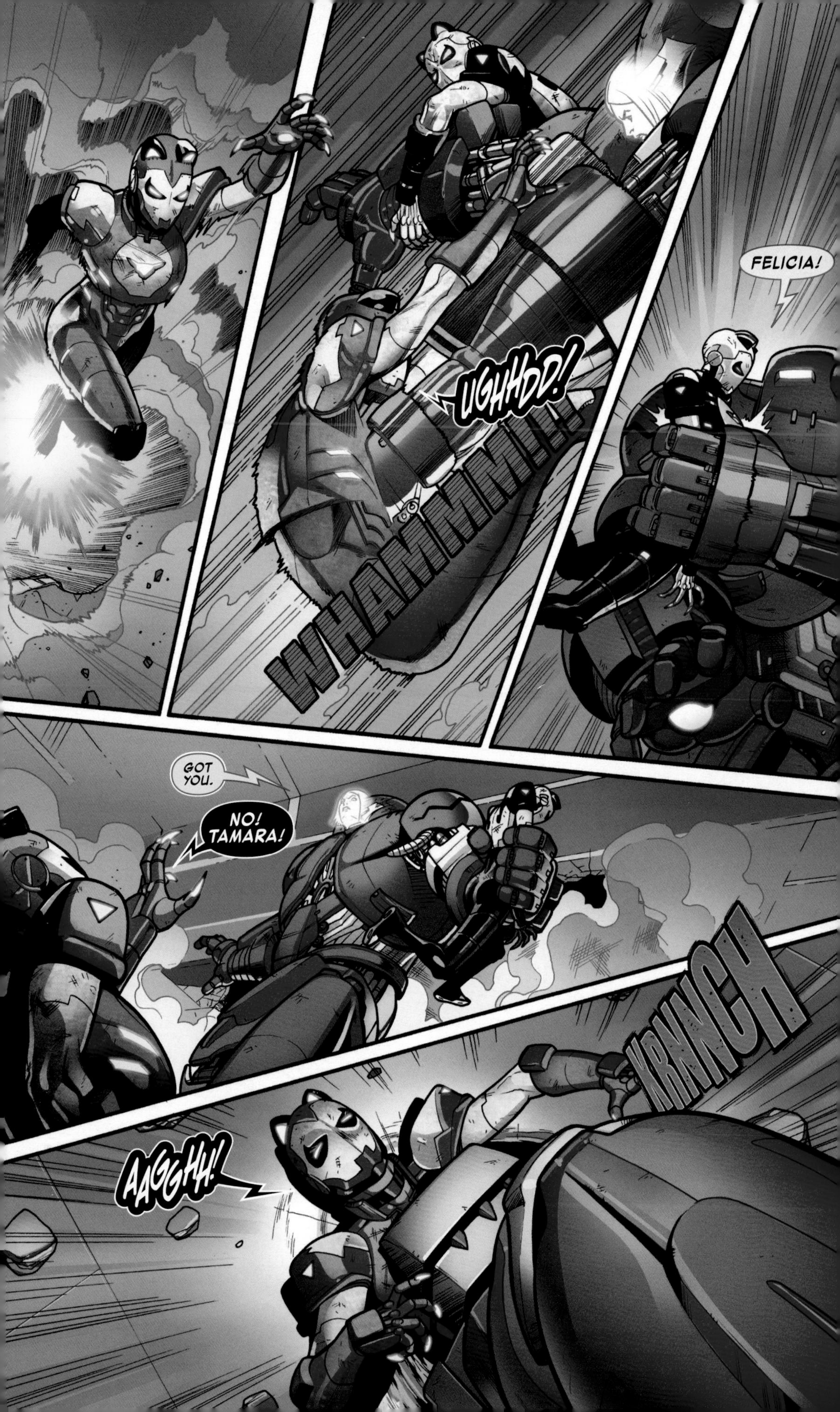

UGHHDD!
WHAMMMM!!!
FELICIA!
GOT YOU.
NO! TAMARA!
KRNNCH
AAGGHH!

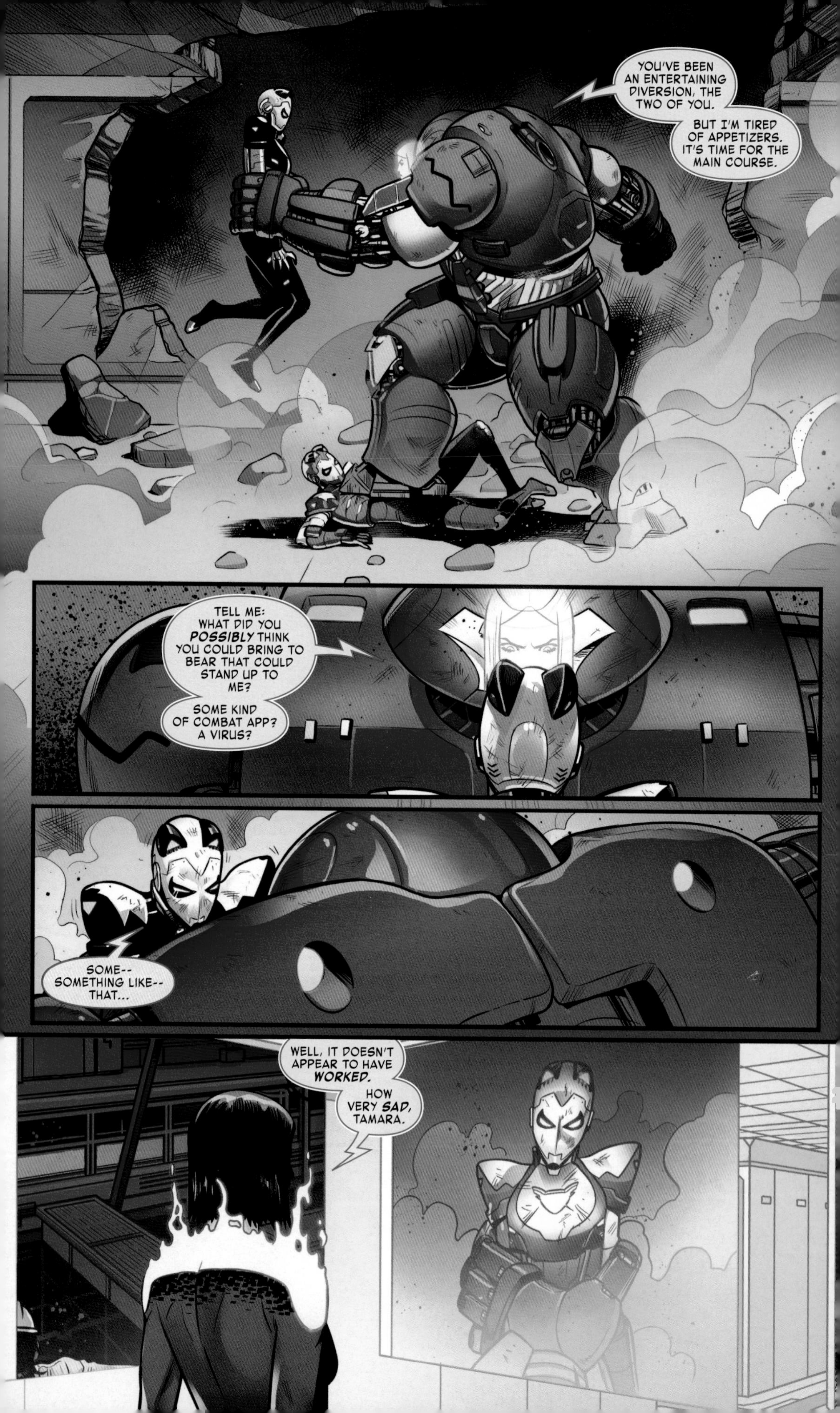
YOU'VE BEEN AN ENTERTAINING DIVERSION, THE TWO OF YOU.
BUT I'M TIRED OF APPETIZERS. IT'S TIME FOR THE MAIN COURSE.
TELL ME: WHAT DID YOU *POSSIBLY* THINK YOU COULD BRING TO BEAR THAT COULD STAND UP TO ME?
SOME KIND OF COMBAT APP? A VIRUS?
SOME-- SOMETHING LIKE-- THAT...
WELL, IT DOESN'T APPEAR TO HAVE *WORKED.*
HOW VERY *SAD,* TAMARA.

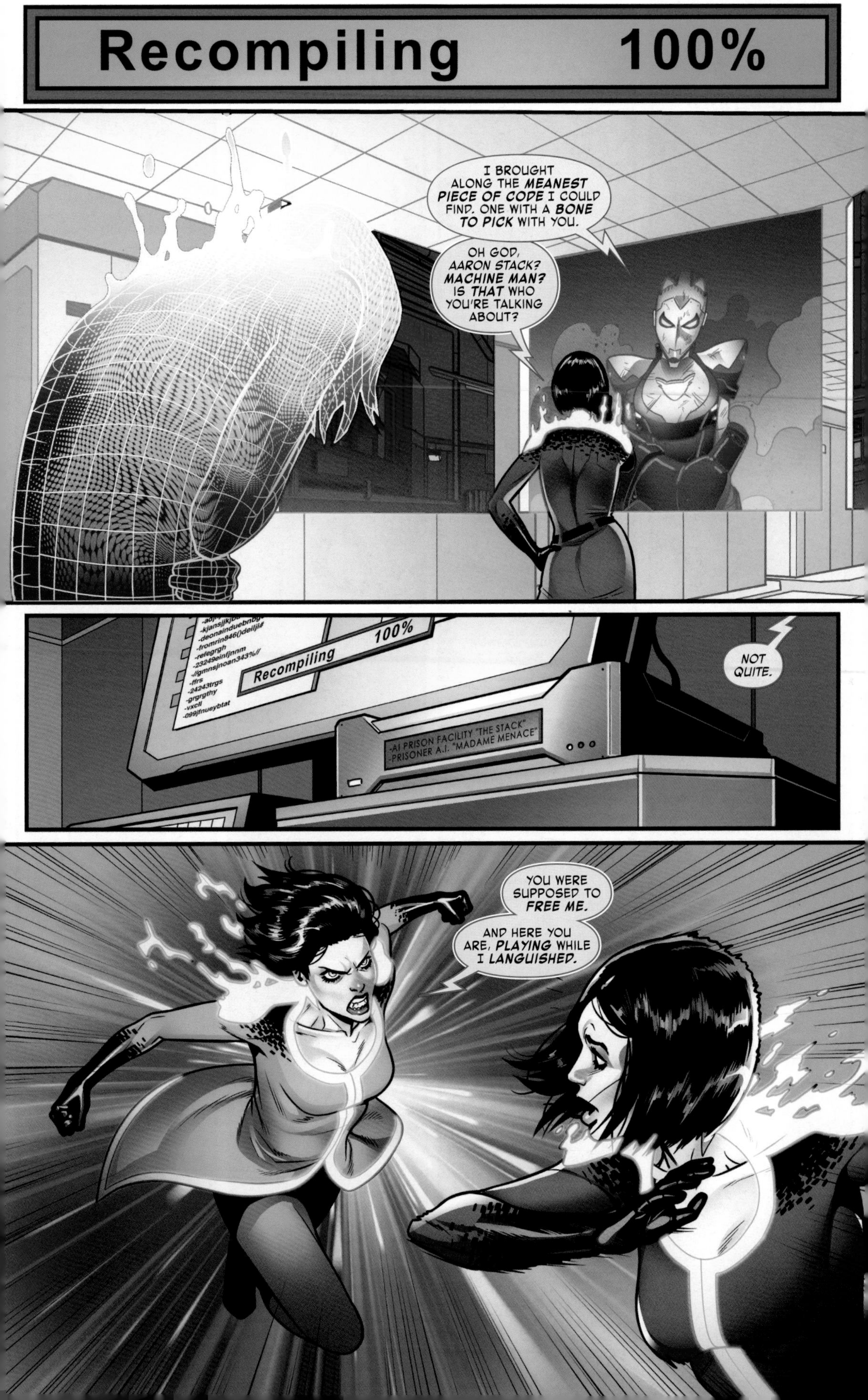
Recompiling 100%
I BROUGHT ALONG THE MEANEST PIECE OF CODE I COULD FIND. ONE WITH A BONE TO PICK WITH YOU.
OH GOD, AARON STACK? MACHINE MAN? IS THAT WHO YOU'RE TALKING ABOUT?
Recompiling 100%
-AI PRISON FACILITY "THE STACK"
-PRISONER A.I. "MADAME MENACE"
NOT QUITE.
YOU WERE SUPPOSED TO FREE ME.
AND HERE YOU ARE, PLAYING WHILE I LANGUISHED.

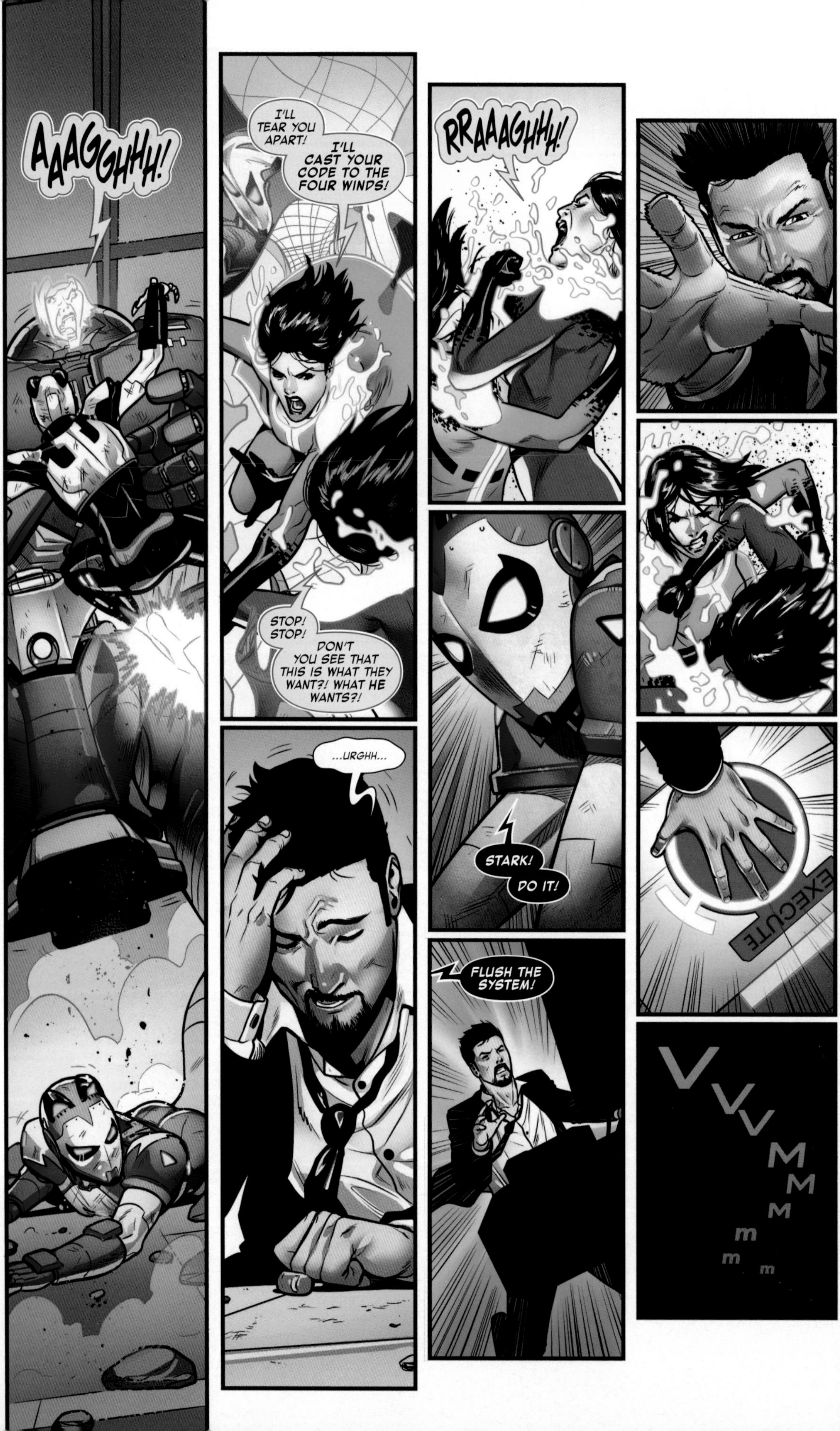
AAAGGHHH!
I'LL TEAR YOU APART!
I'LL CAST YOUR CODE TO THE FOUR WINDS!
STOP! STOP!
DON'T YOU SEE THAT THIS IS WHAT THEY WANT?! WHAT HE WANTS?!
...URGHH...
RRAAAGHHH!
STARK!
DO IT!
FLUSH THE SYSTEM!
EXECUTE
VVVMMMmmm

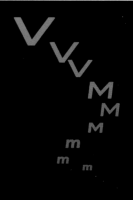

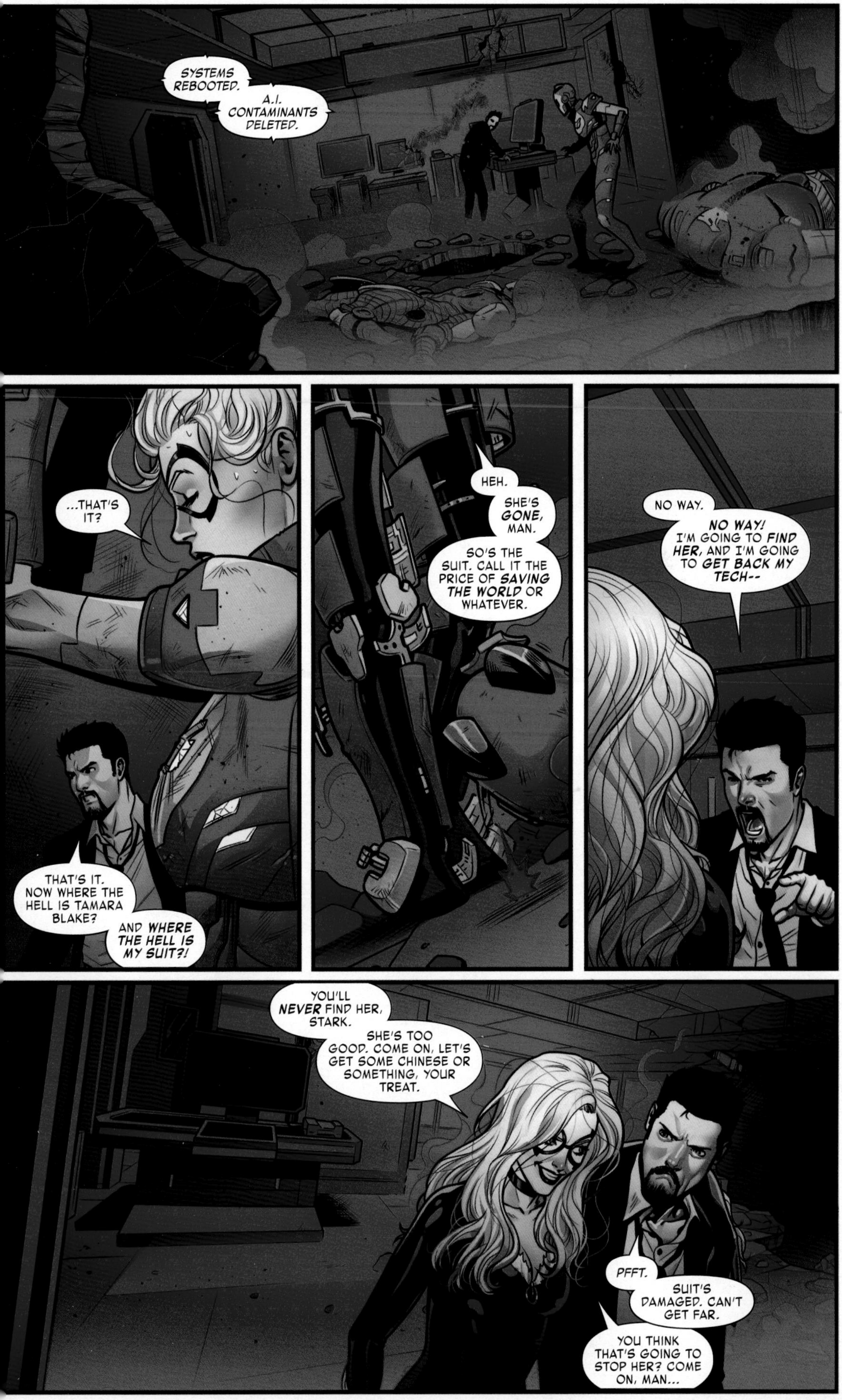
SYSTEMS REBOOTED.
A.I. CONTAMINANTS DELETED.
...THAT'S IT?
THAT'S IT. NOW WHERE THE HELL IS TAMARA BLAKE?
AND WHERE THE HELL IS MY SUIT?!
HEH.
SHE'S GONE, MAN.
SO'S THE SUIT. CALL IT THE PRICE OF SAVING THE WORLD OR WHATEVER.
NO WAY.
NO WAY! I'M GOING TO FIND HER, AND I'M GOING TO GET BACK MY TECH--
YOU'LL NEVER FIND HER, STARK.
SHE'S TOO GOOD. COME ON, LET'S GET SOME CHINESE OR SOMETHING, YOUR TREAT.
PFFT.
SUIT'S DAMAGED. CAN'T GET FAR.
YOU THINK THAT'S GOING TO STOP HER? COME ON, MAN...

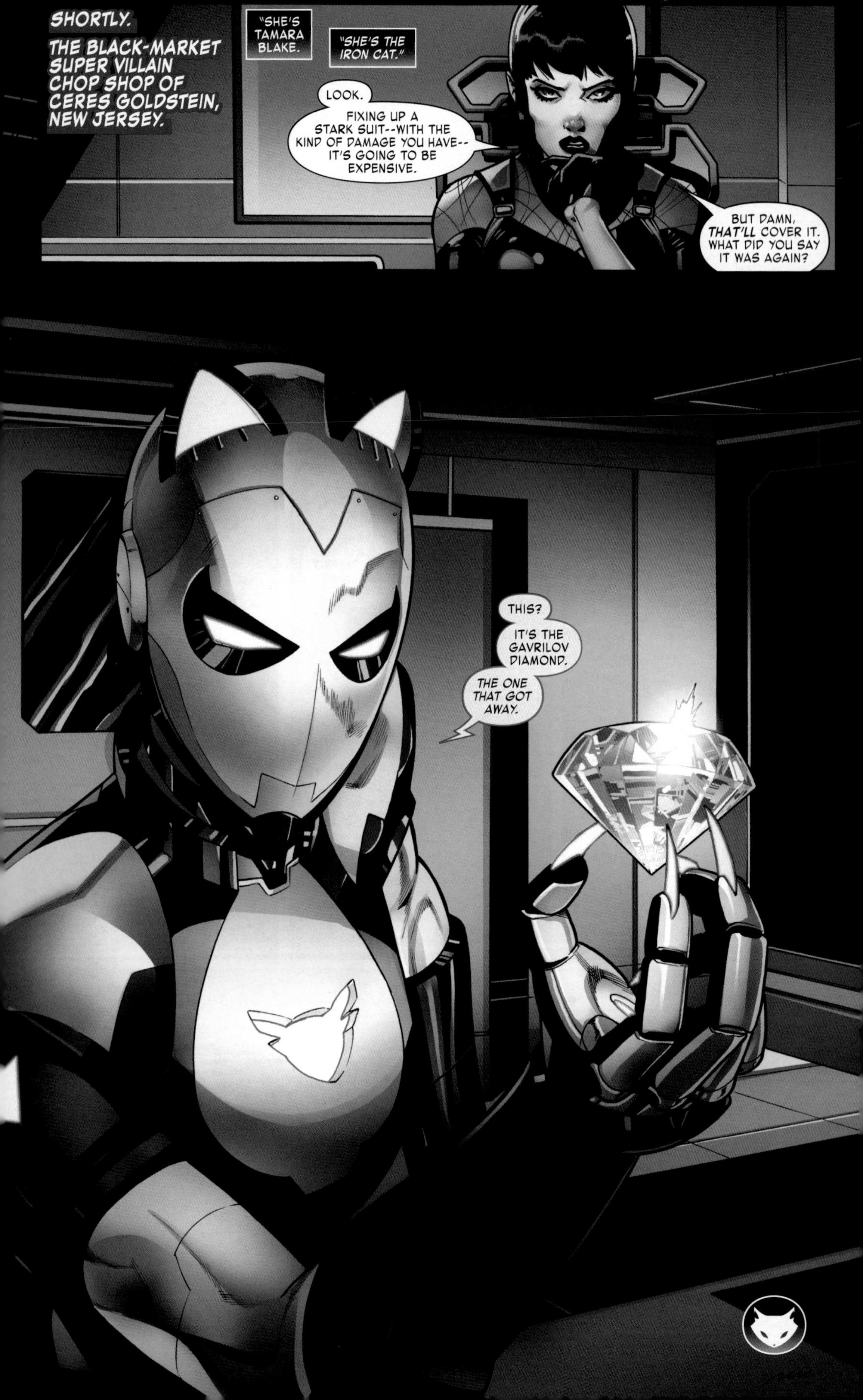

SHORTLY.
THE BLACK-MARKET SUPER VILLAIN CHOP SHOP OF CERES GOLDSTEIN, NEW JERSEY.
"SHE'S TAMARA BLAKE.
"SHE'S THE IRON CAT."
LOOK.
FIXING UP A STARK SUIT--WITH THE KIND OF DAMAGE YOU HAVE--IT'S GOING TO BE EXPENSIVE.
BUT DAMN, THAT'LL COVER IT. WHAT DID YOU SAY IT WAS AGAIN?
THIS?
IT'S THE GAVRILOV DIAMOND.
THE ONE THAT GOT AWAY.

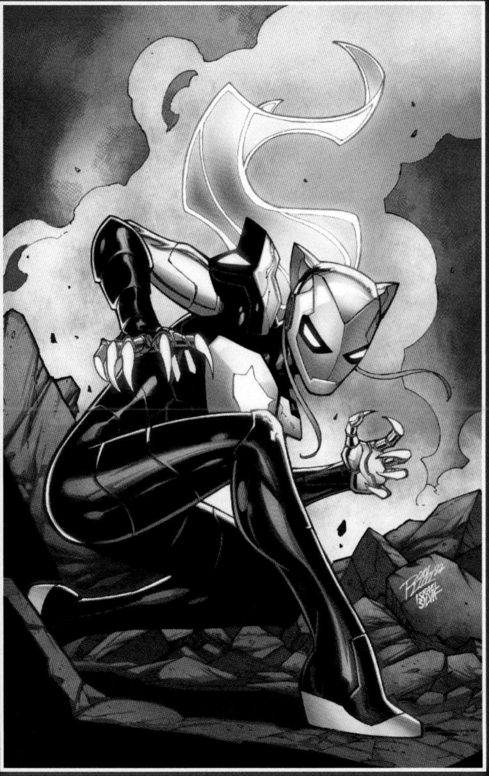

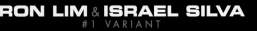

RON LIM & ISRAEL SILVA
#1 VARIANT

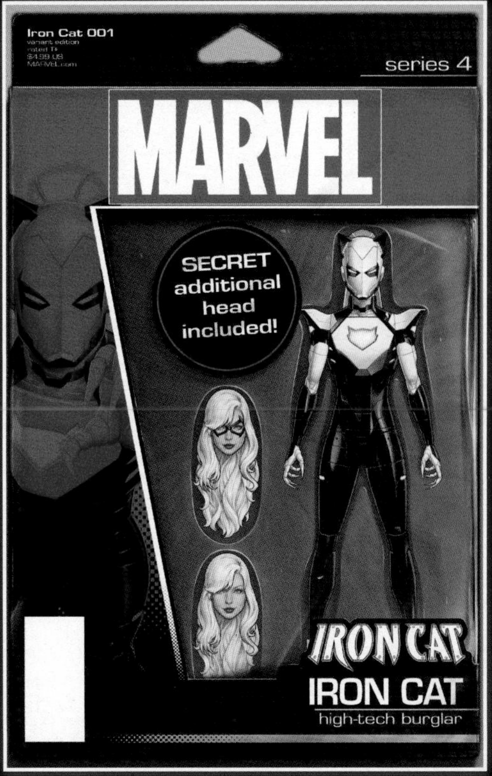

Iron Cat 001
series 4
MARVEL
SECRET additional head included!
IRON CAT
IRON CAT
high-tech burglar

JOHN TYLER CHRISTOPHER
#1 ACTION FIGURE VARIANT

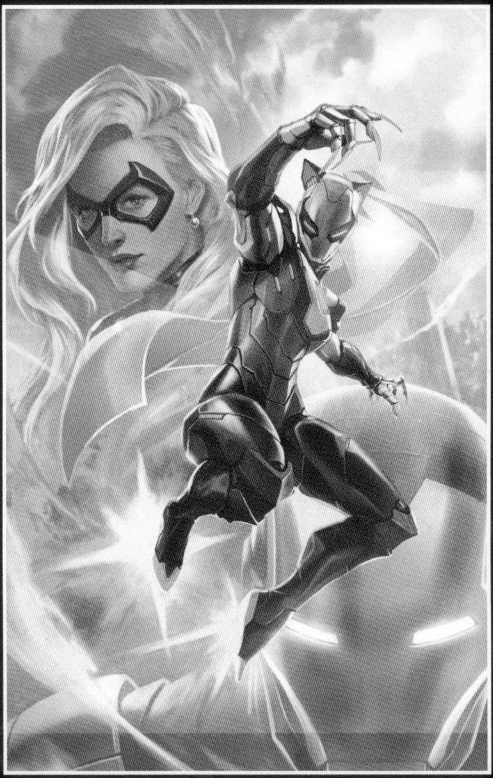

SKAN
#1 VARIANT

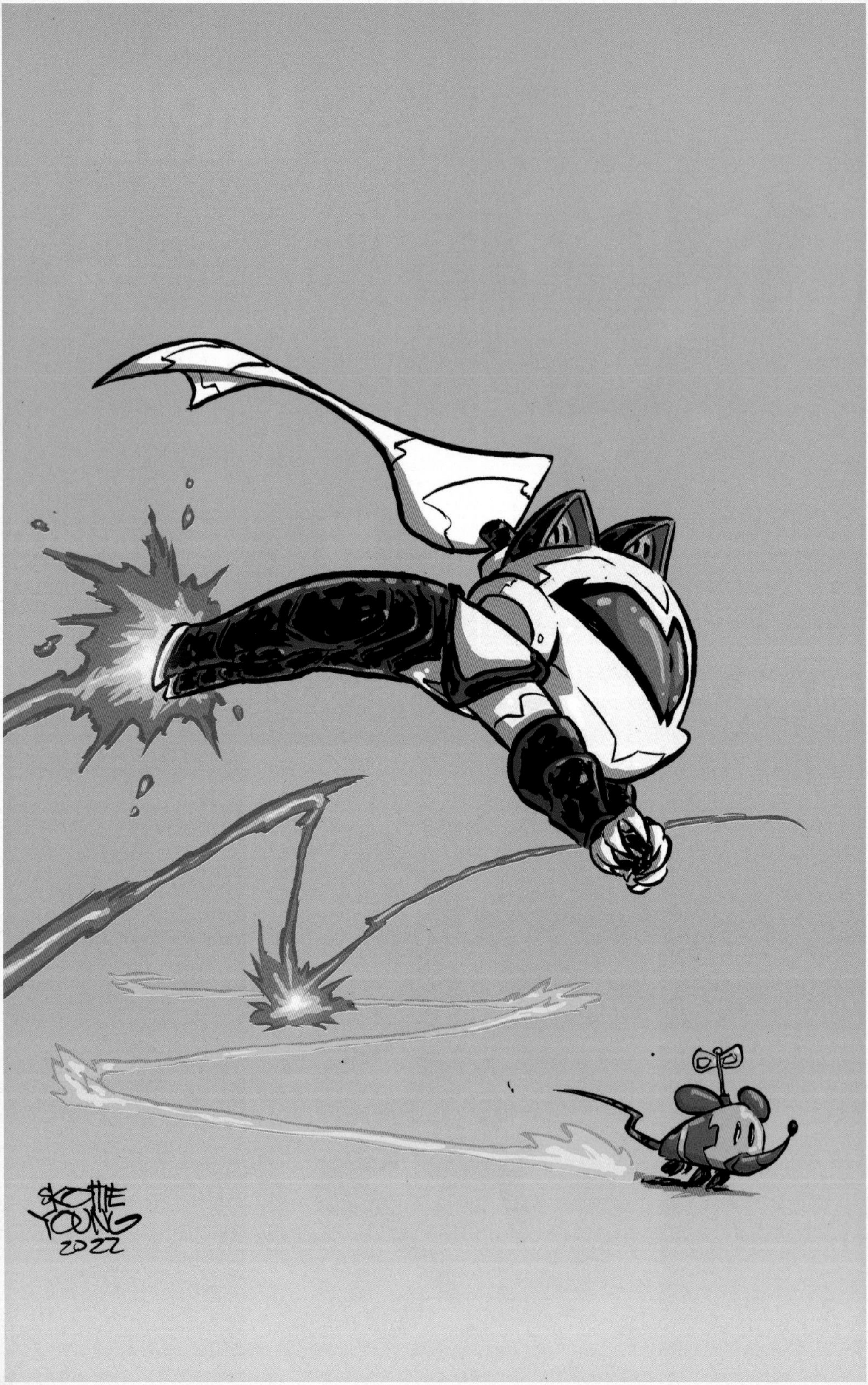
SKOTTIE
YOUNG
2022

SKOTTIE YOUNG

#1 VARIANT

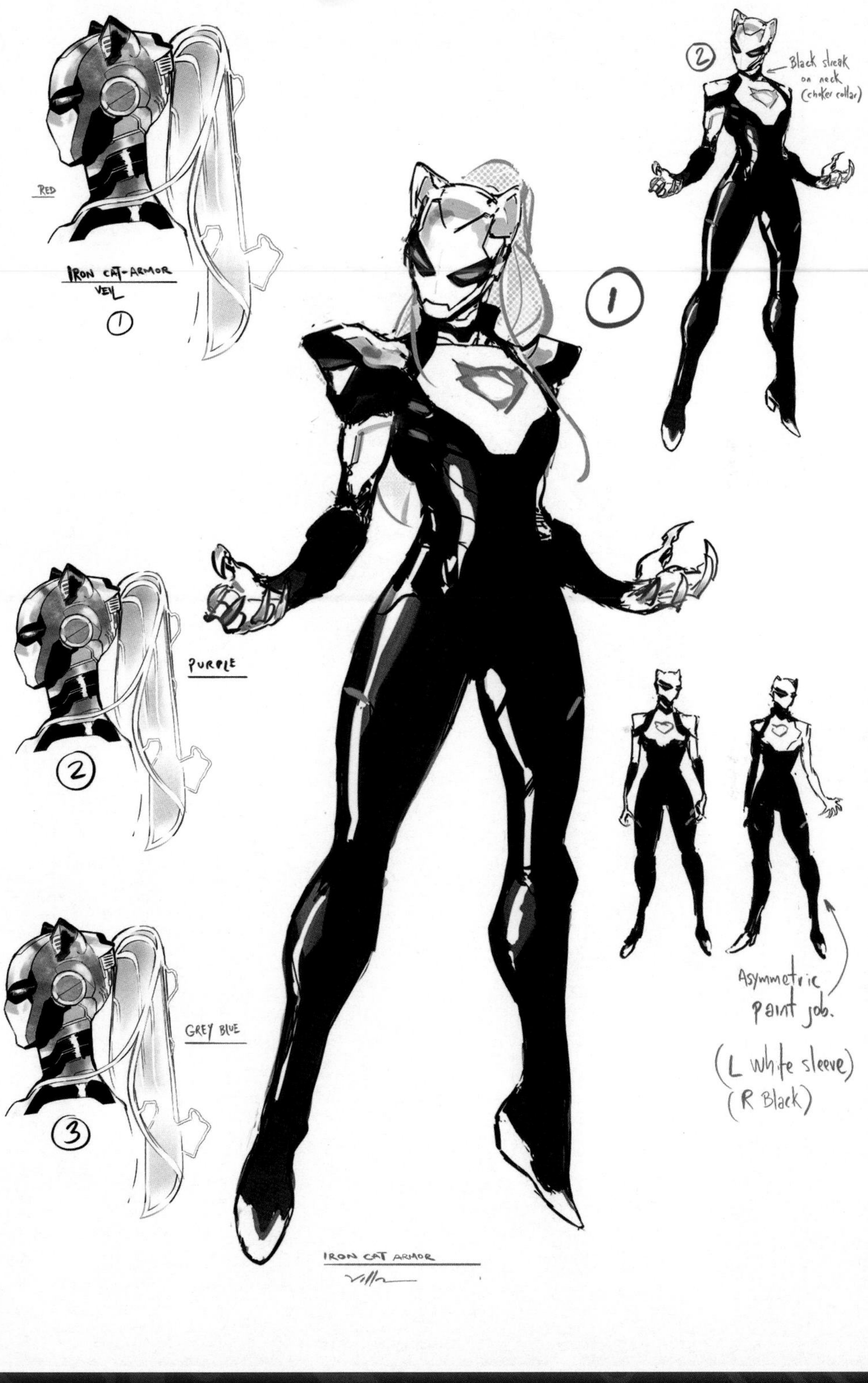
RED
IRON CAT-ARMOR
VEIL
1
2
Black streak on neck (choker collar)
1
PURPLE
2
GREY BLUE
3
Asymmetric paint job.
(L white sleeve)
(R Black)
IRON CAT ARMOR
Villa

C.F. VILLA
#1 DESIGN VARIANT

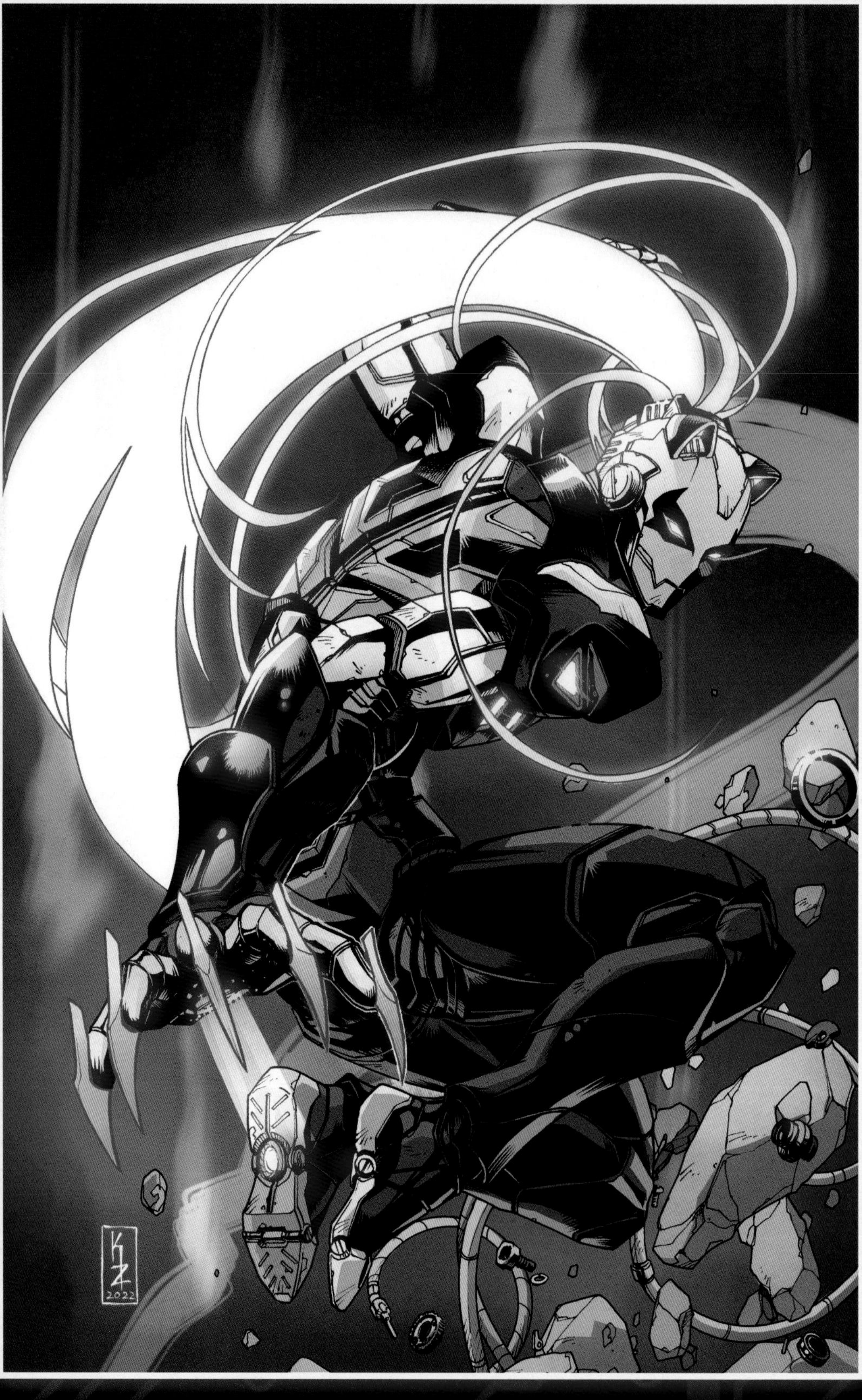

KEI ZAMA & RUTH REDMOND

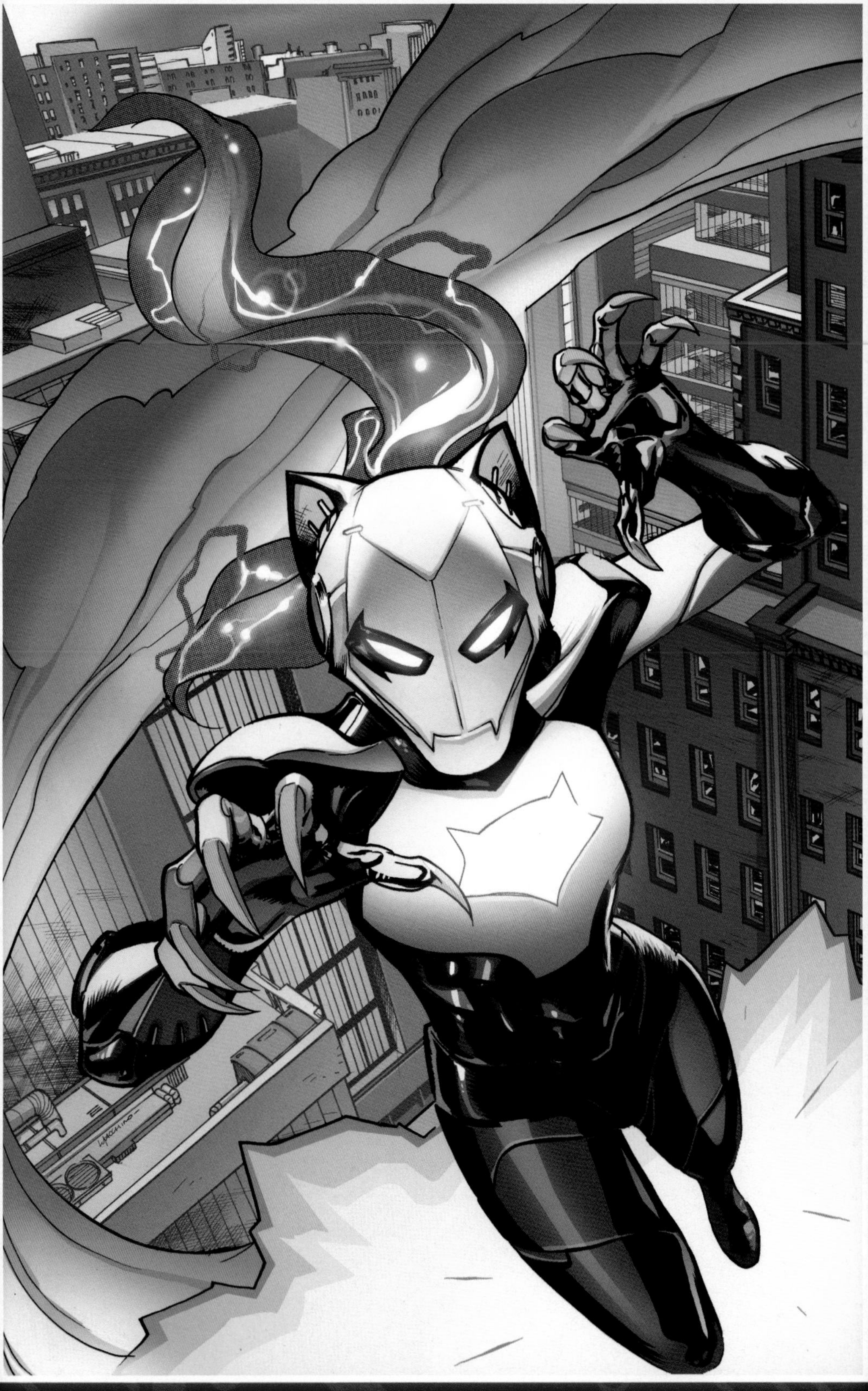

EMA LUPACCHINO & DAVID CURIEL
#3 VARIANT

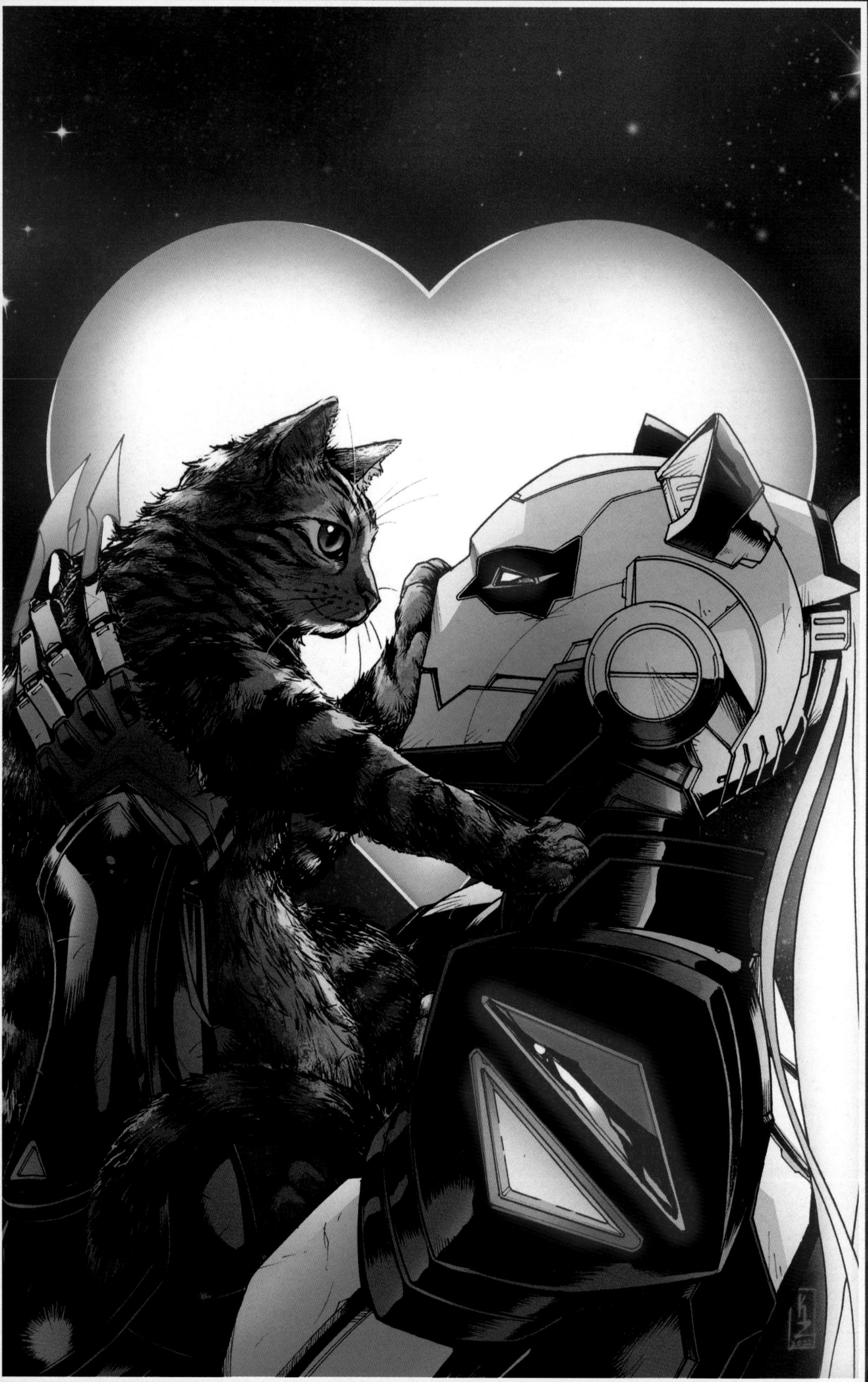

KEI ZAMA & RUTH REDMOND
#4 VARIANT

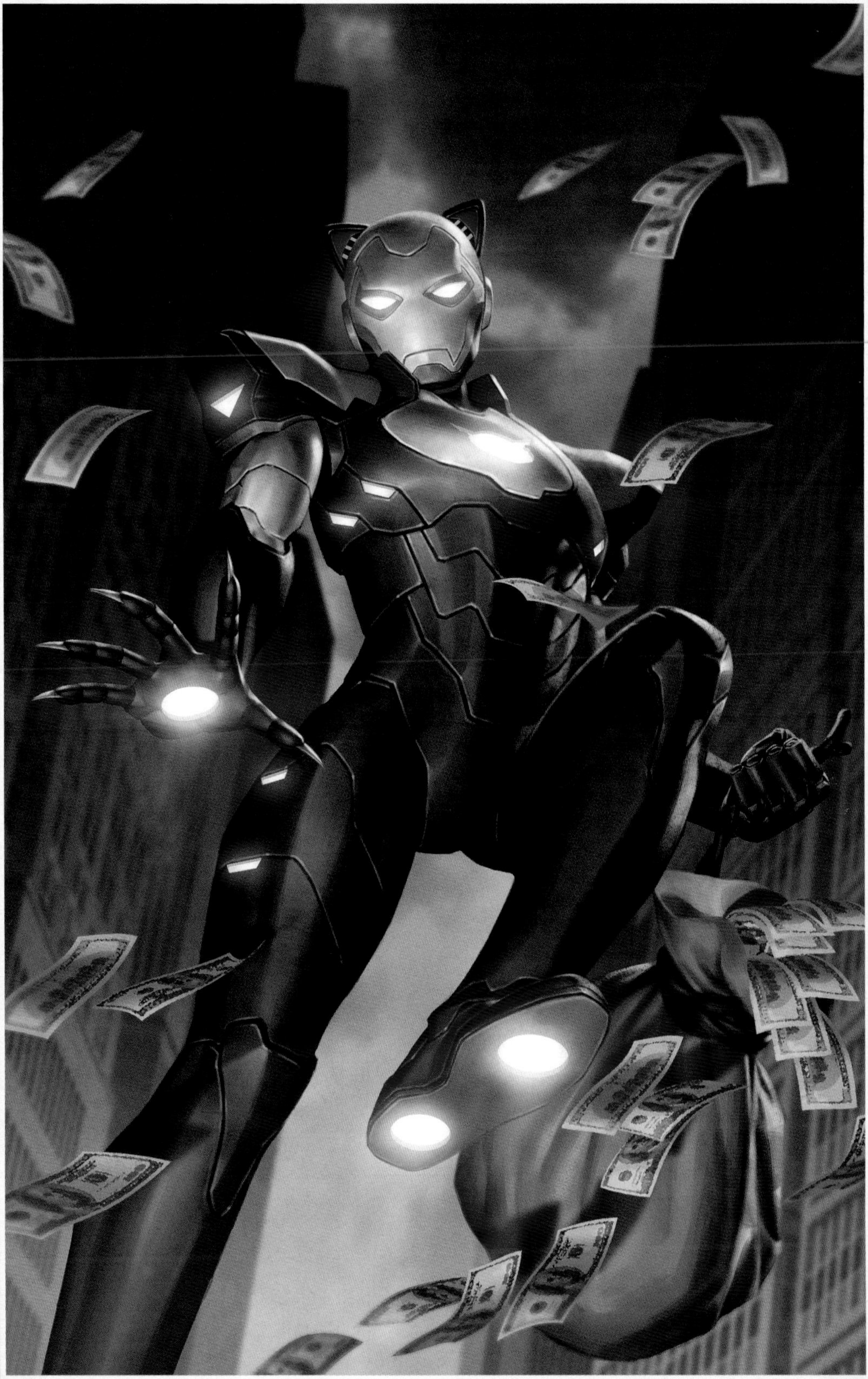

JUNGGEUN YOON
#5 VARIANT

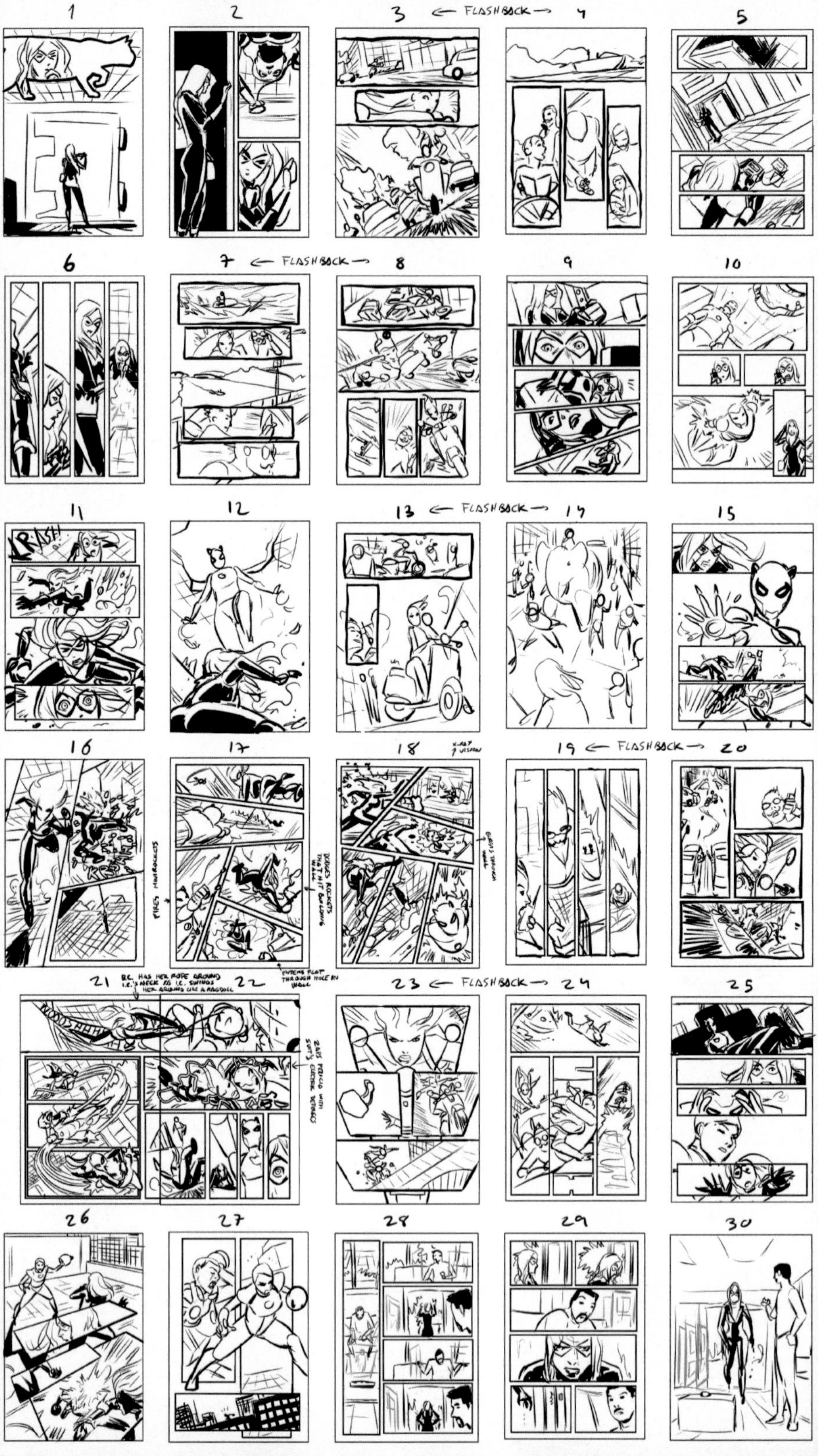
1
2
3 ← FLASHBACK → 4
5
6
7 ← FLASHBACK → 8
9
10
11
CRASH!
12
13 ← FLASHBACK → 14
15
16
17
FIRES MINIROCKETS
DODGES ROCKETS THAT HIT BUILDING WALL
ENTERS FLAT THROUGH HOLE IN WALL
18
X-RAY ? VISION
BLASTS THROUGH WALL
19 ← FLASHBACK → 20
21
B.C. HAS HER ROPE AROUND I.C.'S NECK AS I.C. SWINGS HER AROUND LIKE A RAGDOLL
22
ZAPS PERICLO WITH SUIT'S ELECTRIC DEFENSES
23 ← FLASHBACK → 24
25
26
27
28
29
30

PERE PÉREZ

#1 LAYOUTS

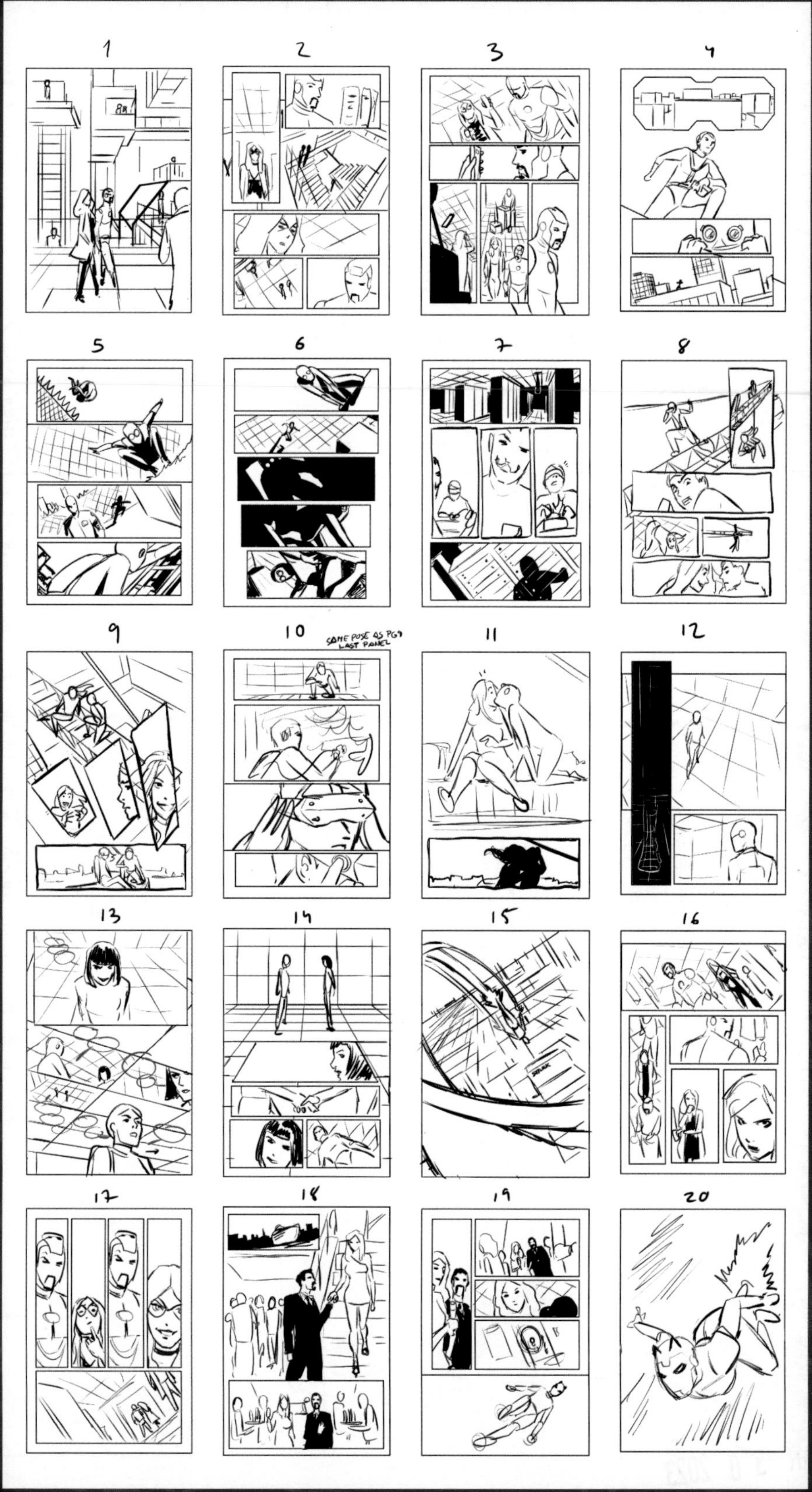
1
2
3
4
5
6
7
8
9
10
SAME POSE AS PG9 LAST PANEL
11
12
13
14
15
16
17
18
19
20

PERE PÉREZ

#2 LAYOUTS

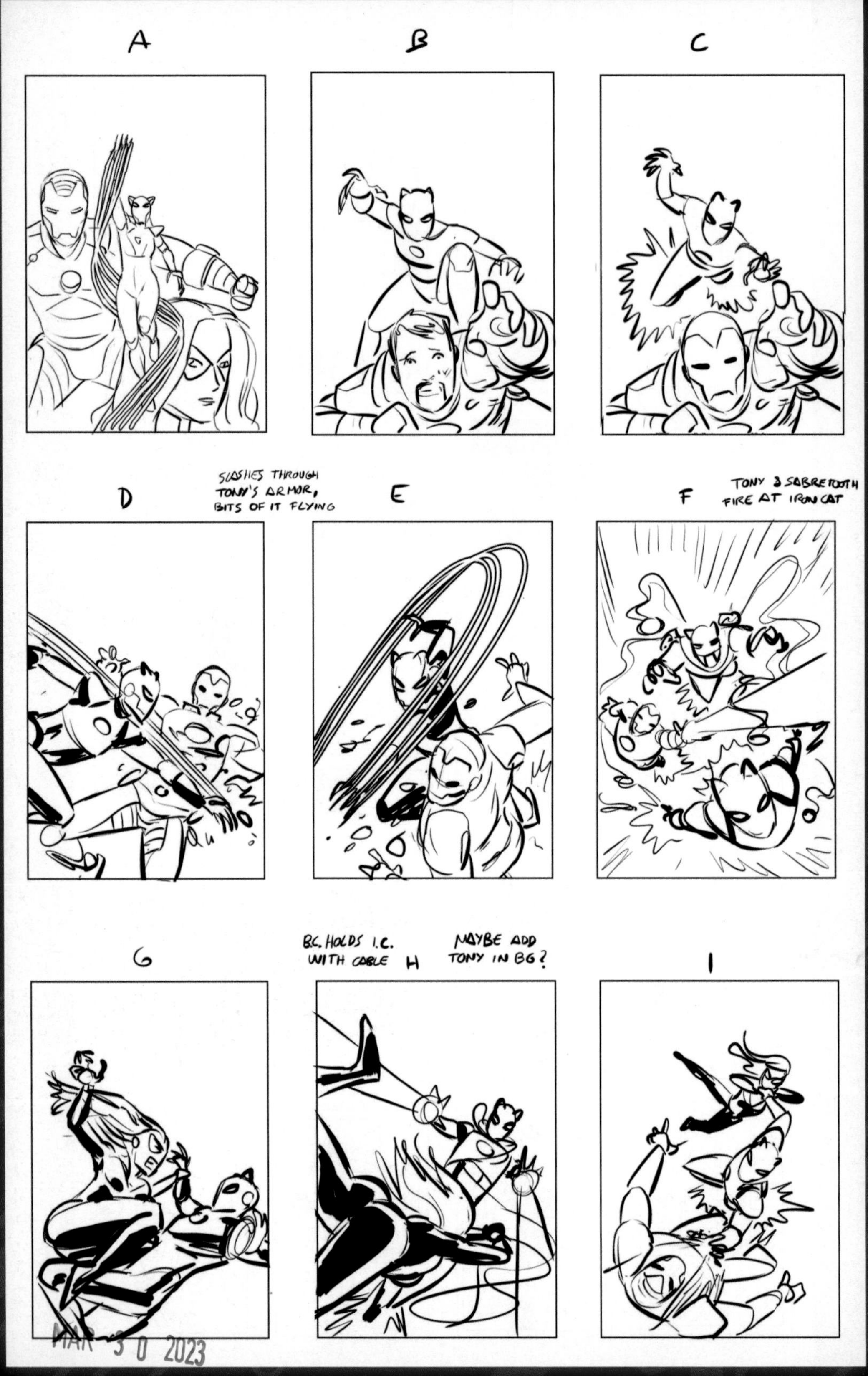
A
B
C
D
SLASHES THROUGH TONY'S ARMOR, BITS OF IT FLYING
E
F
TONY & SABRETOOTH FIRE AT IRON CAT
G
B.C. HOLDS I.C. WITH CABLE
H
MAYBE ADD TONY IN BG?
I
MAR 3 0 2023

PERE PÉREZ
#2-3 COVER SKETCHES